The Role of Law in China's Economic Development, 1978–2011

Jia Hu

The Role of Law in China's Economic Development, 1978–2011

A Study in Law and Political Economy

Springer

Jia Hu
Frankfurt am Main, Germany

ISBN 978-981-99-9910-1 ISBN 978-981-99-9911-8 (eBook)
https://doi.org/10.1007/978-981-99-9911-8

This Springer imprint is published by the registered company Springer Nature Singapore Pte Ltd.
The registered company address is: 152 Beach Road, #21-01/04 Gateway East, Singapore 189721, Singapore

Paper in this product is recyclable.

To my family

Preface

My original interest in this topic emerged many years ago when I was an LL.M. student in Frankfurt. My initial inquiry is about Chinese law's ever-obvious instrumental role for particular purposes, whether political, social, or economic. This observation finally led me to concern about how the law and the economy interact or the role of law in the economy.

Five years into this project, it evolved as the research developed. I started the study by following a conventional approach of deconstructing each economic sector and the related laws. Roughly in the middle of the project, enlightened by Matthias Goldmann's writings concerning the 'paradigm shift', I substantially reshuffled my early results and juxtaposed the development of law and the economy of each of the three decades from 1978 through 2011. These three decades witnessed China's momentous development, and coincidentally, China was governed by three generations of leadership, each of which adopted distinctive developmental strategies.

In addition to the coevolution of law and economy, a study on China's legal education is also crucial to understanding China's legal system. Nevertheless, while China saw an expanding army of practicing lawyers in these decades, the kind of group status described by Weber has yet to take shape on Chinese soil. Hence, my dealings with China's legal education followed a sociological approach, mainly following Bourdieu's concepts of social space and habitus to suggest the potential dispositions of modern Chinese lawyers.

Overall, this approach placed China's economic rise in the context of the changing political and legal environment and integrated law, politics, and the economy into a holistic framework, which ultimately led me to unravel the questions of how China's legal institutions promoted its economic growth and how China's economic conditions have constrained the development of its law.

On the whole, I hope this study will contribute to the debate on law and development in general and to the understanding of how China's law, politics, and economy interacted in particular. Law, to a great extent, appears to be a product of national tradition and culture. Emerging economies such as China, and perhaps many other developing countries, constantly face the difficult choice between directly transplanting the legal system developed by advanced economies and developing a localized legal model, which may take years of painstaking trial and error. Suffice it to say that China has been flexible in this regard and selectively adopted and adapted Western legal institutions to suit its particularities. Hence, I hope these results will contribute to future discussions on the law and development.

This book was written on the riverside of Mainz, where I was lucky enough to dwell for more than five years. In addition to the tranquil environment that I enjoyed while writing the manuscript, my most grateful acknowledgment is due to Prof. Matthias Goldmann, the supervisor of this research. I owe him my foremost intellectual debt, as many of my breakthroughs would never have been made if he were not there for the many intense discussions with me.

Additionally, my hearty thanks go to Prof. Moritz Bälz, the second examiner of the research. His thoughtful suggestions drew my attention to the necessity for some crucial revisions, and his kind comments encouraged me to carry on in the future studies. Furthermore, I would like to express my special thanks to Prof. Li Chen, who has been most generous in sharing his intelligence and time by reviewing the book proposal.

I would also like to acknowledge Benjamin Arens, Grigory Pustovit, Kevin Hinzen, and other members of our routine discussion group. I learned a great deal in discussing my early drafts within this group. Additionally, David Tang was most helpful in offering me constant language advice over the years and proofread Chap. 3 of the work before I submitted it to the faculty.

In preparation for publication, my editor, Lydia Wang, and coordinators, Kowsalya Raghunathan and Avanthika Babu of Springer, offered tremendous help in smoothing the publishing process.

Finally, my most sincere gratitude goes to my family, who have been considerate and patient during these years.

This work is funded by the China Scholarship Council.

Hangzhou, China
April 2023

Jia Hu

Contents

Abbreviations

ABC	Agricultural Bank of China
AMC	Assets Management Company
APC	Agricultural Producer's Cooperative
BIT	Bilateral Investment Treaty
BOC	Bank of China
CCB	China Construction Bank
CCCCP	Central Committee of the Chinese Communist Party
CCP	Chinese Communist Party
CJV	Cooperative Joint Venture
EJV	Equity Joint Venture
FDI	Foreign Direct Investment
FYP	Five Year Plan
GLF	Great Leap Forward
HRS	Household Responsibility System
ICBC	Industrial and Commercial Bank of China
KMT	Kuomingtang
MAT	Mutual Aid Team
MOF	Ministry of Finance
NPC	National People's Congress
PBC	People's Bank of China
PRC	People's Republic of China
SASAC	State-owned Assets Supervision and Administration Commission
SEZ	Special Economic Zone
SOE	State-Owned Enterprise
TVE	Township and Village Enterprise
WFE	Wholly Foreign-Owned Enterprise
WPE	Industrial Enterprises Owned by the Whole People

List of Figures

Chapter 1
Introduction

Abstract The Introduction unveils the major concern of this book—does the law matter to China's economic prosperity? If yes, how has Chinese law achieved this goal? Furthermore, given that China is a country that marched into modernity with thousands of years of strong cultural imprints, this part also briefly overviews the elements that define the characteristics of Chinese society to help unravel the foregoing concerns: China's peculiar political and social traditions, especially of Confucian values outweighing law as the norm of social conduct (1.1), the features of China's unique educational tradition (1.2), and the initial attempt to modernize its legal system (1.3). It ends with a concise framework of the book (1.4).

Just how important is the law to economic prosperity? The significance of the law, or legal institutions, to economic development and sustainability has been taken for granted ever since the global acceptance of the Washington Consensus. The failure of the early attempt by the Law and Development Movement prompted legal scholars, if not to question the role of law in development, to examine the law in a much more nuanced way to understand the relationship between it and economic prosperity. This is the broad picture that the current study fits into.

Nearly half a century into China's economic reforms, the Chinese economy has built diverse economic and legal infrastructures. However, due to unequal regional development, Chinese society has become differentiated and stratified. It is fair to say that the law has waded into the process and left its imprints. This observation presses one to enquire how exactly the law walked through China's economic transformation and wherefrom to re-evaluate the relationship between Chinese law and the economy in particular and the role of law in development in general. Both concerns are vital given that China, a case that any law and development study cannot afford to ignore, is now facing renewed social and economic dilemmas regardless of its early success.

Therefore, this study reviews China's economic reforms over certain past decades and cross-analyses them with the corresponding legal reforms. This inquiry confronts both the internal characteristics and external functions of the law. These two aspects of law refer to the degree of legal formality and rationality and the role of law in different stages of development. Both aspects are significant because they are the

J. Hu, *The Role of Law in China's Economic Development, 1978–2011*,
https://doi.org/10.1007/978-981-99-9911-8_1

clues for unravelling the intertwined mechanism between the law and the society in which it is embedded.

1.1 Political and Social Tradition

Bureaucracy has been one of the defining features of China's political tradition. In Imperial China, this domination was tempered by moral norms distilled mainly from Confucian teachings and was facilitated by literati officials selected via the imperial examination system (Fairbank 1983, pp. 106–134). One might contend that the ancient administrative system was uprooted long ago and that Confucianism has retreated from its official status as an arbiter of social norms. Nevertheless, some consistency with ancient political and social characteristics is still visible in modern China (Harding 1981). Hence, some knowledge of China's historical heritage is indispensable for understanding the organization of the People's Republic of China and modern Chinese society.

First is the consistency of the centralized government with a hierarchical and bureaucratic administrative system, exemplified over two thousand years of history (Wang 1988; Xie 2013). Since 221 BC, when the first Qin emperor united China after a chaotic warring period, China, except for a few disruptions, stood as a unified entity ruled by one central authority until 1912. Though political power transferred from dynasty to dynasty, the dynasties shared similarities in their political systems, especially the centrally organized bureaucratic authority (Fairbank and Goldman 2006). This unique characteristic foreshadowed China's strong political traditions of bureaucracy and central control. Unsurprisingly, these features continue in modern times.

Another dimension is the social consistency that resulted mainly from cultural tradition and can be observed in consistent ideological teaching throughout Chinese history. Unlike Western societies that marched to modernity with a strong mark of religious conflicts, China experienced no comparable conflict throughout its history. During the Warring States period, ancient China had a high moment of a hundred schools blooming (Feng 1952), but from 134 BC, when Emperor Wu of the Han Dynasty adopted Confucianism as the dominant ideology, until the mid-nineteenth century, Chinese society evolved under the dominant influence of Confucianism. Although Confucianism also evolved over time, its essence has remained unchanged, and its signature features, such as submission to authorities and the parental role of governments, are still vivid in modern Chinese society, shaping Chinese people's daily behaviours and choices as well as the role of the government in the present day (Thompson 1988; Overmyer 1986).

On the whole, the political tradition has been consistent in having the government take care of as many things as possible and using Confucianism to nurture and socialize the moral role of an omnipotent government and the moral duty of the people to accept such a government. After thousands of years of socialization with Confucian teachings, it might be odd to see the Chinese people accepting a different ruling style. As we saw decades ago, when the Chinese Communist Party (CCP) came into power and deployed the traditional role of big government, intervening in many aspects of economic and social life, it was natural and easy for people to take such measures in stride.

1.2 Educational Tradition and Its Impact

China's traditional education was headlined by its imperial examination system (kejü zhidu) for selecting civil officials, characterized by a singular emphasis on Confucian teachings (Elman 2013, pp. 280–321). The first examination in history was held in 587 by Emperor Wen of the Sui Dynasty (581–618), and the system then operated for nearly 1300 years before finally being abolished in 1905 by Emperor Guangxu of the Qing Dynasty (1636–1912) (Franke 1960; Jin 1990). Over the centuries, under Confucian teachings, it was stipulated that an able scholar 'should devote [himself] to the service of the state' (Waley 1985, p. 227), and Chinese scholars were trained according to the criteria of the examination. It is no exaggeration to say that traditional Chinese education was centred around the examination system (Chaffee 1985).

Therefore, the focus of the examination was critical in shaping China's educational tradition and the studies of ancient Chinese scholars. Admittedly, both the content and form of the examination changed over a thousand years. Law was a subject of the examination during the Sui and Tang Dynasties (from 581 through 907). In the Song Dynasty (960–1279), the examination centred on reciting classics, suggesting solutions to current affairs, and writing poetry (Ichisada 1981).[1] In the Yuan, Ming, and Qing Dynasties (1271–1912), the contents of the examination were confined to the Four Books and Five Classics (Tu 1990, pp. 123–125)[2] as well as Zhu Xi's commentaries on these classics (Ebrey 1993, pp. 172–177).[3] From the Ming Dynasty onwards, the examination form was confined to stereotyped writings, called eight-legged essays (bagu wen), meaning that examination articles had to be written with eight fixed parts (Elman 2013, p. 61).[4] The impact of the system was so profound that even today, some features of the Confucian style of teaching and learning, for instance, the authoritarian role of the teacher towards his disciples, the worship of books compiled or written by authorities, and the preference for morality over the law as the best way to organize society, are still visible (Hughes 1967, pp. 92 and 99).

A brief review of the examination system reveals that after the Song Dynasty, legal knowledge was no longer used to select civil officials (Chang 1994, pp. 309–310; Elman 2013, p. 312).[5] In fact, no discipline except Confucianism mattered to ancient Chinese scholars because mastering Confucianism was the only path to advance one's social and political status, and the examination was almost the only channel for ordinary people to ascend in the social hierarchy. Hence, the law dropped out of favour among ancient Chinese scholars, and such negligence of the law lasted until China started to modernize its education system in the late nineteenth century.[6]

Waking up after two bitter defeats in the Opium Wars, the Qing court began to realize the inability of China's traditional Confucian education to compete with Western countries. Thus, it sent young Chinese students to learn from the West under the Self-Strengthening Movement from the 1860s through the 1890s (Schwartz 1964). Although this effort ended unsuccessfully, it systematically opened the first page of China's learning from the West. Following in its footsteps, the second chapter of sending students abroad opened around the 1910s with the help of the Boxer Indemnity Scholarship. Over a thousand students were selected and sent to Western countries, mainly the United States and England (Wang 1972). Unlike the students in the first attempt, recipients of this funding turned out to be highly successful, and many of them became the backbone of China's early modernization (Chen and Tian 1991, pp. 188–190 and 197–202).[7] However, one characteristic about the subject matter chosen by those students was evident—probably because China had consistently been defeated in recent history, these students overwhelmingly chose natural sciences, engineering, and medicine as their majors, and very few enrolled in social science fields such as law (Chen et al. 2007, pp. 188–190).[8] The skills they acquired in earlier-industrialized countries were of great importance to China's early technological and economic development. However, China soon paid the price of the lack of human resources in social sciences.

In addition to sending students to learn from the West, another attempt to modernize China's education system involved establishing modern universities and colleges, which commenced at the end of the nineteenth century (Cohen 1974, pp. 171–184). Moreover, with the ongoing arrival of missionaries since the mid-nineteenth century, many missionary schools were established at different educational levels, most of which were located in eastern port cities (Fairbank 1983, pp. 328–355).[9] These schools and colleges taught by foreign missionaries helped China educate its first cohort of students with English abilities and knowledge other than Confucian teachings. This wealth of resources was later inherited by the Communist Party after the Civil War.

Thus, China's education system around 1949 had several outstanding features. First, after several waves of learning from Western movements until 1949, China possessed a number of scholars who had been educated in Western countries and specialized particularly in the natural sciences and engineering. Second, after decades of advancement, by 1949, China had established hundreds of universities, which paved the way for the development of modern education. Third, social sciences and the law were primarily ignored in ancient and contemporary times, and these programmes therefore had to be built from scratch.

1.3 Early Attempt at Legal Modernization

The first legal reform effort in China's recent history was initiated in 1902, one year after the Qing Empire signed the Boxer Protocol.[10] It was part of the New Policies of the late Qing Dynasty, also called Cixi's New Policies. This series of reforms was initiated to salvage the legal system and to quell social disturbances caused by external aggression and domestic uprisings and revolts (Ichiko 1980, pp. 375–415). Emperor Guanxu (1871–1908) appointed Shen Jiaben (1840–1913), the then vice minister of justice (Li 2000), and Wu Tingfang (1842–1922), the first ethnic Chinese barrister trained at University College London (Norton-Kyshe 1971; Pomerantz-Zhang 1992), as the secretaries of enactment in 1902.

At the time, there was a debate, known as the 'rite-law debate', over the guiding ideology of the reform, with two rival forces led by Zhang Zhidong (1837–1909) and Shen Jiaben. The former represented China's conservative element, advocating reform within the framework of Chinese culture (Li 1999; Zhang 2017). The Shen-Wu team, on the other hand, favoured Western legal ideas such as equal gender rights and property rights. Essentially, it was a conflict between rite-oriented Chinese culture and rights-oriented Western legal ideas.

This legislative effort resulted in the emergence of several key codes, including the 1906 Constitutional Outline Made by the Imperial Order (1906); the Current Criminal Code of Qing (1910), which abolished inhumane corporal punishments; the New Criminal Code of Qing (1906–1911); the Commercial Code of Qing (1903–1911); and the Civil Code of Qing (1907–1911). It was indeed a fruitful effort in terms of the legal volumes enacted in this period. However, as the dates of many of these codes show, most had been completed when imperial rule was overthrown by the 1911 Revolution[11] and were thereafter abandoned.

Following the victory in the Xinhai Revolution (1911), Sun Yat-sen (also called Sun Zhongshan, 1866–1925), the leader of the revolution (Schiffrin 1968), outlined the Provisional Constitution of the Republic of China in 1912. However, the Provision was barely effective in practice due to the factional warring era that followed the revolution, with each rival warlord having his own constitution (Nathan 1976, 1983, pp. 259–283). This divisive period ended in 1928 when the Kuomintang (KMT) triumphed in its military campaign and formed the Nanjing Government. In 1931, the newly established government issued the Provisional Constitution of the Political Tutelage Period, the supreme law of the period that lasted until the sanctioning of the Constitution of the Republic of China in 1946. From 1928 through 1946, the KMT promulgated six principal codes—the Code of Criminal Procedure (1928), Civil Code (1929), Code of Civil Procedure (1930), Administrative Laws (1933), Criminal Code (1935), and Constitution (1946)—which were historically called the 'Six Codes' and were repealed by the Communist Party in 1949 (Gilpatrick 1950).

Upon establishing the People's Republic of China, the ruling Party issued its first Constitution in 1954. This was later replaced by the 1975 Constitution, which featured the political movements of the time, such as the dictatorship of the proletariat over the capitalist in cultural and educational areas (Article 12) and the use of Big Character poster (dazibao) for propaganda (Article 13), a hallmark of the Cultural Revolution (1966–1976). These era-specific articles were deleted from the 1978 Constitution.

Under the new regime, legislation occurred only sporadically in the early decades,[12] and a systematic effort to build up the legal system commenced only as late as 1978, after Deng penned an article titled *Emancipating the Mind, Seeking Truth from Facts, Forwarding with Solidarity* (Deng 1978, pp. 140–153). This article launched a nationwide debate over the criteria of truth. In it, Deng echoed the idea of 'seeking truth from facts', which first appeared in a newspaper editorial, '*Practice Is the Only Criterion in Examining Truth*' (Hu 1978). While ostensibly focused on truth criteria, Deng was, in fact, directly reacting to the then pervasive ideology of the 'Two Whatevers', a political slogan proclaimed by Hua Guofeng (1921–2008), Mao's successor, who served as chairman of the CCP from October 1976 to June 1981 (Fontana 1982). The 'Two Whatevers' indicated a political commitment that 'we will resolutely uphold whatever policy decisions Chairman Mao made, and unswervingly follow whatever instructions Chairman Mao gave' (Editorial 1977). Deng's attack on this ideology effectively sabotaged Hua's attempt to use Mao's charisma to consolidate his own political clout (Fewsmith 2001, pp. 44–46).

More importantly, this article also marked the Party's change of opinion on the legal system. As Deng suggested, to protect China's political structure, it was essential to strengthen the notion of 'rule by law'.[13] His idea about the relation of the law to China's politics and the economy was as follows (Deng 1978, pp. 146–147).[14]

First, he admitted that Chinese society lacked the basic concept of law and that there was confusion between the law and leaders' words. As he pointed out, '[the populace] are still taking the leaders' words as law and treating behaviours as illegal if they were against the leaders' words, or see the law changes if the leader changes his or her words'. He urged the importance of institutionalizing the law and 'making sure the institution and the laws will not be changed due to the change of leaders or their opinions'.

Second, he admitted that China's then legal system was incomplete and stated that many laws should be promulgated soon. He expected 'the relationship between the state and the enterprises, enterprises and enterprises, enterprises and individuals clarified by the laws and their disputes to be settled by law'. To achieve this effect, Deng encouraged concentrating the effort on legislating the 'Criminal Code, Civil Code, litigation laws, and other necessary laws …'.

Third, by proclaiming the fast-forwarding style of legislative work, he recognized that a considerable workload lay ahead and proposed a broad-brush style of legislation in the beginning, to be refined later. The passage below demonstrates his general idea about constructing China's legal system:

> At present, the workload of legislation is overwhelming. Hence, [we can have] laws with more general articles first and refine them step by step. [On some issues], we can first stipulate local laws in some regions and promulgate national laws after experiment and improvement. Then, we can revise the laws one at a time, and there is no need to wait for a complete package [of the law]. In all, it is better to have laws than not and to have them soon than slowly. Also, we should put more effort into studying international law.

His remarks laid down the roadmap of legislative work for the coming decades. Laws started to emerge from 1979 onwards, and the legal system became ever more comprehensive, complete, and complicated as time passed.

1.4 Framework of the Book

This study opens with a theoretical discussion on the relationship between political structure, legal thought, and the economy. Undergirded by Max Weber's conceptual constructs of legal domination and formal rational law, it delves into the legal and political institutions crucial to economic development and their potential social costs, with a brief excursion into the American legal transformations in the nineteenth century (Chap. 2).

Before exploring China's economic development, the study first demonstrates the social and economic transformations undertaken by the Mao regime and the legal infrastructure during that time to present the economic and legal situations from which the economic reform emerged (Chap. 3).

After clarifying the theoretical models and historical background, it then examines the evolving political pursuit of economic results and the related legal development in recent decades. The goal is to understand the dynamic relationship between China's political economy and the law by examining legal transformations since 1978 (Chaps. 4 through 6). Each of these three chapters unfolds with the following sections.

The section on the external functions of the law examines the interplay between the law, political power, and the economy. This part incorporates a general political economy background, the actual economic reforms, and the emergence of related legal systems for each period. Indicators, such as selective legislation and alternate usage of law and policy to regulate economic activities, are employed to reveal the intended external functions of the law. Therefore, this section evaluates the extent of the law's autonomy in each of the three generations of leadership.

The section on the internal characteristics of the law aims to assess the rationality of the law on the basis of focused case studies. These sections select specific legal fields (contract law in the 1980s, company law in the 1990s, and labour contract law in the 2000s) that were essential to each period's economic reforms and then examine the formal rationality of the law by evaluating its predictability and calculability. It also considers the formality of the law in action by studying the reasoning processes of a few selected judicial cases to determine whether legal judgements were result-oriented.

The section on the formation of the legal profession aims to understand the style of legal thinking of Chinese legal experts. It focuses on the learning materials, teaching methods, and styles of China's bar exams to determine the characteristics of the legal knowledge that Chinese legal professionals receive in law schools and, therefore, the mode of legal reasoning.

Finally, each chapter ends with a summary of the institutional interactions between the law's internal characteristics and its external relations with the state and the economy. These summaries highlight the institutional structures that bolstered China's social and economic transformation and the elements cultivated by China's legal professionals in these periods.

The study concludes that China's shifts in political economy had an unmistakable impact on its legal transformations—a coordinated paradigmatic shift of the law and the political economy. This result negates a straightforward understanding of the relationship between the law and the economy because of the implied complicated interaction between the two, which requires a more nuanced and contextualized study.

Notes

1. The form of reciting classics and poetry writing was abolished in 1071 by the famous Song reformer Wang Anshi (1021–1086).
2. The four books are Great Learning, Doctrine of the Mean, Analects, and Mencius, and the Five Classics are Classic of Poetry, Book of Documents, Book of Rites, Book of Changes, and Spring and Autumn Annals. These are authoritative books of Confucianism written before 300 BC.
3. Zhu Xi (1130–1200) was a neo-Confucian sage who wrote commentaries on the Four Books (sishu jizhu), which since the Yuan Dynasty (1271–1368) have become standard commentaries and official references for the examination. For a contextualized reflection on Zhu Xi's philosophy, please refer to Gardner (1986).
4. The eight legs are Break open the topic (poti), Receiving the topic (chengti), Beginning discussion (qijiang), Initial leg (ruti), Transition leg (qigu), Middle leg (zhonggu), Later leg (hougu), and Conclusion (dajie or shugu). However, the ossified form of writing and very confined contents of the examination have also been blamed for China's backwardness in recent history for the origin, format introduction, and cognitive issues.
5. Legal questions appeared in late Qing examinations, although they were peripheral in the examination system.
6. For a more detailed discussion of China's legal education efforts, see the legal education section in Chaps. 4, 5 and 6 of this study.
7. To name but a few, Qian Xuesen (physicist), Qian Zhongshu (literature), Nobel Laureate Yang Zhenning (physicist), and Feng Youlan (philosopher) were all among its recipients.
8. Among the first cohort of 180 students from 1909 to 1911, only four enrolled in law.
9. From the late nineteenth century onwards, missionary schools opened in China from middle school to university. Many of them were inherited by the Communist Party and transformed into modern universities. Famous among them are Saint John's University (established in 1879, currently East China University of Political and Science), Soochow University (opened in 1900, now Suzhou University), and Yenching University (established in 1919, later integrated into Peking University).
10. It was signed between the Qing Empire and eleven western powers (the British Empire, France, Germany, Japan, Russia, the United States, Italy, Austro-Hungary, Belgium, Spain, and the Netherlands) after China's defeat in suppressing the Boxer Rebellion (also called the Yihetuan Movement), an anti-Christian, antiforeign, anticolonial uprising.
11. It was called the Xinhai Revolution and lasted from the Wuchan Uprising on 10 October 1911 to the abdication of Puyi, the last emperor of imperial China, on 12 February 1912. Because 1911 was the year of the Xinhai, according to the sexagenary cycle of the traditional Chinese calendar, it was therefore also called the Xinhai Revolution.
12. Legislative work from 1949 to 1978 is introduced in Chap. 3 of this study.
13. In this article, the term Deng used is translated literally as 'legal institution' (法制). The idea of 'the rule of law' (法治) officially appeared during the Jiang administration in the 1990s.
14. The quotations are translated from Deng's original text *Emancipating the Mind, Seeking Truth from Facts, Forwarding with Solidarity* (my translation).

References

Chaffee JW (1985) The thorny gates of learning in sung China. Cambridge University Press, Cambridge
Chang WG (1994) Legal education in Qing China. In: Elman B and Woodside A (eds) Education and society in late imperial China. University of California Press, Oakland
Chen XX and Tian ZP (1991) Zhongguo jindai jiaoyu shiliao huibian liuxuejiaoyu/Collected historical materials of China's modern education: overseas education. Shanghai Education Publishing House, Shanghai
Chen YH, Chen XX, and Tian ZP (2007) (eds) Zhongguo jindai jiaoyu shiliao huibian: liuxue jiaoyu/ Collection of historical resources of China's modern history of education: overseas education. Shanghai Educational Publishing House, Shanghai
Cohen PA (1974) Between tradition and modernity: Wang T'ao and reform in late Ch'ing China. Harvard University Press, Cambridge
Deng XP (1978) Jiefang sixiang, shishiqiushi, tuanjie yizhi xiangqian kan/Emancipating the mind, seeking truth from facts, forwarding with solidarity. In: (1993) Deng Xiaoping wenxuan, di er juan/The selected works of Deng Xiaoping, vol 2. People's Publishing House, Beijing
Ebrey PB (1993) Chinese civilization and society: a sourcebook, 2nd edn. The Free Press, Washington DC
Editorial (1977) Xuehao wenjian zhuazhu gang/Mastering the files and grasping the gist. People's Daily 7 February, p.1
Elman BA (2013) Civil examinations and meritocracy in late imperial China. Harvard University Press, Cambridge
Fairbank JK (1983) The United States and China, 4th edn. Harvard University Press, Cambridge
Fairbank JK and Goldman M (2006) China: a new history. Harvard University Press, Cambridge
Feng YL (1952) A history of Chinese philosophy (trans: Derk Bodde). Princeton University Press, Princeton
Fewsmith J (2001) Elite politics in contemporary China. Sharpe, Armonk
Fontana DG (1982) Background to the fall of Hua Guofeng. Asian Survey 22(3):237–260
Franke W (1960) The reform and abolition of the traditional Chinese examination system. Harvard University Press, Cambridge
Gardner DK (1986) Chu Hsi and the ta-hsueh: neo-confucian reflection on the confucian canon. Harvard University Press, Cambridge
Gilpatrick MP (1950) The status of law and lawmaking procedure under the Kuomintang 1925–46. The Far Eastern Quarterly 10(1):38–55
Harding H (1981) Organizing China: the problem of bureaucracy 1949–1976. Stanford University Press, Redwood
Hu FM (1978) Shijian shi jianyan zhenli de weiyi biaozhun/Practice is the only criterion for examining truth. Guangming Daily 11 May, p. 1
Hughes ER (1967) Epistemological methods in Chinese Philosophy. In: Moore C (ed) The Chinese mind. University of Hawaii Press, Honolulu
Ichiko C (1980) Political and institutional reform 1901–1911. In: Fairbank JK and Liu K-c (eds) The Cambridge history of China, vol 11. Cambridge University Press, Cambridge
Ichisada M (1981) China's examination hell: the civil service examinations of imperial China (trans: Schirokauer C). Yale University Press, New Haven
Jin Z (1990) Kejü zhidu yu zhongguo wenhua/The imperial examination system and the Chinese Culture. Shanghai People's Publishing House, Shanghai
Li ZH (1999) The western is the substance, and the Chinese is for application. Contemporary Chinese Thought 31(2):32–39
Li GL (2000) Shen Jiaben zhuang/A biography of Shen Jiaben. Law Press, Beijing
Nathan A (1976) Peking politics, 1918–1923: factionalism and the failure of constitutionalism. University of California Press, Oakland

Nathan A (1983) A constitutional republic: the Peking government, 1916–1928. In: Fairbank JK (ed) The Cambridge history of China, vol 12. Cambridge University Press, Cambridge
Norton-Kyshe JW (1971) History of the laws and courts of Hong Kong from the earliest period to 1898. Noronha and Company, Hong Kong
Overmyer D (1986) Religions of China: the world as a living system. Harper and Row, New York
Pomerantz-Zhang L (1992) Wu Tingfang (1842–1922): reform and modernization in modern Chinese history. Hong Kong University Press, Hong Kong
Schiffrin HA (1968) Sun Yat-sen and the origins of the Chinese revolution. University of California Press, Oakland
Schwartz B (1964) In search of wealth and power: Yan Fu and the west. Harvard University Press, Cambridge
Thompson LG (1988) Chinese religion: an introduction, 4th edn. Wadsworth, Belmont
Tu W-M (1990) The Confucian tradition in Chinese history. In: Ropp PS (ed) Heritage of China: contemporary perspective on Chinese civilization. University of California Press, Oakland
Waley A (1985) The analects of Confucius. Vintage, New York
Wang SH (1972) Gengzi difang peikuan/The local boxer indemnity. Collected Papers of the Institute of Modern History Academia Sinica 3:25–57
Wang YN (1988) Zhongguo dizhu jingji xingtai yu zhongguo guanliao zhengzhi yanjiu, di si juan/Formation of China's landlord economy and a study on China's bureaucratic politics. In: Wangyanan Wenji, vol 4. Fujian Education Press, Fuzhou
Xie BC (2013) Brief history of the official system in China (trans: Chen MR and Wilson AR). Path International, Seattle
Zhang ZD (2017) Quanxue pian/To encourage learning. Blossom Press, Beijing

Chapter 2
Law and Political Economy

Abstract The second chapter sketches the methodological framework for the thesis. It challenges the conventional view of law as an instrument for political will by recapitulating Max Weber's study of the role of formal rational law in the rise of Western capitalism. (2.1) In light of the rising inequalities following China's economic reforms, this section introduces the literature on the economic constitutions of the U.S. during the late twentieth century (2.2), which is undergirded by a review of the literature on the relationship between law and capitalism in this period. (2.3) The chapter ends with a theoretical overview of the role of legal professionals, which Weber considered essential in studying the law. (2.4) Overall, this chapter theoretically clarifies that the relation between law and economy is a complicated matter entailing a context-dependent interpretation.

2.1 Formal Rational Law and the Rise of Capitalism

Admittedly, China's economy has experienced remarkable development since its opening-up reforms. However, this growth was not achieved under the guidance of a finely crafted blueprint. Rather, Deng Xiaoping's words about China's development strategy, 'groping for stones while crossing the river' (Vogel 2011, p. 391),[1] suggest that the ideology behind China's reform and opening-up policy has followed a context-based strategy. It therefore implies the potential of constant policy changes to respond to the transitions of society and the economy.

This contingent economic strategy situated the state and the law at centre stage. Unlike Western democratic societies, which feature the separation of powers, China has a unique one-party-rule political system, where the state holds dominant power over virtually all aspects of social and economic life. Therefore, the political reality sets a somewhat different scene for understanding the relationship between law and the economy. Compared to Western scholarship on this topic, the study of China's case must stress the state's role in order to understand the role of law in China's social and economic transformation.

J. Hu, *The Role of Law in China's Economic Development, 1978–2011*,
https://doi.org/10.1007/978-981-99-9911-8_2

Having laid bare China's economic development strategy and the state's dominant power, one could reasonably speculate that the role of law in the economy would be responsive to the political will in controlling economic affairs. In other words, the shifts in the role of law would be strongly associated with political economic shifts in different stages of economic development. This is where the current study takes an interest and intends to map the dynamics of the coevolution of law and the economy under the directions of the party-state.

Given that China has endorsed Marxist ideology since Mao's era, this analysis employs a structuralist approach and related theoretical framework for methodological purposes. Marxist ideology regarding the role of the state, economy, and law implies that the Chinese government would view the law as a superstructure decided by its material base—the development of the economy. The clarification of China's orthodox political-economic ideology also reveals the government's goes-without-saying attitude towards its instrumental use of the law and the reality that the development of the law in the Chinese context has largely revolved around the transformation of the economy. Before delving into the concrete legal and economic developments over the selected decades, in this chapter, we will first sketch the general contour of the theories relevant to the present study.

As the study takes on issues of the dynamics of law in the context of political economy, it falls well into the field of the sociology of law. On this topic, Max Weber's theoretical accounts of the interrelations between formal rational law and the rise of capitalism offer a structural starting point for uncovering the dynamics of law and the political economy of a given society and therefore could support the structural analysis of China's recent legal and economic codevelopment. Furthermore, Weber's study on the status group indicates legal professionals' defining role in social transformation due to their specialized training and expertise, which directs our attention to the legal education system in which Chinese lawyers were trained.

Empirically, the economic system coupled with formal rational law tends to be governed by a small government or called a laissez-faire economy. Nevertheless, the social and economic ramifications of such alignment were vivid in terms of the rising social complications seen in early-twentieth-century America, which ushered in a substantive turn of law and the rise of the welfare economy. The American transformation therefore presaged, to a certain extent, the story of China. Following China's liberalization of its economy and the formalization of the legal system, Chinese society found itself facing growing social stratification and inequalities, a situation similar to the earlier experience of American society. Therefore, this chapter also touches on the American legal transformation after the heyday of U.S. industrialization as a foil for analysing China's realistic turn of the law in the later stage of its economic reform.

2.1.1 Max Weber in Context

Max Weber wrote widely on the sociology of law in terms of relationships between domination (Herrschaft), law, and the economy. As his study demonstrates, these three spheres are closely related. In particular, the modernization of domination requires an equally modernized legal system to support it, which means that the law must be formal and rational. In a similar vein, the rise of Western capitalism, or the Western style of industrialization, requires a predictable and calculable legal system for support. In this section, the main emphasis is on the theoretical reconstruction of Weber's account of the relationships between domination, law, the economy, and the role of legal professionals in those relationships.

Born in 1864, Weber studied law in Heidelberg and Berlin and wrote his doctoral and habilitation theses on legal history and economics (Ringer 2004, p. 1).[2] The late nineteenth century, when Weber reached his intellectual maturity, was considered the golden age of German Historicism, an intellectual current that witnessed the rise of prominent figures such as Ranke, Dilthey, Rickert, Last, and Simmel, whose writings Weber was believed to have read and been influenced by (Beiser 2011, pp. 511–516).

German Historicism was, epistemologically, a fundamental shift from the Enlightenment. It rejected the paradigm of universality in understanding social, political, and moral issues and regarded the particular social environment in which people lived as relative, changing, and particular (Beiser 2011, pp. 10–13). Therefore, for historicists, contingent and context-dependent factors, such as culture, time, and space, became the primary factors in understanding human actions and societies. This preference for nonuniversal elements in understanding human societies ultimately resulted in a methodological dispute between German historicists and Austrian economists—the *Methodenstreit* at the end of the nineteenth century, also called the Carl Menger and Gustav Schmoller dispute (Louzek 2011).

As an economist, Menger insisted on the necessity of general theory for social studies. He argued that the generalization of social aspects, such as forming general concepts, could help us understand the infinite nature of our society by singling out the particularities of social phenomena and building connections among these factors. Such a general theory, to Menger, was the natural law for understanding. On the other hand, the old historical school refuted Menger's general theoretical approach to social science, considering it too abstract and artificial and arguing that it ignored many aspects of real life. Instead, historicists considered socially constructed concepts to be the reflection of realities (Beiser 2011, pp. 521–527).

Appealing to his neo-Kantian epistemology, Weber disagreed with Menger over his natural law idea of general theory, which Weber perceived as an a priori approach to understanding reality rather than reality per se. In rejecting Schmoller, Weber argued that concepts are not the reflection of things. Rather, concepts are cognitive instruments that we use to understand the world around us, not an end in themselves (Beiser 2011, pp. 521–527).

Eventually, Weber proposed the 'ideal type' to reconcile the divergence between positivism's insistence upon general law and historicism's stress of distinctive aspects of a particular social phenomenon. Thus, the 'ideal type' is a cognitive device that combines the features of general theory and substantive particularities. It is a general theory that can be universally applied while simultaneously addressing social particularities and hence avoiding decontextualization. The goal of the 'ideal type', Weber argued, was to reveal not the general features but the particularities of a specific social phenomenon (Beiser 2011, pp. 544–549). The development of the 'ideal type', hence, constituted Weber's reaction to the intellectual background that he was born into and grew up with; later, it became the critical methodology throughout his studies of types of domination and law in interpreting different civilizations.

2.1.2 Ideal Types of Domination and the Economy

According to Weber, '"[d]omination" is the probability that a command with a given specific content will be obeyed by a given group of persons' (Weber 1978, p. 53). It refers to the situation in which 'the manifested will (command) of the ruler or rulers is meant to influence the conduct of one or more others (the ruled) and actually does influence it in such a way that their conduct to a socially relevant degree occurs as if the ruled had made the content of the command the maxim of their conduct for its very own sake' (Weber 1978, p. 946). Weber's construction of domination was greatly influenced by Jellinek's study of the state (Weber 1978, p. XCIX). To Jellinek, the 'relations of domination', or the social relations of command and obedience, were the basis of the study of the state, and Weber grafted these ideas onto the study of state and economic relationships (Weber 1978, p. XCIX). Integrating his early studies on ancient and medieval polities and economies, Weber formulated his ideal types of domination, namely, traditional, charismatic, and legal domination,[3] and delved into the relationships between political structures and the economy of each type of domination.

2.1.2.1 Traditional Domination and the Economy

Traditional domination refers to the rulership seen in primary societies, which usually apply age-old rules that people believe in or deem sacred or divine. In such societies, the dominators are selected in accordance with traditional rules from which they derive their authority or the legitimacy of their domination. While the masters receive their legitimate status from traditional rules, the dominated show their obedience or loyalty to the ruler(s) rather than to the traditional rules (Weber 1978, pp. 226–227). In other words, once the dominator is designated, the domination relationship between the ruler and the ruled is personal.

In Weber's typology, he distinguished three types of traditional domination according to their organizational structures. In summary, as defined by Weber, patriarchalism is the primitive form of domination in traditional societies that operates without working staff (Weber 1978, p. 231). The key characteristic of patriarchalism is that the dominator receives his rulership status via acknowledged traditions, and the actual domination in such societies 'must definitely be exercized as a joint right … of all members' (Weber 1978, p. 231). That is, the power of the master, to a great extent, is checked by the members of the society, whose political willingness assumes a role in reality.

The other two types of domination in traditional society are prebendalism and partimonialism. They differ from patriarchalism in that they operate with staff and differ from each other in how they support the administrative staff.

When societies are ruled in the form of prebendalism, their administrative staff receive benefices for maintenance (Weber 1978, p. 235). The staff are 'purely personal instruments of the master' (Weber 1978, p. 231), and therefore, the domination operates at the discretion of the master, as does the appropriation of the benefices. As the master controls the administration, the staff and the master form an interpersonal tie, which allows the staff limited autonomy over their benefits and thus security. The extreme form of prebendalism, in which such personal control of staff plays a major role in the master's domination, is called sultanism.

In the domination of patrimonialism, the administrative staff possess greater power, as the discretion of the master is limited to 'selecting his administrative staff', and the staff control the appropriations of positions, the means of administration, and the governing power (Weber 1978, p. 232). In patrimonialism, the staff are supported by 'fief', and their offices can be inherited. In comparison to prebendalism, the staff in a patrimonial domination system enjoy a certain level of property security as well as official positions (Weber 1978, p. 1074).

In a traditional society, domination is established on the basis of particular values per the time-honoured traditions of the given society; these traditional values also impact economic activities. Also important to the traditional economy is the administrative practice of the regime, typical features of which are lack of technically trained impersonal staff with sufficient administrative skills, lack of the formal rational regulations essential for economic calculation, and lack of rules to curb individual arbitrariness, either of the staff or of the ruler, in managing the economy (Weber 1978, pp. 194–199 and 237–239). Furthermore, these regimes typically show a strong tendency towards substantive outcomes, i.e., consideration of particular utility or value, in making economic decisions. Such characteristics of traditional domination impede rational calculation and curb economic dynamics, thus constraining the growth of economic rationality and the rise of capitalism (Weber 1978, pp. 239–240).

2.1.2.2 Charismatic Domination and the Economy

Charismatic domination derives its legitimacy from the charisma of the leader. It is transitional and disappears with the decease of the charismatic leader. As Weber put it, the term 'charisma' applies to 'a certain quality of an individual personality by virtue of which he is considered extraordinary and treated as endowed with supernatural, superhuman, or at least exceptional powers or qualities. … [and is] regarded as of divine origin or exemplary' (Weber 1978, p. 241). This idea was secularized from the Christian church (Haley 1980).[4]

In the ideal type of charismatic domination, the leader is deemed divine by the dominated. Such worship is granted to the leader as an individual. The ruled obey the master because they believe that he possesses some kind of superpower that could lead them to a promising future. It is from such 'belief' that the domination of the charismatic leader is legitimized. In turn, once the leader passes away or is proven incapable of meeting the expectations of the dominated, his charisma disappears or is jeopardized. Therefore, to maintain his domination, the charismatic leader 'must work miracles. ... [And] if the people withdraw their recognition, the master becomes a mere private person...'. (Weber 1978, pp. 1114–1115).

Personal charisma is almost impossible to transfer; hence, the legitimacy of charismatic domination cannot be inherited. Such domination is transitory and can appear in different types of societies, most likely in periods of social transition. Unlike traditional domination, which differs from modern rulership with its administrative structures, the defining feature of charismatic domination is the source of its legitimacy and its noninheritable nature—the obedience in such domination is conveyed to the charismatic leader as an individual, not to the administration. With respect to the organization of the administration, as charismatic ruling can appear in almost any type of society, the structure of the staff has no signature features (Bendix 1967).

In charismatic domination, where personal loyalty dominates the state institution and the operation of society, rationality gives way to emotions. As a result, in economic spheres, decisions are made less on the basis of economic calculations and more on the basis of obedience to the charismatic leader. Therefore, the charismatic authority prevents logical analysis and breeds emotional calculations, a style of thought that stands in opposition to rationality, which is a feature of modern societies and facilitates economic prosperity. Additionally, when an individual assumes centre stage in the domination relationship and there are no preestablished impersonal rules, the risk of arbitrariness rises significantly, as the personal satisfaction of the charismatic leader influences the system of ruling, increasing the difficulty of predicting economic consequences (Weber 1978, pp. 242–245).

2.1.2.3 Legal Domination and the Economy

Unlike the previous two types of domination, in which authority originates from personal relations, legal domination is impersonal. In other words, in legal domination, the dominator, like the dominated, is subject to established rules. The ruled convey their obedience to confirmed impersonal rules, not to the superior as an individual. Moreover, this system differs from traditional domination in that the master in traditional domination also derives his authority from externally established rules, but in those time-honoured traditions, the obedience is to the master as an individual, not to the impersonal rules (Weber 1978, pp. 217–220).

Therefore, to achieve legal domination, a society should possess a preestablished system of impersonal rules or an operative legal order consisting of a set of laws.

However, constructing a legal order does not necessarily lead to legal domination. A legal order suggests the existence of an established rule system that the government applies to the ruled. In addition to the existence of such an order system, legal domination requires a rather subtle element called 'belief'. This means the ruled have faith in the established legal order and recognize its rules as legitimate (Bendix 1977, p. 390).

Given that obedience is granted to impersonal rules, legal domination also features in a peculiar administrative system called bureaucracy. In other words, to achieve legal domination, a society must build bureaus filled with trained technical staff capable of logical and rational conduct. Moreover, unlike the staff maintained in traditional domination systems, the staff in a legal domination system are contract-based free agents. They are trained with particular skills required for operation in such a society. The relationship between the staff and the authority is impersonal because the staff must follow established rules, not personal orders. That is, the staff are responsible and loyal to impersonal rules, not to their superior (Weber 1978, pp. 220–223).

In other words, legal domination is distinct because of its modern legal system and bureaucratic administrative staff, both of which are unimportant in charismatic and traditional domination styles. Moreover, these two key characteristics are crucial to the economy. In fact, the rise of the modern administrative state, as will be discussed below, reveals the close relationship between the domination structure and the economy. Indeed, Weber implied the characteristics of domination that are essential to a capitalist economy—the legal domination equipped with preestablished logical, formal, and rational rules for economic activities and staffed with technically trained personnel—when he negated the economic functions of traditional and charismatic domination systems. These characteristics are indispensable to the rise of the modern capitalist economy because such formal rational rules can institutionalize economic actions and provide calculable guarantees for economic behaviours (Trubek 1972).

A capitalist economy needs a calculable and predictable ruling environment, which means that the traditional and charismatic styles of domination, due to their strong tendency towards arbitrariness and incalculability in rule application, cannot cultivate and boost capitalist economic activities. In contrast, in its reliance on its impersonal preestablished rules, legal domination stands out as the system capable of delivering calculability and predictability to economic actions and, therefore, as conducive to the rise of capitalism (Trubek 1972).

To a great extent, legal domination and the capitalist economy form a reciprocal system: The structure of domination, by and large, is the result of particular economic development stages, but it also influences the advancement of the economy in the given society (Rheinstein 1954, p. 323). In other words, legalism, with its calculable rules, facilitates capitalist activities and therefore provides the foundation for the rise of capitalism. In turn, the capitalist economy, with the strengthening of the power of the capitalist class and the stratification of society, needs the consolidation of the rule of law to maintain the status quo and justifying its economic interests (Horwitz

1977). A case in point is the rise of American legal formalism against the progress of industrialization, which is examined in the following section.

2.1.2.4 The Structures of Domination and the Economy—A Synthetic Comment

It is worth reiterating at this point that although Weber constructed the three types of domination based on his historical studies, these ideal types of domination are conceptual constructs for understanding political structures. Therefore, they are not specific to a certain historical period. They are separate from each other by their own peculiar characteristics, and they overlap, in one way or another, because the characteristics of each ideal type may coexist under certain circumstances (Szelenyi 2016, p. 6). Nevertheless, these conceptual devices are helpful in examining the relationship between the power structure and the economy.

While the basic power structure between the dominator and the dominated remains, the administrative organization that matters to economic activities differs significantly between traditional and legal domination. As mentioned above, the key difference in the administrative structure of the two economies is whether the 'means of administration' are impersonal (Kronman 1983, pp. 64–67).[5] This involves the status of the staff and the nature of the office.

In the traditional economy, the staff have personal loyalty to the master and the office and are in service to loyal or privileged groups. The economy in these societies is usually organized as a household economy, or *oikio* (Kronman 1983, p. 44), which can function without administrative staff, as in patriarchalism, or with personal staff supported by inalienable properties, either noninheritable, as in prebendalism, or inheritable, as in patrimonialism. Whichever form is adopted, the staff and the office are in private relation to the ruler, and the economy exists to satisfy daily wants and 'is rooted in the need to meet ongoing, routine demands' (Weber 1978, p. 1111).

In contrast, legal domination shields the staff from personal relationships, which could minimize the ruler's influence on the staff. Additionally, official duties are separated from private life, which could eliminate the impact of the staff on the official duties so that the staff can work 'without hatred or passion' (Weber 1978, p. 225). Moreover, the scope of power in legal domination is decided not by the incumbent but by impersonal and abstract rules. These characteristics of impersonality, or the exclusion of factors outside official duties, could provide a high level of the administrative predictability and calculability that are essential to profit-oriented economic activities.

Nevertheless, the economically productive formal rational administrative structure, or rational bureaucracy, comes with personal and social costs (Sayer 1991). The cornerstone of Weber's legal domination, widely seen in his treatment of 'definitions, classifications, typologies' in *Economy and Society,* is the feature of formality and rationality (Marcuse 1971, pp. 132–151). The impersonal character of legal domination—treating people impersonally—will rob subjects of individual freedom (Mommsen 1965) and treat concrete human beings in abstract terms—a rational system that is, in effect, irrational (Löwith 1993, pp. 62–67). To a great extent, such a system, if not doomed, has difficulty maintaining its ideal functionalities (Parsons 1942), as substantive concerns always slip in when human beings are involved (Löwith 1993, pp. 62–67). A possible consequence is that traditionalist substantive factors may penetrate the supposedly rational bureaucratic machine (Parsons 1942).

Weber was pessimistic about modernism (Weber 1947, pp.155–156), and such rational bureaucracy, in his eyes, was like 'the shell (also Gehäuse) on a snail's back'—a burden that we cannot live without (Sayer 1991, p. 144). In other words, the pros and cons of modernity that we both enjoy and endure are 'something can be true, although and in as much as it is neither beautiful, nor holy, nor good' (Löwith 1993, p. 72). These impersonal characteristics of legal domination indicate the value-neutrality of the bureaucratic system, which combines with the equally value-free legal system—the formal rational law that makes legal domination possible and hence essential to the modern economy.

2.1.3 'Ideal Type' of Law

The modern Western legal tradition can be traced back to the Gregorian Reform, which led to the separation of ecclesiastical and secular polities and resulted in the systematization of the canon law and secular law systems. The latter, composed of multiple legal sources, such as feudal law, mercantile law, and royal law, after generations of consciously responding to the changing social and economic environment by legalizing customized behaviour patterns, finally emerged as a sophisticated and integral legal tradition grounded in its society (Berman 1983).

The further evolution of law and society led to the emergence of 'legalism', which is regarded as the main critical indicator of modernization (Parson 1966, p. 26). This idea centres the law while measuring the advancement of society, and whether or not it is actually the case, the crucial role of law in social transformation is beyond dispute. By and large, the achievement of legalism is conditional on several factors. Among other things, the law in such a society must assume autonomy, meaning it must be differentiated from other social spheres. Moreover, legal rules in society should supersede other norms systems, such as ethnic or religious values, and the society must be under an administration that responds only to established rules. Additionally, the legal system must be formal and rational and should be logically constructed by trained legal experts (Trubek 1972, pp. 736–739). Such a society tends to be dominated by autonomous legal rules and is commonly considered a modernized society. This section shifts attention to the legal phenomenon in social development and examines the 'formal rational law' that Weber deemed crucial to the rise of Western capitalism.

2.1.3.1 Formal Rational Law

Law is crucial to Weber, as he saw the law as a critical factor in the rise of capitalism in Western societies. Unlike Marx (Collins 1982), Weber did not see the law as a superstructure that reflects the material basis of society. In Weber's account, the relationship between law and the economy has a much broader role, as the law was also involved in the process of industrialization and facilitated the rise of capitalism. However, this role of law in the economy does not imply that Weber assigned economic value to the law. On the contrary, Weber, a neo-Kantian, strongly believed that law as a social fact belongs to the empirical world, and the meaning of the law is subjective and associated with the value system of the person who is involved with the law, either in making or in applying it (Berman 1987).[6] As Weber put it, 'in our context, the concept of law will be defined as an order which depends on an enforcement staff. In other connections, different definitions may well be appropriate' (Rheinstein 1954, p. 6). This distinction between objective fact and subjective value, as described by Kronman (1983), was a 'will-centred', 'positivistic theory of value' (p. 36).

To understand the characteristics of the law that contribute to the capitalist economy, Weber constructed four ideal types of law as projection modes to decipher the role of the law in the rise of European capitalism, thus classifying the legal system into four different types according to its formality and rationality. In his construct, the ideal type of law conducive to the rise of Western capitalism had three characteristics; namely, it was logical, formal, and rational (Weber 1978, pp. 654–658).

Before any further analysis of the four ideal types of law, it is essential to point out that Weber's philosophical idea of the law was that the law should be free of all types of value consideration (Weber 2012), and his concern was for the formal aspects of the law, not the substantive contents. Also crucial is to delineate the two dimensions of the legal model in Weber's discussion. Weber's idea of the law consisted of two sets of characteristics—formal and substantive and rational and irrational; these are determined by how the law was made and found in a given society. Below, we consider the meaning of the two pairs.

2.1.3.2 Formal Versus Substantive

The formal characteristic of the law can be further divided into two kinds. The first type adheres to external, tangible data, i.e., seals, signatures, and particular symbolic performance with fixed meaning. It is called rigorous legal formalism. The other type does relies not on perceptible data for reference but rather on 'logical analysis of meaning', and abstract rules are therefore formulated and applied (Rheinstein 1954, p. 63). On the other hand, the substantive quality of law suggests that laws are made to pursue particular values or ad hoc political, economic, or religious results. Therefore, such a law cannot be universally applied. Moreover, a legal system with substantive quality indicates a low level of social differentiation in which the law is vulnerable to the intervention of external forces and therefore lacks autonomy.

These two types of laws are differentiated by the universality of their application—whether the law can be universally applied to all cases or is applicable only to particular ones. It also implies Weber's idea on the relationships between law and value. To Weber, the law should and could be free of value pursuit in achieving its formal quality (Weber 2012). This type of law emerges in advanced societies that have achieved a high level of social differentiation—the legal system as a separate social system is differentiated from other social spheres, such as economics, politics, and religion. Hence, the formal characteristic of law refers to the autonomy of law, suggesting that laws should be free of the intervention of external forces, such as political power or religion. Moreover, with a high level of formality, the legal system operates without the potential interference of other powers, thereby achieving a high degree of autonomy.

In a legal system with formal characteristics, the lawmaking process is free of external value considerations and therefore is guided by general rules or principles that are themselves the law. In other words, rules outside the given legal systems, such as religious values or particular political concerns, should not influence the formation of the law. The law should consist of general rules that are capable of universal application. In a similar vein, legal decisions should be reached by logically applying abstract rules to concrete cases with deductive reasoning, and in the process of legal reasoning, only general characteristics of facts should be taken into account. In other words, legal decisions should be made according to criteria intrinsic to the legal system, and only general factors of concrete cases should be considered (Rheinstein 1954, p. 63). Thus, factors outside the law, such as political or economic considerations, should not be involved in making legal decisions, and legal decisions should not be result-oriented. This indicates the degree of differentiation of the legal system from other social spheres, such as politics and religion.

On the other hand, in a legal system with a strong substantive propensity, the making of the law tends to be guided by particular external purposes, i.e., in pursuit of rapid economic growth or particular political aspirations. In other words, lawmaking is done to achieve preset goals that are usually intended to achieve specific social or economic results. Therefore, the law probably consists of substantive rules designed to achieve equally substantive outcomes. By the same token, legal decisions are reached by considering particular desired results. That is, particular elements and substantive results of cases are crucial in the process of legal reasoning in a substantive legal system. The specific purpose of the law oftentimes plays a role in reaching legal decisions. Alternatively, considerations outside the law, if relevant to the purpose of the law, can influence the lawfinding process.

2.1.3.3 Rational Versus Irrational

The rationality of the law depends on whether it can be understood intellectually. In the Weberian system, the rational quality of the law depends on its predictability and calculability in performing relevant actions, and the degree of rationality depends on how, in a legal system, laws are made and applied (Rheinstein 1954, pp. 61–64).

Rationality indicates that the activities in a legal system, either lawmaking or lawfinding, are guided by rational considerations and constituted by general rules. Generality indicates that the laws are composed of general, not ad hoc, rules, which can be applied to all related cases. These contrast with rules made by prophetic revelation, oracles, or ordeals, which are considered irrational or beyond the control of human reason. Rational-legal thought, associated with characteristics such as logic and consistency, tends to 'proceed upon the basis of general principles and maintain consistency in avoiding contradictions within itself' (Rheinstein 1954, p. liv).

Hence, a rational-legal system is composed of abstract legal principles or propositions derived from a process of generalization from concrete cases by means of reduction and sublimation—a process that moves from particularities to generalities and thus achieves universality (Rheinstein 1954, pp. 62–63).

Explicitly, when the law is made under the guidance of general rules, not rules beyond intellect or reason, such as ordeal or oracle, and insofar as the contents of the law are composed of intellectually understandable rules, the law should be regarded as rational. In a similar vein, rational-legal decisions are those reached by logically applying abstract rules to concrete cases via deductive techniques. In contrast, when legal decisions are made arbitrarily or emotionally, without conscious and logical reasoning, or when they are based on ethical or political considerations outside the law, the application of the law should be regarded as irrational. Rationality is crucial to Weber's concept of law because it provides predictability and calculability to the law, which is conducive to economic activities.

In addition to the two pairs of attributes, Weber emphasized the 'logical' feature of the law, which indicates the internal quality of the legal system (Rheinstein 1954, pp. 198–223). This concept has two strands of meaning: the internal coherence of the legal system and the use of legal reasoning as a technique. The legal system, to be logical, must be consciously constructed by trained legal specialists with the help of systematic and logical techniques, and legal decisions should be made by logical deductions based on established rules or principles. While 'logical' is connected with 'formal' and 'rational' as one of the critical elements of Weber's ideal type of Western law, it differs from the other two in that it refers to a certain level of technique that is indispensable in achieving the formal and rational characters of law. Therefore, the emergence of a logically constructed legal system is conditioned on the existence of a group of highly skilled legal experts, a topic that will be discussed in Sect. 2.4.

2.1.3.4 The Four Ideal Types of the Law

With the above understanding of the two sets of key concepts of Weber's idea of law, it is time to decompose his four ideal types of law, which are built by different combinations of the above two pairs of characteristics. The four types of law, as Weber presented them, are logically formal rational law, formal irrational law, substantive rational law, and substantive irrational law.

Formal irrational law refers to legal situations in which the process of lawmaking or lawfinding adopts means that are beyond intelligent control (Rheinstein 1954,

p. 63). For instance, oracles, instead of general rules, are an integral part of the rule system and are referred to as criteria for making legal decisions. Irrationality could also emerge in a regime under charismatic rule, where personal emotion supersedes rational calculation. Hence, while the rules in such a system are to some extent formal, they are beyond intellectual reasoning and thus unpredictable and incalculable. On the other hand, substantive irrational law indicates a rule system that applies factors from outside its system, and other considerations, such as ethical, religious, or political factors, are weighed and used to reach legal decisions (Rheinstein 1954, p. 63). This differs from formal irrational law in that the rules applied in concrete cases are not general norms that are free of any particular considerations external to the rules in use. Weber referred to ancient Chinese law as an example (Weber 1978, p. 818) and described it as '*khadi justice*' (Marsh 2000, p. 294).

Rational-legal activities can be formal or substantive, according to the norms they are based on. Thus, the system would be called formal if the legal activities are based on general rules and substantive insofar as the norms are ad hoc (Rheinstein 1954, p. xlviii). Hence, substantive rationality occurs when the rule system is composed of particularistic or not general universally applicable norms. In such a system, legal decisions are made by considering factors that are external to the law, for instance, utility or emotional reasons (Rheinstein 1954, pp. 63–64).

Formal rationality exists when lawmaking and lawfinding are based on general and abstract norms derived from the process of generalization and proceed through means that are conscious, reasonable, and therefore intellectually knowable, as in modern European law. A formal rational-legal system considers both substantive and procedural law, viz., both kinds of law are conceived in a general manner so they can be universally implemented and determined. In Weber's words, legal activities are logically formal and rational insofar as 'the legally relevant facts are determined in the process of logical interpretation of the meaning and as fixed legal concepts are thus created and applied in the form of strictly abstract rules' (Rheinstein 1954, p. xlix).

If Weber's account of the four ideal types of the law is not too immense and obscure to construe, it appears elusive and difficult to draw boundaries between different pure types. While the four types are structurally clear, the meanings of formal and rational sometimes overlap (Kronman 1983, p. 79), and the distinction between formal and substantive characteristics is relative (Rheinstein 1954, pp. 61–65).

In his philosophical recounting of Weber's work, Kronman pointed out that the confusion of Weber's classification of the four ideal types of law arises because Weber tried to use two pairs of characteristics to describe, in fact, three kinds of distinctions among the many different types of legal thought (Kronman 1983, p. 79). The three variables he identified in Weber's idea of law are as follows: the nature of the law, which distinguishes legal systems that stress general rules from those that emphasize particular decisions; the basis of legal decisions, with different legal systems that employ 'the logical interpretation of meaning' or 'adhere to external characteristics of the facts' (Kronman 1983, p. 79); and the autonomy of the legal system, which separates legal systems that divide law and morality from those that merge them (Schwartz 1984; Trubek 1985). Therefore, it is clear that when a legal system is made up of general rules, it applies a 'logical interpretation of meaning' in making legal decisions and distinguishes legal norms from nonlegal ones (Kronman 1983, p. 79). This is what the Weberian system of logical, formal, and rational implies.

As mentioned, Weber made a clear distinction between fact and value, and law, as value-free fact, possesses no intrinsic value itself. The above introduction explains why Weber preferred formal rational law to other types of legal thought for modern society. Nevertheless, a legal system hollowing intrinsic values would appear vulnerable to manipulation by whatever power triumphed in a specific time and space. The history of the American legal transformation and the U.S. enthusiasm for legal formalism hence offered fertile soil for reviewing the theoretical construct of Weber's sociology of law in particular and the role of law in the economy in general.

2.2 Legal Formalism and the Laissez-Faire Economy

Since an abstract account of Weber's sociology of law is somewhat decontextualized, let us now turn to the coevolution of law and the economy during the era of American industrialization (approximately the 1850s through the New Deal), which is a typical case for examining the dynamics of the rise of legal formalism and economic transformation.

In the United States, throughout the nineteenth century, the law transformed from an instrumental role in promoting mercantile ends in the antebellum period to a facilitating role for framing an apolitical image of the law in relation to the economy against the backdrop of industrialization (Horwitz 1977). In the late nineteenth century, the formalistic turn of the law ultimately backfired because it was out of touch with social reality and was criticized by progressive scholars who advocated a realistic turn of the law.

While it is a country-specific legal history, the legal evolution of U.S. society is a worthy reference for countries undertaking fundamental economic transformations. Moreover, the concerns expressed by legal realists in facing the social and economic aftermath of the outreach of legal formalism also provide a critical perspective on Weber's endorsement of formal rational law.

2.2.1 The Political and Economic Foundations of Formalistic Law

On its path towards independence, American society was immersed in ideas such as 'the Laws of Nature', liberty and consent as well as equality (The Declaration of Independence 1776). The Lockean liberal ideas expressed in the Declaration of Independence formed a shared understanding that the government was a 'night watchman' staying vigilant to protect individual rights rather than intervening without consent

(Locke 1698). Referring to Locke's idea of consent, Alexander Hamilton wrote, '[n]o laws have any validity or binding force without the consent and approbation of the people' (Hamilton 1961, p. 105). Furthermore, in Number Ten of the Federalist, Madison depicted the 'tyranny of the majority' and proposed a form of government that would be controlled by procedure, expressing an ideal of constructing a stable and legal regime by controlling mass democratic powers. This political vision was later translated into the U.S. Constitution and legal institutions and shaped the common ideal of the state being a passive protector and refraining from unwanted intervention. This was an affirmation of legal institutions after overthrowing the old social order established by the British Empire.

American society throughout the nineteenth century was guarded by the 'small state' and experienced its heyday of industrialization—a period often called the Gilded Age. It was also the time when American society experienced an all-encompassing transformation from an economic structure to one of immigration and urbanization: Technologies and production modes advanced against the backdrop of industrial transformation (Nichols and Unger 2017), and this advance was followed by a high demand for unskilled workers. The increase in wages (Long 1960, p. 144) attracted an influx of millions of immigrants from Europe and China (Chen 2000)[7] between the 1870s and 1920s (Archdeacon 1984; Martin 2010). The economic expansion resulted in substantive social and economic differentiation as income inequalities were entrenched by the economic structure (Fraser 2015; Zinn 2005). The concentration of economic capital was transmitted to the accumulation of political capital, and to prevent the redistribution of wealth, the winners of industrialization managed to institutionalize their wealth by reshaping the law to entrench their economic interests (Horwitz 1977).

Although different from Weber's continental legal system, the legal formalism in the common law system also proved to be crucial to capitalist industrialization. The transformation of the American economy and legal system explored by Horwitz demonstrates that American law in the early nineteenth century favoured substantive justice in economic activities by adopting a paternalistic and protective law to guarantee individual justice. Nevertheless, when the instrumental paradigm of the law could no longer serve the interests of the economically advantaged, their demand for legal services shifted to consolidating their vested economic interests via a politically neutral legal design. The capitalist class hence pursued legal formalism (Horwitz 1977).

In a substantive approach, Horwitz traced the transformation of the law through the lens of the distribution of wealth and power in American society and argued that the entrepreneurial and commercial groups that had benefited from instrumentally wielding the law for their economic and political interests (Horwitz 1977) had adopted a formalist approach to law and the economy by the end of the Civil War. This shift helped the wealthy entrench the status quo of social differentiation and guarded American society through the Gilded Age (Horwitz 1977, pp. 253–254). With the transformation of the legal system, the economic relationships between disproportionate groups were legally institutionalized. As a result, American legal formalism strengthened the interests of the economically and politically powerful by granting them more extensive discretion in legal interpretation—an endeavour to further entrench the economically disadvantaged group (Horwitz 1977, pp. 253–266).

Nevertheless, Horwitz's thesis on law and economic transformation sparked a flurry of scholarly criticism. For instance, Novak (1996) argued against the instrumental view of law and claimed that the law in the prewar era was used in an orderly manner by the government 'for the common good' (p. 13). Equally opposed to Horwitz's economic interpretation of the law was Karsten's writing. In his *Heart versus Head*, Karsten (1997) sided with judges, contending that their judgements were produced either by English precedent or by following their religious beliefs; neither involved pursuing economic results for the elites. However controversial the motivation of lawyers and the judiciary regarding the role of law in the economy, the dominant role of formalist law in postbellum America's laissez-faire economy is not in dispute. The dominance of legal formalism coincided with the thriving free-market economy in American history, suggesting an internal mechanism between formalistic law and the laissez-faire economy.

2.2.2 Legal Formalism in the Context of the Laissez-Faire Economy

As mentioned, in justifying the Declaration of Independence, Thomas Jefferson appealed to the 'law of nature' as the source of law, which served as the dominant legal thought in eighteenth-century America (Wilson 1967, pp.126–147). In other words, American legal thought, from the foundation of the nation through the many decades to come, was underpinned by divine or higher laws that appeared to be natural and universal. The assumption of God's law or higher law became the foundation of 'the immutable maxims of reason and justice' (Dickinson 1766, p. 4). This is crucial in that divine law, unlike secular norms, is much more resistant to change owing to its transcendent characteristics and therefore helped entrench the then prevailing legal concepts and rationales.

The legal thought formulated in the antebellum period was conventionally called classical legal thought or legal formalism; this period was also termed laissez-faire constitutionalism (Hall 1989, pp. 190 and 222), meaning the idea that legal provisions should not bear value tendencies and should stay impartial (Siegel 2002, p. 632). Wiecek (1998) defined classical legal thought as 'a way of thinking about law ... [as] abstract, formal, conceptualistic, categorical, and (sometimes) deductive' (p. 4). These abstract and general legal concepts would facilitate maintaining concept-oriented legal reasoning under a value-free façade—a systematic legal system capable of logical reasoning without appealing to substantive factors nor opting for particular substantive results, at least on the surface. Hence, the formalistic legal system presented the law as a kind of 'science' that was neutral and had nothing to do with value and politics.

The 'scientific' transformation of the American legal system was, first, a reaction to the then chaotic writ system. Inherited from the British legal tradition, the American legal system initially operated with an action-form-based writ system (Nelson 1979, pp. 69–88). The decline of the writ system took place around the mid-nineteenth century (Nelson 1979, pp. 69–88); during the second half of the nineteenth century, the American legal system was reformulated on the basis of more general and categorical legal concepts (Horwitz 1992). The legal treaties and literature that emerged during this period became more systematic and abstract by eliminating elements that were considered contradictory to a systematic legal approach (Horwitz 1992, pp. 12–13). For instance, the introduction of contract law was organized under the idea of 'will', and rules revolved around general categories referring to components of contractual behaviours (Horwitz 1992, Chap. 2).

The building blocks of a formalistic legal system consist of highly abstract legal concepts, or, to use Kennedy's term, the 'conceptual apparatus' (Kennedy 2006, p. ix). These general categories of legal concepts then facilitate the unique legal reasoning process, which is also called categorical thinking. In the judicial process, these highly sublimated legal concepts and principles are measured to reach judgement without considering specific results. Hence, the judicial process is also referred to as lawfinding rather than lawmaking, and in a legal procedure, the substantive consequence of a case is not the court's concern (Kennedy 2006, p. ix). In other words, legal procedure outweighs substantive consequences in legal formalism.

Nevertheless, such legal thinking is accused of reductionism, as it eliminates substantive factors of concrete cases in legal reasoning—a form of detachment from reality. Moreover, such formalistic legal reasoning implies that legal principles and laws at the time are universally applicable and objectively scientific without time and space concerns. Hence, it generates a legal perception that law is absolute and certain (Wiecek 1998, p. 11); it strips the law of its social trappings and structures the supposedly socially mobile rules into a rigid framework that denies the socially evolutionary nature of the law (Wiecek 1998, pp. 12–14).

The rise of legal formalism was accompanied by the idea of a neutral state and a laissez-faire economy (Hoyos 2013, pp. 86–104). Formalistic law was the way to legitimize political and economic arrangements by delinking politics from the law—making the law a 'neutral arbiter' that did not take sides in economic life (Horwitz 1992, p. 9). The economic parallel to the liberal neutral state was the classical laissez-faire economy, prevailing through the rise of American industrialization. As mentioned above, the free-market economy in nineteenth-century America resulted in the simultaneous concentration of wealth and the stratification of American society, which contributed to the formation of groups with unequal economic and political power—the economic elites and the common people (Horwitz 1992). Under the paradigm of legal formalism, even if a society faces class polarization, a neutral state remains hands-off and does not intervene to rebalance differentiated groups.

In economic terms, a neutral state helps maintain the status quo and refrains from addressing economic inequalities and social consequences. Such political-economic ideology certainly suits the wealthy group, as they enjoy the upper hand in social and economic interactions with the working class. As a result, the formal impartiality of the nonintervening state, in effect, favoured those economically and politically advantaged groups by turning a blind eye to unequal social and economic consequences (Horwitz 1992, pp. 20–27). Such liberal political ideas gripped American society from the founding of the nation until the age of the New Deal (Hartz 1983).

While legal formalism put a neutral veil over the state, the immediate economic outcome of applying formal law revealed its biased nature. A revealing case of the use of formal law to neutralize the state's role in protecting the rich was *Pollock v. Farmers' Loan and Trust Co.* (1895). By invalidating the Wilson-Gorman Act, the supreme court accepted the concept of direct and indirect taxes and took the side of the wealthy group. To this judicial decision, Justice Brown wrote his dissenting opinion that 'the decision involves nothing less than the surrender of the taxing power to the moneyed class' (Pollock v Farmers' Loan and Trust Co. (1895) 158 U.S. 601).

2.2.3 *The* Lochner *Case—The Pinnacle of Legal Formalism*

The idea of legal formalism travelled to its extreme when, in the case of *Lochner v. New York* (1905), general legal propositions were upheld at the cost of detaching the law from the very soil where it is supposed to take root. In summary, the New York Bakeshop Act (1895) set maximum working hours for bakers, while Lochner, an owner of a bakery, was found to employ bakers to work more than the limited hours, hence violating the state law (Lochner v New York (1905) 198 U.S. 45). In this case, one controversy was whether the New York state regulation for the working hours of bakers violated the rights of freedom of contract that were guaranteed under the Fourteenth Amendment of the U.S. Constitution. In the judgement, the majority of the judges held that the state law was 'an arbitrary interference with the freedom of contract' (Lochner v New York (1905) 198 U.S. 45).

Justice Holmes opened his dissenting opinion by pointing out that the case was 'decided upon an economic theory which a large part of the country does not entertain' (Lochner v New York (1905) 198 U.S. 45). This view was again powerfully expressed by Pound in his *Liberty of Contract,* in which he argued that in an age where giant corporations had assumed disproportionate economic power, 'to every one acquainted at first hand with actual industrial conditions', the academic theory of 'equal rights' behind the freedom of contract was a fallacy 'in the fact of practical conditions of inequality', and the legal thought behind it was 'an individualist conception of justice, which … exaggerates private rights at the expense of public right' (Pound 1909, P. 457). The judgement was considered to be an instance of judges, under the influence of laissez-faire economic thought, actively seeking favourable economic results for enterprises (Benedict 1985, p. 295; Soifer 1987, p. 250). The formalistic legal reasoning, in this case, was vividly exemplified by the judges applying a formal abstract legal proposition to the case in a mechanical manner; although case particularities, such as the long working hours, would harm bakers' health, they were not considered a relevant factor in making the decision.

In this case, freedom of contract represents the legal institution that proclaims free economic transactions under the norm of 'will' and in which the state should not intervene. This is a general interpretation of contractual freedom, which guarantees the universal and impartial application of the form of contract regardless of the actual situation of each party—the law, therefore, gained a neutral and apolitical façade. Under this rationale, the *Lochner* case was decided. Nevertheless, behind the pursuit of contractual freedom was the laissez-faire ideology of political economy that took capitalist society to its apex, where the minimum role of the state was advocated. On the economic front, the idea of a 'small state' situates the government in a place where it is better to leave the market to regulate itself. However, as Holmes put it, 'general propositions do not decide concrete cases', and under legal formalism, judges enjoy the leeway to interpret abstract rules creatively (Lochner v New York (1905) 198 U.S. 45).

2.2.4 The Crisis of Legal Formalism

The formal rational law proclaimed by Weber assumes the central stage of legal development in modern society, as this is deemed the hallmark of modernization (Parsons 1966). The concept of the autonomy of law or autonomous law can essentially be traced back to Weber's emphasis on the law's internal qualities and its insulation from the society in which the law is embedded. In the Weberian system, the law achieves its external functions, i.e., facilitating economic activities, via the perfection of its internal qualities, namely, being formal and rational. His belief in the clear division between the law and value thus prevented him from considering social needs in building the link between formal rational laws and the rise of capitalism.

As mentioned above, in the Weberian system, bringing external considerations, whether political or economic, into the law would ultimately undermine the law's external functions because such considerations would reduce the law's generalities and thus diminish its universal character. Worse still, by stripping the law of its formal character, the key ability of the law to facilitate economic activities, substantive concerns would intrude into the process of legal reasoning and eventually open the law 'to manipulation by various interests' and reduce 'its predictability' (Trubek 1986, p. 590). Thus, the ideal type of law that Weber acclaimed, logical, formal, and rational, is a closed system that is not responsive to society's appeals. In other words, it is a legal system that prevents particularities or values from penetrating its inner structure and therefrom achieves an autonomous status in society. However, the pursuit of internal qualities of the law put the law in peril, as two types of crisis can emerge in such a rigid autonomous legal system.

First, while the lawmaking process can cut out value pursuit and constitute a formal system through technical strategies, such purity is impossible to achieve in applying the law to concrete cases (Kennedy 1976). The formal and rational characters of law in Weber's system are not two separate features but are mutually dependent. Law's formal character ensures a certain level of rationality, as excluding particularities from the law guarantees its predictability and calculability. However, as discussed above, a pure type of formal law cannot, in reality, be immune to substantive concerns. The application of law in real life inevitably brings in substantial considerations. That is, the very nature of law's formality in turn reduces its formality. This inner paradox of formal law invites the following inquiry: If some element of substantiveness is unavoidable, perhaps a more practical concern is how, or at what stage, substantive elements can be injected in a way that best serves the integrity of the law.

Moreover, the more formal the legal system appears to be, the greater leeway is left to individuals who wield the power to apply the law. The system therefore grants individuals the power to apply personal values or interest considerations in making legal decisions and hence undermines the predictability and calculability that are essential to the formal system that Weber held dear (Kennedy 1976). It has been argued that the Weberian formal rational-legal system without inherent value pursuit actually maximized the liberty of individuals in applying rules, as within such a value-free legal system, individuals who hold vital political or economic capital can more easily gain the upper hand and inject their personal values while applying the laws; however, this freedom is not equally distributed to all parties in the society. Therefore, such a formal rational-legal system, in effect, puts the majority in a less free position and is vulnerable to coercion in a 'formal legal' disguise. Such liberty invites inequality, especially in authoritarian domination systems, as Weber noted:

> a legal order which contains ever so few mandatory and prohibitory norms and ever so many "freedoms" and "empowerments" can nonetheless in its practical effects facilitate a quantitative and qualitative increase not only of coercion in general but quite specifically of authoritarian coercion (Weber 1978, p. 731).

While Weber endorsed formal rational law as the hallmark of modernity, he likened formal law to bureaucracy, which creates an 'iron cage', empty of meaning and emotion, like 'a shell of bondage which man will perhaps be forced to inhabit someday, as powerless as the fellahs of ancient Egypt' (Weber 1978, p. 1402).

Second, the nonresponsiveness of the law to external social needs puts the law in danger of being socially irrelevant. Formal rational law stands out with its calculability and predictability for the propensity to facilitate economic activities. While its rigidity serves modernization and marks legal modernity, its inflexibility ushers in fragmented substantive rationality due to constant responses to changing social and economic needs. Additionally, a formalist legal system has structural deficiencies that ultimately erode its integrity when substantive considerations unavoidably penetrate the formal rational mode of law.

2.3 The Socially Responsive Law and the Welfare Economy

2.3.1 *The Rise of the Administrative State*

At the turn of the twentieth century, American society had evolved into an unequal economy, with giant corporations possessing economic power that dwarfed smaller businesses and labourers. Laissez-faire economic thought supports a self-regulated market and prefers that the state remain neutral and refrain from intervention. However, reflection on the naturalness of the market came with force in the early twentieth century; the work by Robert L. Hale (1923) was seminal.

The very idea underscoring the classical laissez-faire approach was challenged by Hale's claim (1923) that the economic system under 'laissez-faire is, in reality, permeated with coercive restrictions of individual freedom, and with restrictions ... out of conformity with any formula of "equal opportunity" or "preserving the equal rights of others"' (p. 470). Hale's criticism strongly questioned the premise of the laissez-faire economy by demonstrating that the market economy was not a spontaneous order and that transactions were coercive due to the unequal property and entitlement held by each party. By stripping the market of its façade of voluntariness, Hale revealed the artificial nature of the economic system—the market as a social construct was formed by institutions with hidden coercive powers.

When the nature of the economic system was revealed, the role of the state in economic affairs could no longer be hidden under the name of neutrality. Surfacing with the role of the state was the mechanism between government and the economy as well as the role of law in the scenario. While the scope of the administrative state could be much broader, this study focuses on its relation to economic affairs, on which the administrative state was mainly divided over the regulation of public interests or business interests (McCraw 1975).

The state's intervention in social affairs, economic or not, expanded during the Progressive Era (late nineteenth century), as Americans tempered their fast-changing society following industrialization, urbanization, and immigration (Grisinger 2013, pp. 368–369). These economic and social transformations led government to intervene in the form of issuing regulations for railroads, immigration, social welfare, etc. (Grisinger 2013, pp. 368–369). This tendency culminated in the New Deal era, which marked a significant shift in the state's role in economic and social life (Hartz 1983). The growing role of the state surfaced in the bureaucratic system and governmental agencies that made and administered economic policies. Hence, new tensions ushered in questions such as how the regulative state would shape its policies and what would impact its decisions.

The aforementioned dichotomy of the public and business interests of the administrative state in economic areas was of particular concern in later decades, especially when the state's involvement in social life was constantly found to be manipulated by interest groups. These concerns then drew attention to legitimacy issues regarding administrative agencies and procedures; both rose along with the expanding influence of the state (Grisinger 2009). Ultimately, as concerns over administrative procedures accumulated, the U.S. legally institutionalized the power of administrative officials by enacting the Administrative Procedure Act in 1946.

2.3.2 *The Realist Critique of Formalism*

Parallel to the changing role of the state was the evolution of legal thought. Culminating in the *Lochner* ruling, the formal justice endorsed by classical legal thought was criticized as 'the violence... hidden in abstractions' (Menand 2001, p. 440) and failed to deliver substantive justice. A tide of progressive legal thought attacked classical legal thought for its static nature and nonresponsiveness to social reality, arguing that the law had lost track of society (Hovenkamp 1995). The idea of social Darwinism was raised, as were concerns about reforming society to help individuals live better lives (Hovenkamp 1995).

The failure of legal formalism to respond to changing social and economic needs was, in fact, entrenched in its abstract norms and pattern of reasoning. Decades of formalistic legal tradition had cultivated generations of legal professionals with an orthodox legal mentality who saw law and legal reasoning as an autonomous field that differed from political ideology (Horwitz 1992, p. 193). The idea of separating the law and social values was under attack by legal realism, an intellectual current that proclaimed that the law should consider social concerns (Freeman 2014, pp. 823–839).

Before the *Lochner* case appeared before the Supreme Court, Justice Holmes, by criticizing legal formalism, suggested the separation of law and politics and pointed out that the law has social roots (Holmes 1897). Soon after the *Lochner* ruling, in 1909, Pound led a movement that advocated a sociological understanding of the law, or 'sociological jurisprudence', arguing that the law should be connected to society and made more responsive to social needs (Pound 1909). Later, he criticized the mechanical application of formal law to concrete cases without considering the social consequences (Pound 1910).

By tracing the processes and elements that influenced judicial decisions, Justice Cardozo noted in *The Nature of the Judicial Process* (1921) that the law is not transcendental and was deeply rooted in the society where it grows. Echoing Holmes's idea that 'the life of the law has not been logic; it has been experienced' (Holmes 2009, p. 3), Cardozo commented that '[a judge] must get his knowledge just as the legislator gets it, from experience and study and reflection; in brief, from life itself' (Cardozo 1921, p. 113). By tracing changes in the American economic transformation and law, legal historian Morton Horwitz also concluded that 'the development of law cannot be understood independently of its social context' (Horwitz 1992, p. II vii).

Going beyond the dichotomy of legal formalism and realism, Brian Tamanaha suggested that judicial decisions were made under the impact of social and political position as well as the law's own logic, from which he proffered a 'balanced realism'—taking into consideration aspects of both legal formalism and realism (Tamanaha 2009, p. 197).

2.3.3 The Substantive Turn of the Law

Legal realism aims to make the law more responsive to societal needs. However, opening legal boundaries to substantive concerns risks dragging the law into the abyss of substantiveness, which is similar to Weber's ideal type of substantive rational law (Rheinstein 1954, pp. 63 and 303). To address the tension between the integrity and openness of legal institutions, Philippe Nonet and Philip Selznick (2001), in *Law and Society in Transition: Toward Responsive Law*, proposed a model called 'responsive law'.

As formal law retreats from responding to social needs and therefore protects its integrity, it pays the price of insulating itself from the society in which it is embedded. It also retreats from the role of active social control by eliminating its function of being socially responsible. In contrast, responsive law takes responsibility as a social force for actively reacting to external social needs. To avoid blindness and degeneration into legal opportunism, responsive law uses the 'purposiveness' of the law as guidance for its openness (Nonet and Selznick 2001, p. 78).

Hence, the key to responsive law lies in the design of a mechanism that can mediate the integrity and the power of the law. To do so, first, the 'purpose' of the law must be institutionalized. In one account, for 'purpose' to mediate the tension between the law's integrity and openness, the law's purpose must first be generalized (Nonet and Selznick 2001, pp. 78–79). The 'generalization of law's objectives' makes the law flexible in responding to social needs and grants more discretion in making legal decisions. Moreover, eliminating 'artificial reasons' facilitates legal rationalization. Additionally, it prevents officials from hiding behind the rules and holds them accountable (Nonet and Selznick 2001, pp. 82–83).

A key mechanism in bridging general goals and specific objectives is the interplay between the principle and the rules of the law. Rules must constantly be updated to ensure their social relevance, and principles offer guidance for updating rules. This interplay of rule and principle therefore maintains the integrity of the law and opens the boundary of the law to make it responsible. This internal mechanism between rules and principles, or the ability to 'translate general purposes into specific objectives', also helps the purpose of the law gain authority (Nonet and Selznick 2001, pp. 80–83).

To meet the purposive requirement of the law, legal institutions, as the rule makers, must remain open to external social needs. This requires the law to be competent in the face of social changes and thus to make itself socially relevant. Moreover, it refers to the second key element of responsive law—procedural concerns, or 'legal and political participation' (Nonet and Selznick 2001, p. 95). Procedural concern emphasizes activeness in the legal process in reacting to social needs. In such an institutional arrangement, private groups or special-purpose institutions, those formerly excluded from the process of lawmaking, receive legal entitlement, which grants them the right to bring public concerns, i.e., environmental policies, to legal forums, such as courts. By doing so, these groups are made capable of legally challenging existing rules and thus opening the legal process to rule-changing. In addition, legal institutions should be capable of self-correcting when facing unlawful or unjust situations (Nonet and

Selznick 2001, p. 107). This involves a quest for new legal skills, namely, the 'articulation of principles of institutional design and institutional diagnosis' (Nonet and Selznick 2001, p. 111).

This process of participation put the legal order to the test by requiring the law to be capable of informing 'itself of the range of issues and interests it affects, … the ability to comprehend the group structure of society' (Nonet and Selznick 2001, p. 98). Ultimately, responsive law calls for the competence of legal institutions, by either lawmaking or lawfinding, for the law must contribute and respond to social needs (Nonet and Selznick 2001, p. 56). Purposive reasoning breaks the boundary of formal legal reasoning, which builds law into empirical science. The government in this model of responsive law assumes dual roles, both as a political actor to decide what goals to pursue and resources to assign and as a legal actor to establish institutions and mechanisms to fulfil the above goals (Nonet and Selznick 2001, pp. 112–113).

Nevertheless, the responsive model, as Teubner pointed out (1983), overly emphasized the internal dynamics of the law and paid little attention to the external dimensions—the mechanism of the law's interaction with other social systems. He considered this the major deficiency of the 'responsive law' model and argued that while responsive law captures the central part of modern sociolegal development, it might not be, as Nonet and Philip Selznick asserted, an advanced stage of legal development. Instead, it may potentially be a temporary stage of legal development (Teubner 1983, pp. 246–257).

2.4 The Role of Legal Professionals

As Weber argued, the rationalization of the law and the legal system entails specialized legal knowledge. This understanding convinced him that legal professionals, rather than economic or other social factors, should directly shape the law (Weber 1978, p. 776), and specialized training is essential for legal professionals to acquire the knowledge to apply complicated legal rules and principles (Rheinstein 1954, pp. 198–223; Weber 1978, pp. 775–776). In other words, the character and development of the law depend primarily on the character of legal professionals, as individuals and as a group.[8] Furthermore, the law and legal professionals could form a closed circle from which the specialized legal group, with their legal training and expertise and exclusive legal knowledge, could technically prevent legal nonspecialists from influencing legal affairs (Weber 1978, pp. 302–307).

Naturally, the significant influence of legal professionals on the formulation and application of the law thus positioned legal education—specifically the type of legal education—as the starting point from which to learn the characteristics of the law in a given society. Thus, in his account of legal training, Weber discussed two types: the law as a science and the law as a craft, referring to theoretical training and practical training, respectively.

Weber believed that the character of the law is directly connected with the type of legal education that legal professionals receive. In his discussion of the types of legal education, Weber attributed the legal rationality that he perceived in the continental legal system to the legal training that was common there and thought of the guild-like common law training style as the stark counterforce in rationalizing the law (Rheinstein 1954, p. 202). In other words, to Weber, whether the legal system in a given society was formal and rational was closely related to the form of legal education offered in that society.

Following Weber's idea about legal training, this section is devoted to two distinct styles of legal training: the practically oriented common law tradition and the academic style of legal training that prevails in civil law systems. The discussion dwells mainly on two aspects of legal study: the characteristics of legal concepts and the style of legal reasoning. These aspects are the critical pillars of legal education.

2.4.1 Characteristics of Empirical Legal Training—Law as a 'Craft'

Taking the English legal tradition as an example, Weber asserted that guild organizations could not offer 'rational-legal training or theory' and therefore could by no means cultivate formalistic legal thinking (Rheinstein 1954, p. 202).

Starting from the historical background of the emergence of the 'attorney', Weber sketched the rise of a specialized group, attorneys, that was conditioned upon the procedural rationalization of the loyal court in the medieval age. From this point, Weber established the link between forming a particular professional group and the skills that were exclusive to it.

He stated that the type of legal training that is purely empirical and monopolized by guild organizations, as taught by lawyers via practice, produces legal concepts, and the style of legal thinking associated with this training has distinctive characteristics of specialization.

Legal concepts formed through practising in particular cases would ineluctably be substantive in nature. Such characteristics of the legal concept are decided by the process of how it is derived. Case law reasoning starts by comparing cases to identify the similarities and differences between them. In this process, the result of such comparison is the emergence of the 'legal concept' if it is accepted (Levi 1948, part II). Hence, the legal concept in the common law tradition was born in the process of case comparison by the courts in searching for appropriate terms.

The legal concepts so formed feature external substantive concerns and are ready for change if needed, such as to serve the interests of different clients (Rheinstein 1954, p. 201). As a result, the legal system filled with substantively oriented legal concepts tended to be fragmented, which, in turn, prevented the formation of a systematic system of legal knowledge and a comprehensive understanding of the law.

The nature of the legal concept and the legal system it formed impacted the process of legal reasoning, which, in the common law tradition, characteristically starts from precedent and employs analogy to reach legal decisions (Levi 1948).It thus features a process 'from the particular to the particular' (Rheinstein 1954, p. 202). As such, no commitment is made to draw general legal propositions from particular cases (Rheinstein 1954, pp. 201–202).

Taken together, with nonabstract legal norms and analogy-dependent legal skills, the law and the legal system have a large margin of flexibility in use. They hardly experience a rationalization process, which is indispensable in shaping modern formalist law. In such a system, legal practice is concerned with client utility or substantive results. Furthermore, with practitioners assuming a central role as legal educators, the economic concern is always present in influencing the current contents or form of the law (Rheinstein 1954, pp. 202–203). Furthermore, the legal professionals thus trained who formed a web of legal knowledge consisting of substantive legal concepts and became adept at analogical analysis would benefit most if codification of the law were prevented. Any adaptation of the form of the law would require legal practitioners to renew their received legal training. As it happened, English lawyers did indeed successfully prevent codification (Sunderland 1926). In other words, the law and the legal professionals formed an interest group, as opposition to formalization of the law would best serve the interests of practice-oriented legal professionals, and the characteristics of legal training as such ensured the character of the law—a 'reproduction' effect of education on the law, to borrow Bourdieu's term (Bourdieu and Passeron 1977).

2.4.2 Characteristics of Academic Legal Training—Law as 'Science'

Whereas the monopoly of legal training in a guild-like system is in the hand of lawyers, universities hold the door to the profession of law in the civil law tradition. In such a system, practical training in the law, while still a necessary step in accessing the legal profession, retreats to a secondary place. Two key aspects in university legal training stand out in contrast to craft-like legal training—the formality of legal knowledge and the reasoning mode or thinking style for legal issues that is an essential precondition to rationalization of the law.

As in craft-like legal training, two key aspects are essential to the rationalization of the law—the teaching of legal concepts and the cultivation of rational-legal thinking. The former teaches rigorous and abstract legal concepts, which are, in turn, the critical ingredient for the development of formal rational reasoning skills. Hence, the two parts are interdependent and evolve synchronously. Together, they facilitate the process of the rationalization of the law.

Legal concepts taught by academic training, usually monopolized by universities, are often based on carefully crafted textbooks. The concepts thus taught tend to be uniform and rigorous. Nevertheless, the character of uniformity guarantees that the legal concepts will be consistently understood and applied in legal practice. Moreover, the feature of rigor can ensure the scientific and logical use of legal concepts. These characteristics of the legal concepts in academic legal training, as Weber noted, can be attributed to the original purpose of compiling these books (or the sacred books in Weber's example). The purpose is not to teach practical legal skills but to sustain 'the needs of the uninhibited intellectualism of scholars' (Weber 1978, p. 789). Therefore, these concepts are usually highly abstract.

These highly abstract norms are the primary starting point for forming logical, systematic legal thinking. Ideally, law students taught to understand and apply abstract norms tend to apply these concepts in their thinking, which is key to shaping their propensity for formal and rational-legal reasoning. To a certain extent, they are prone to produce abstract ideas in handling concrete cases, which, in turn, facilitates their subsequent rational and systematic thinking style.

A legal system that consists of abstract and rigorous legal concepts and entails logic and rational-legal reasoning could eliminate the influence of external substantive factors on the formulation of laws. The same effect could also apply to the field of legal practice. Consequently, the abstract and rational nature of the law, in addition to where it is embedded in a systematic legal system, could facilitate a wide range of applications of the law in social life (Weber 1978, p. 789).

Indeed, abstract reasoning entails real-world examination. The exact role of legal professionals, whether they are trained in practice or university, can be determined only when we examine reality. Similarly, the role of law in China's economic transformation cannot be well understood by pure theoretical speculation or by merely drawing from other countries' experiences. To form a contextualized understanding of China's legal and economic transformation since 1978, one must obtain an overview of society and the economy prior to the reform.

Notes

1. The term could also be translated as 'crossing the river by feeling the stones', which contains a slightly different meaning than Vogel's translation but is closer to the original Chinese meaning.
2. His doctoral thesis was entitled *The History of Commercial Partnerships in the Middle Ages* (1889) and his Habilitation was titled *Roman Agrarian History and Its Significance for Public and Private Law* (1891).
3. Arguably, there were four types of domination in Weber's discussion, and the fourth is the 'will of the dominated'. See Szelenyi (2016).
4. Weber's sociological use of 'charisma' is believed to be indebted to Rudolph Sohm's discussion of the charismatic organization in his *Kirchenrecht*; for a short account, see Haley (1980).
5. 'Means of administration' was regarded as an extension of Marx's means of production in relation to economic production. For a philosophical discussion of the term, see Kronman (1983).
6. Weber's sharp distinction between fact and value in law was well elucidated in Berman (1987).
7. Chinese labourers were concentrated primarily in California. However, their willingness to accept low wages angered workers of other ethnic origin and finally led to Congress passing the Chinese Exclusion Act in 1882, which banned Chinese labourers from entering the US.

8. Weber's methodology of individualism would inevitably lead him to place the role of the individual at the centre in this process. However, in light of the development of modern psychology, group conscience is a factor that one cannot afford to ignore if the issue is to be discussed with rigor. However, this topic is beyond the scope of this thesis.

References

Archdeacon TJ (1984) Becoming American: an ethnic history. Free Press, New York
Beiser F (2011) The German historicist tradition. Oxford University Press, Oxford
Bendix R (1967) Reflections on charismatic leadership. Asian Survey 7(6):341–352
Bendix R (1977) Max Weber: an intellectual portrait. University of California Press, Oakland
Benedict ML (1985) Laissez-faire and liberty: a re-evaluation of the meaning and origins of laissez-faire constitutionalism. Law and History Review 3(2):293–331
Berman HJ (1983) Law and revolution: the formation of the western legal tradition. Harvard University Press, Cambridge
Berman HJ (1987) Some false premises of Max Weber's sociology of law. Washington University Law Quarterly 65(4):758–770
Bourdieu P and Passeron J-C (1977) Reproduction in education, society and culture. Sage, Thousand Oaks
Cardozo BN (1921) The nature of the judicial process. Yale University Press, New Haven
Chen Y (2000) Chinese San Francisco, 1850–1943: a trans-pacific community. Stanford University Press, Redwood City
Collins H (1982) Marxism and law. Oxford University Press, Oxford
Dickinson J (1766) An address to the committee of correspondence in Barbados. William Bradford, Philadelphia
Fraser S (2015) The age of acquiescence: the life and death of American resistance to organized wealth and power. Little, Brown and Company, Boston
Freeman MDA (2014) Lloyd's introduction to jurisprudence, 9th edn. Sweet and Maxwell, London
Grisinger JL (2009) Law in action: the attorney general's committee on administrative procedure. Journal of Policy History 20(3):379–418
Grisinger JL (2013) Law and the administrative state. In: Hadden SE and Brophy AL (eds) A companion to American legal history. Wiley, Hoboken
Hale RL (1923) Coercion and distribution in a supposedly non-coercive state. Political Science Quarterly 38(3):470–494
Haley P (1980) Rudolph Sohm on charisma. The Journal of Religion 60(2):185–197
Hall KL (1989) The magic mirror: law in American history. Oxford University Press, Oxford
Hamilton A (1961) The farmer refuted. In: Syrett HC and Cooke JE (eds) The papers of Alexander Hamilton 1768–1778, vol 1. Columbia University Press, New York
Hartz L (1983) The liberal tradition in America: an interpretation of American political thought since the revolution. Harcourt Brace Jovanovich, San Diego
Holmes OW (1897) The path of the law. Harvard Law Review 110(5):991–1009
Holmes OW (2009) The common law. Harvard University Press, Cambridge
Horwitz MJ (1977) The transformation of American law 1780–1860. Harvard University Press, Cambridge
Horwitz MJ (1992) The transformation of American law 1870–1960: the crisis of legal orthodoxy. Oxford University Press, Oxford
Hovenkamp H (1995) The mind and heart of progressive legal thought. Iowa Law Review 81(1):149–160
Hoyos RJ (2013) Beyond classical legal thought: law and governance in postbellum America, 1865–1920. In: Hadden SE and Brophy AL (eds) a companion to American legal history. Wiley, Hoboken

Karsten P (1997) Heart versus head: judge-made law in nineteenth-century America. University of North Carolina Press, Chapel Hill
Kennedy D (1976) Form and substance in private law adjudication. Harvard Law Review 89(8):1685–1778
Kennedy D (2006) The rise and fall of classical legal thought. Beard Books, Washington DC
Kronman AT (1983) Max Weber. Edward Arnold, London
Levi EH (1948) An introduction to legal reasoning. The University of Chicago Law Review 15(3):501–574
Lochner v New York (1905) 198 U.S. 45
Locke J (1698) Two treatises of government. Laslett P (ed) (1988). Cambridge University Press, Cambridge
Long CD (1960) Wages and earnings in the United States, 1860–1890. National Bureau of Economic Research, Cambridge
Louzek M (2011) The battle of methods in economics: the classical methodenstreit – Menger vs. Schmoller. The American Journal of Economics and Sociology 70(2):439–463
Löwith K (1993) Max Weber and Karl Marx. Routledge, London
Marcuse H (1971) Industrialization and capitalism in the works of Max Weber. In: Stammer O (ed) Max Weber and sociology today: explorations in interpretative sociology. Harper and Row, New York
Marsh RM (2000) Weber's misunderstanding of traditional Chinese law. American Journal of Sociology 106(2):281–302
Martin SF (2010) A nation of immigrants. Cambridge University Press, Cambridge
McCraw TK (1975) Regulation in America: a review article. Business History Review 49(2):159–183
Menand L (2001) The metaphysical club. Farrar, Straus and Giroux, New York
Mommsen W (1965) Max Weber's political sociology and his philosophy of world history. International Social Science Journal 17(1):23–45
Nelson WE (1979) Americanization of the common law: the impact of legal change on Massachusetts society 1760–1830. Harvard University Press, Cambridge
Nichols CM and Unger NC (2017) A companion to the gilded age and progressive era. Wiley, Hoboken
Nonet P and Selznick P (2001) Law and society in transition: toward responsive law, 2nd edn. Transaction Publisher, Piscataway
Novak WJ (1996) The people's welfare: law and regulation in nineteenth-century America. University of North Carolina Press, Chapel Hill
Parsons T (1942) Max Weber and the contemporary political crisis I: the sociological analysis of power and authority structure. Review of Politics 4(1):61–76
Parsons T (1966) Societies: evolutionary and comparative perspectives. Prentice Hall, Hoboken
Pollock v Farmers' Loan and Trust (1895) 158 U.S. 601
Pound R (1909) Liberty of contract. The Yale Law Journal 18(7):454–487
Pound R (1910) Law in books and law in action. American Law Review 44(1):12–36
Rheinstein M (1954) Max Weber on law in economy and society. Harvard University Press, Cambridge
Ringer F (2004) Max Weber: an intellectual biography. University of Chicago Press, Chicago
Sayer D (1991) Capitalism and modernity: an excursus on Marx and Weber. Routledge, London
Schwartz NL (1984) Max Weber's philosophy. The Yale Law Journal 93(7):1385–1398
Siegel SA (2002) The revision thickens. Law and History Review 20(3):631–638
Soifer A (1987) The paradox of paternalism and laissez-faire constitutionalism: United States Supreme Court, 1888–1921. Law and History Review 5(1):249–279
Sunderland ER (1926) The English struggle for procedural reform. Harvard Law Review 39(6):725–748
Szelenyi I (2016) Weber's theory of domination and post-communist capitalism. Theory and Society 45(1):1–24

Tamanaha BZ (2009) Beyond the formalist-realist divide: the role of politics in judging. Princeton University Press, Princeton

Teubner G (1983) Substantive and reflexive elements in modern law. Law and Society Review 17(2):239–285

Trubek MD (1972) Max Weber on law and the rise of capitalism. Wisconsin Law Review 1972 (3):720–753

Trubek DM (1985) Reconstructing Max Weber's sociology of law. Stanford Law Review 37(3):919–936

Trubek DM (1986) Max Weber's tragic modernism and the study of law in society. Law and Society Review 20(4): 573–598

Vogel E (2011) Deng Xiaoping and the transformation of China. Harvard University Press, Cambridge

Weber M (1947) Science as a vocation. In: Gerth HH and Mills CW (eds) From Max Weber: essays in sociology. Routledge, London

Weber M (1978) Economy and society: an outline of interpretive sociology (eds: Roth G and Wittich C). University of California Press, Oakland

Weber M (2012) The "objectivity" of knowledge in social science and social policy. In: Bruun HH and Whimster S (eds) Max Weber: collected methodological writings. Taylor and Francis, Oxfordshire

Wiecek WM (1998) The lost world of classical legal thought: law and ideology in America 1886–1937. Oxford University Press, Oxford

Wilson J (1967) The law of nature. In: McCloskey RG (ed) The works of James Wilson, vol 1. Harvard University Press, Cambridge

Zinn H (2005) A people's history of the United States. HarperCollins, New York

Chapter 3
The Economy and the Rule System Before the Reform

Abstract This chapter provides a broad-brush account of China's economic and legal transformations prior to Deng Xiaoping's opening-up strategy. It reviews how the Chinese economy evolved from a decentralized economy to a centralized socialist economy in the 1950s, the subsequent radical acceleration of industrialization via movements such as the Great Leap Forward and the People's Commune, and the failure of these campaigns that ultimately triggered the disastrous ten years of the Cultural Revolution. (3.1) The second part of this chapter outlines the legal development in this period. It appears that the legal system at the time was a mixture of political orders, party resolutions, and administrative directives following the abolishment of the Six Codes promulgated by the Kuomingtang (KMT). Likewise, rather than professional judges, the courts were overseen by Party cadres who were tasked with crushing counterrevolutionaries, mimicking the Soviet style. (3.2).

3.1 Political Economy from 1949 to 1976

The People's Republic of China was established upon a unique political and economic structure in a messy economic situation with underdeveloped infrastructures due to years of warfare (Feuerwerker 1983, pp. 28–127; Zhang 1986a).[1] It was a society that combined a thousand years of a centralized bureaucratic ruling tradition with a semifeudal and semicapitalist political structure that resulted from constant defeats in wars with Western powers since the mid-nineteenth century (Fairbank 1953; Zhang 1993).[2] This hybrid political structure was also reflected in the economy. China's economy by then was a mixture of many somewhat different economic components (Perkins 1975). First, the feudal economy was still dominant (Myers 1980; Xie 2013).[3] This was primarily because China had a large number of poor peasants who were mostly landless and thus were economically and physically tied to landlords or rich peasants who possessed large amounts of land. In 1949, agriculture still accounted for over 80% of China's economy (Ma and Sun 1981, p. 103). Second, foreign capital represented a significant portion of the economy following the opening up of coastal cities as a consequence of successive military defeats since

J. Hu, *The Role of Law in China's Economic Development, 1978–2011*,
https://doi.org/10.1007/978-981-99-9911-8_3

the First Opium War in 1842; thus, foreign capital poured into China through the mid-nineteenth century.

Also operating in China at the time were bureaucratic capital and national capital, with the former developed under Kuomingtang (KMT) rule and the latter struggling for decades to compete with foreign and bureaucratic capital (Chen 1964; Coble 1986; Wilbur 1984).[4] In addition, throughout the country, numerous craftsmen were working as 'individual entrepreneurs' who represented a non-negligible economic force. These very different economic components coexisted in China for decades until a new regime came to power in 1949 (Perkins 1975; Xu and Wu 2003, p. 731).

Externally, the international environment of the time was unfriendly to China due to ideological differences and its intervention in the Korean War in 1950. Since 1950, the U.S. had enforced an embargo against China, which was joined by other Western powers in 1952 and was not lifted until 1972.[5] Therefore, in the initial years of reorganization, the Chinese government faced a much-constrained international economic environment and a domestic economic structure that conflicted with its socialist ideology.

To build China into a socialist country, the government had to fundamentally reinstitute these coexisting multiple economic components. However, given the internal and external economic difficulties, the socialist transformation could not proceed all-out from the beginning. Hence, the government took a few years to rebuild the country ideologically and economically.

3.1.1 Reorganizing the National Economy, 1949–1952

As briefly introduced above, to transform the highly diverse economic structure into a socialist one, the new government had three primary tasks in the early years, by and large: nationalizing the most significant economic segments to lay the foundation of the national economy; restructuring the financial sector to curb the hyperinflation resulting from years of warfare; and reforming the land system nationwide to equalize landownership (Cheng 1982; Eckstein 1977; Lyons 1987).

Regarding the national economic system, the new government's first step was to restore it by targeting the bureaucratic capital left by the KMT government and foreign capital. When the so-called New China was built, crucial components of China's national economy were foreign capital, bureaucratic capital, and national capital. The first two initially were important to the Party because they held the largest share of the economy, functioning as the lifelines of the economy (Dong 1996, p. 29).[6] To nationalize them, the new government deployed two different strategies.

First, regarding foreign capital, the authorities' strategies could be summarized as 'forcing out'. As mentioned above, foreign capital had been entering China since the mid-nineteenth century. Due to their privileged status under international treaties and their better financial situation,[7] foreign capitalists had mostly controlled the industries that were significant to the country, including heavy industry; public transportation, such as railways, airlines, and waterways; and some light industry, such as the food and textile industries (Wu 1955). In other words, foreign capital had penetrated and controlled multiple sectors of the Chinese economy. It was estimated that it constituted, in total, 71.6% of China's industrial capital before the Second World War (Wu 1955, pp. 105–107). To force out foreign capital, the Party ostensibly allowed these businesses to operate as usual. However, the privileges they had obtained under previous international treaties were eliminated. Additionally, heavy restrictions and taxes were imposed upon them, making it difficult to run businesses profitably. Consequently, some applied to close their corporations; others transferred their assets to the authority, often without compensation.

Second, a direct confiscation policy was applied to so-called bureaucratic capital. Two major components formed China's bureaucratic capital—national monopoly capital and part of foreign capital that the KMT had confiscated from Japan after its surrender in 1945. Like foreign capital, bureaucratic capital enjoyed a wide range of control over certain economic sectors, from the financial sector and heavy industry to light industry and public transportation (Wu 1955, pp. 27–29). On the eve of the Communist Party's declaration of victory in the Civil War, these KMT-owned enterprises accounted for two-thirds of China's total industrial output (Xue 1960, pp. 27–29). The Communist Party started confiscating these enterprises immediately after it assumed control in Beijing, and by the end of 1952, together with foreign capital, they had been acquired by the new regime and thus became the cornerstone of New China's national economy.

Another major task in this period was to reform the financial sector, which was extremely urgent given that high inflation had been engulfing China for over a decade and reached a devastating level when the new leaders were seated in Beijing (Chen 1949, pp. 29–31; Zhang 1986a). Although the Communist Party had inherited the national banking system left by the KMT, the fundamental task of reforming the financial system was nationalizing numerous private banks. It was reported at the end of 1949 that 446 private banks existed in six major cities in mainland China (Cheng 1963, p. 63), and it took the new government several steps to accomplish the task.

The first step was to withdraw state funds from private banks and deposit them in the Central Bank of China (the People's Bank). This approach pushed many private banks to bankruptcy, and consequently, more than half of them had disappeared by the end of 1950 (Cheng 1954, p. 42). Later, another array of privately owned banks closed after the government implemented the requirement to increase the capitalization ratio, which many private banks found impossible to do. The remaining banks, which usually had a relatively sound financial foundation, were encouraged or, more precisely, pressured to form a joint operation with state banks, a proposal that was put forwards in a joint conference attended by different financial parties and convened by Party authority in August 1950 (Central Finance and Economics Committee 1950, pp. 358–361). Hence, by the end of 1952, all of these private money houses had merged with state banks and been formed into five units under the name 'joint administration'.[8] However, notwithstanding the superficial title of 'joint administration', the top directors were all high-ranking cadres of the People's Bank of China, which had, in effect, prevented private entities from operating anywhere in the entire banking sector (Cheng 1954).

The third crucial task that the authority accomplished in this period was land reform (Shue 1980; Wang 1988).[9] The reason for undertaking the reform was, as Liu Shaoqi, the then vice president of the PRC, pointed out, 'the extreme unreasonableness of China's land system' (Liu 1950, p. 254), and the purpose of the reform was to redistribute the land and eradicate the landlord class from China (Liu 1950, pp. 251–268). Hence, as announced by Article 1 of the Land Reform Law, the basic ideology behind the movement was to abolish 'feudal exploitative landownership'. In general, the reform had two key aspects: reallocating the ownership of land and other farming properties and reshuffling the class status of peasants.

The overall strategy of the land reform was first to classify the peasants, according to the amount of land they owned, into four categories, namely, landlords, rich peasants, middle peasants, and poor peasants (Government Administration Council 1951, pp. 92–108). According to some field investigations, the combined number of landlords and rich peasants accounted for less than 10% of the total rural population, yet they possessed 70–80% of the total land (Liu 1950, p. 254). Therefore, the critical step of the reform was to confiscate land and other farming assets, such as draught animals and agricultural implements, owned by the landlords and rich peasants. These properties were then redistributed by local authorities among landless poor peasants—those defined as middle and poor peasants. It was announced, however, that a limited share of land would be allowed to landlords and rich peasants for their own livelihoods (Oi 1989).[10] After the reform, over 300 million peasants equally shared 46,667,000 hectares of land (Liao 2008, p. 38).

3.1.2 The Socialist Transformation, 1953–1956

After the preliminary rearrangement of the national economy, the next goal of the Party was to accomplish the promise it had made to the Chinese people to build a socialist economy. From 1953 through 1956, a nationwide movement called the socialist transformation of the means of production engulfed both rural agricultural economies and urban industrial and commercial businesses (Cheng 1982; Eckstein 1977; Lyons 1987). This movement had three major economic components in China: agriculture, craftsmanship, and national capitalists—those left untouched in the first round of the reorganization. This transformation was the most sweeping structural adjustment to the economy that happened in New China within its first three decades; upon completion, it had effectively wiped out the whole class of Chinese capitalists. More crucially, unlike the previous years of the nationalization movement, it was backed by the 1954 Constitution and thus legally transformed the entire Chinese economy into a socialist one (Article 5–10).

3.1.2.1 The Agricultural Sector

This movement started in the agricultural sector. The rural area by then had just finished its first movement – land reform. The immediate beneficiaries of the land reform were the great majority of middle and poor peasants, who constituted over 90% of the rural population (Xue 1960, p. 2) and had formerly been landless or owned only minimal amounts of land but now possessed shares of land equal to those owned by the previous landlords and rich peasants (Land Reform Law 1950, Article 10). As one can imagine, achieving a national-level equitable division of land among all Chinese peasants meant that land boundaries had to be redrawn and parcels divided into small pieces for allocation. As a result, arable land was extremely dispersed into the hands of millions after the reform. Despite all the happiness of acquiring land, many peasants eventually found that their minimal farming knowledge and lack of implements greatly hindered their farming activities (Xi 1992, p. 61). Poor agricultural production performance thus followed very soon. This situation could not be tolerated by the authority, given that poor agricultural outputs would hinder China's pace of industrialization, and it was against this backdrop that rural China started the next stage—collectivization reform.

A gradual approach was adopted to change this situation. 'Gradualism' here implies that in this transformation, peasants gradually lost control of landownership and farming tools. Step by step, China's individual farming was transformed into collective farming (Friedman et al. 1989, Chaps. 8–9). The strategy was first to pool land, facilities, and labour by organizing mutual aid teams (MAT), which usually consisted of three to five households. This was the initial stage of collectivization, for, naturally, as its name reveals, it was a form of organizing individual peasants to work together. However, each peasant involved in the MATs still held the title to their land and implements (CCCCP 1951, p. 452; Shue 1980). Later, this system developed into the lower agricultural producers' cooperatives (APC), a higher stage of collectivization. At this stage, although the peasants still had landownership in name, they lost actual control over their land, draught animals, and other farming assets, which became the property of their related cooperatives. These pooled means of production were used collectively, and as compensation, peasants could receive certain dividends according to their shares of land and implements as well as the labour they contributed (Standing Committee of the National People's Congress 1955, p. 303). In the final stage, which was called advanced APCs, the peasants who joined the advanced APCs were asked to transfer the ownership of their land and major farming equipment to the APCs, and each was allowed to keep only a small private plot for subsistence purposes. Dividends were abolished because the peasants no longer held the title to their properties. Remuneration was paid according to the amount of labour that each peasant contributed (Regulation of Advanced Agricultural Cooperatives 1956, Article 30–38). Thus, by the end of the agricultural transformation, peasants had lost their ownership of the means of production and become wage labourers in a sense. The transformation was initially implemented in stages. However, by 1955, this gradual approach had accelerated, and rural China finished its socialist transformation by the end of 1956, with over 96.3% of rural households having joined either MATs or APCs and 87.7% of them belonging to advanced APCs (Xue 1960, p. 147).

3.1.2.2 Craftsmanship

Another branch of the transformation took place in craftsmanship between 1953 and 1956. Although it was a less significant element in China's economy than agriculture and capitalist industry and commerce, its total contribution to China's economy was still worth the attention of the authority. It was estimated that in the early 1950s, approximately ten million craftsmen were working individually (some were individual households), contributing over ten billion *yuan* to the national economy (Zhu 1953, pp. 550–554). A complete socialist transformation of the nation would have to incorporate this army of private craftsmen. To eliminate private ownership and establish collective ownership, the authority first had to group them. However, unlike the agricultural and capitalist industries, craftsmanship in China, as an individual economy, was scattered throughout the whole country. Therefore, it was not an easy task to organize and pool these workers together and socialize them collectively (Xue 1960, pp. 54–99). Thus, the approach applied to this group was mainly the use of propaganda and persuasion to guide craftsmen to join cooperatives voluntarily; these strategies were supplemented by offering financial support and preferential policy treatment (Liu 1953, pp. 559–564). The transformation strategy featured three steps towards gradually eliminating and transforming private ownership into collective ownership, as in the agricultural sector.

The most primitive stage involved 'supply and marketing groups', which generally comprised three to five households (Liu 1953, pp. 559–564). It was a primitive stage of cooperation in that each household within the group enjoyed a wide range of freedom in the process of production. For instance, production was still organized within families or apprenticeships, as it had been previously. Each unit also enjoyed freedom to purchase raw materials. The ownership of tools and other productive implements was still largely private, although some equipment, such as large machines, was collectively owned. Production could be organized for state orders, or self-marketing could be performed by each unit. The distribution of profits could be conducted through unified accounting within the whole group, or each household could account for its profits and losses. Overall, freedom throughout the whole process of production was the key feature of the 'supply and marketing groups', which guaranteed that they would be easily accepted by craftsmen. Thus, the first stage was smoothly carried out.

After the first stage of collectivization was completed, what followed was developing these groups into 'supply and marketing cooperatives', which differed from the previous form in several aspects. First, circulation was controlled. Raw materials, production processes, and sales in this stage were no longer the prerogative of each household. Instead, they had to buy raw materials from state-run agencies and sell finished products to them afterwards. In other words, production itself was no longer under private control. Second, the cooperatives started to operate as independent entities possessing properties such as machines and tools. Third, membership in these cooperatives was no longer open to households only; individuals were allowed to join under their own names. Thus, the former family-based structure of production began to wane. Nevertheless, the process of production was still primarily undertaken separately, with only a few exceptions (Xue 1960, pp. 85–99).

The most advanced form of collectivizing craftsmen was 'handicraft producer cooperatives', where membership was open only to individuals. As the final stage of the transformation of the trade, the means of production were entirely collectively owned. That is, private ownership was abolished, production was centrally organized according to state plans, and unified accounting and labour-based profit distribution were widely applied (Dong and Wu 2011, pp. 225–226). At this stage, production was wholly intertwined with state-owned enterprises operating under the planned economy. By the end of 1956, 91.7% of craftsmen in China had been absorbed into some form of handicraft cooperative (Zhou 1959, p. 36), and the output value of this sector constituted 9.1% of the gross output value of industry and agriculture and 16.6% of the total industrial output value (Zhu 1957, p. 5).

3.1.2.3 The National Capitalist Economy

The most obvious branch of the socialist transformation was privately owned industrial and commercial enterprises, which accounted for the most significant share of the urban economy after the Party had addressed foreign and bureaucratic capital. National capitalists,[11] as mentioned above, were one of the components of China's capitalist economy when the Party came to power. In contrast to the fate of foreign and bureaucratic capitalists, who either had their assets confiscated or fled from China in the first three years, national capitalists were relatively 'lucky' and were protected by the regime when the other two types of capital had been eliminated. However, protection was never a long-term strategy for national capitalists (Mao 1950, pp. 223–226).[12] 'Utilization, restriction, and transformation' were the concrete steps and approaches to dealing with the national capitalists laid down officially in the 1954 Constitution (Article 10).

'Utilization' was the strategy applied from 1949 until the end of the Korean War in 1952. It was characterized by placing production orders with private enterprises and purchasing finished products from them later. Thus, private enterprises survived, and some even thrived. The state also benefited from a secure material supply and an expanded pool of revenue. This was particularly helpful to both parties during the Korean War, as the increasing demand for military supplies brought private enterprises huge profits, and the state secured its military materiel. As a result, from 1949 to 1952, the output value of private industrial enterprises increased by 54%, and retail sales of private commerce enjoyed 20% growth (Xue 1960, pp. 108–109).

However, when the war was drawing to a close in 1952, the strategy of 'restriction' was implemented (Bo 1997, pp. 166–189). The adoption of the utilization policy in the early years was driven by a need for economic and political stability when the regime had just come to power. However, when the land reform in rural areas and the financial reform in the urban sector ended, the economic and political situation of the regime had become relatively stable. By the end of 1951, misconduct by national capitalists was widely reported (Bo 1997, pp. 166–167), and the policy towards private enterprises was changed. A campaign named Five Antis soon followed, with ostensible justifications such as combating illegal activities conducted by capitalists. The movement intended to combat the 'five evils' conducted by national capitalists, namely, bribery, theft of state property, tax evasion, cheating on government contracts, and stealing state information (Bo 1997, p. 170). During the campaign, in nine major cities, over three-fourths of the private enterprises that were investigated were found to be guilty of some sort of misbehaviour (Bo 1952, pp. 152–153). Consequently, hefty fines were imposed upon them. Through this campaign, a large amount of private capital (liquid assets) was diverted into government pockets, contributing greatly to the increase in government revenue in 1952 (Bo 1953, pp. 32–52; Teiwes 1979). Unable to shoulder the financial burdens of the huge fines, many private enterprises ran out of capital to continue operating, and their fate was thus sealed. For those that made it through the Five Antis movement, the follow-up policy was 'buying off'.

The previous two stages, utilization and restriction, had still been the elementary stage of socialization. The fundamental transformation started in 1954 with the use of a strategy that combined political pressure and the 'buying off' policy. In this stage, the actual takeover of private enterprises was carried out in two aspects: capital and personnel. First, formerly privately owned enterprises became public–private joint ventures by liquidating private capitalists' assets and investing state capital. Second, in addition to controlling a large portion of shares, government officials were assigned to top positions in these enterprises and thus in practice controlled their daily management, production, and personnel (Government Administration Council 1954, p. 390). The real owners, the former national capitalists, held insignificant positions allocated by the government and thus lost control over their enterprises. The unfolding of the movement first took place in individual enterprises one by one. In 1956, in the nationwide atmosphere of accelerating the socialist transformation, the transformation of national capital started to be carried out on a trade scale—one trade after another was transformed collectively. By the end of 1956, over 99% of private enterprises had been transformed into government-controlled joint ventures. The trade-wide transformation was completed by 'paying off' the national capitalists. First, the total value of the holdings of private capitalists was assessed (State Council 1956a, pp. 108–110), and they were then paid by the state at a fixed interest rate (ranging from 1 to 6%, depending on each case's particular situation) on their shares for ten years (State Council 1956b, pp. 106–107). This payment came from the net revenue of the transformed enterprises, and when the payments ended, the business owners lost their enterprises entirely to the state (Xue 1960). Thus, in effect, the whole class of national capitalists had been wiped out by the eve of 1957.

At the end of 1956, the state claimed the complete success of socialism over capitalism. By 1957, 97.5% of peasant households had joined cooperatives, 90.2% of craftsmen had become part of collectives, and the ratio of the output value of public industrial enterprises accounted for 99.9% of the economy (Xue 1960, pp. 147–148). This was the period in which China welcomed its relatively successful economic reformation. Even though the majority of Chinese people had lost their ownership of the land and the means of production to the state, the overall economic performance in this period was improved.

3.1.3 The People's Commune and Great Leap Forward, 1958–1962

Paralleling the socialist transformation was China's first economic Five-Year Plan (hereafter FYP, 1953–1957), a relatively successful economic plan that was followed by major disasters (Eckstein 1977, pp. 191–200). As a socialist country, China was under the direct influence of the Soviet Union, which was reasonable because the two countries shared common ideologies associated with socialism (Clubb 1971; Ellison 1982). China adopted the Soviet mode of economic development and strongly emphasized industrial development, especially heavy industry. The general goal of the first Five Year Plan was 'to concentrate on the industrial construction that was centred on the 156 construction units that were facilitated by the Soviet Union ...., to build a preliminary foundation for the socialist industrialization...' (National People's Congress 1955, pp. 354–355). It was claimed that the economic plan was a great success (Editorial 1958a, p.1), and the just-finished and equally successful socialist transformation gave the Party leaders, especially Mao Zedong, great confidence. They became bold enough to push the economic reorganization to a higher stage, aiming at rapidly transforming China from an agrarian society into a socialist industrial society (Editorial 1958a, p.1). Mao Zedong launched a movement called the 'Three Red Banners' in 1958. The three red banners referred to the General Line of socialist construction, the Great Leap Forward (GLF), and the People's Commune. The General Line was intended to rally the Chinese people to 'go all out, aim high, and get greater, faster, and better economical results to build socialism' (Liu 1958, p. 263). Following such extreme zeal, however, were waves of economic turmoil and disasters.

3.1.3.1 The People's Commune

In August 1958, the Central Committee of the Party (CCCCP) passed a resolution on issues concerning building the People's Commune. It claimed that 'the form of Agriculture Production Cooperatives which usually consisted of a few dozens or hundreds of rural households, could no longer fulfil the demand for commune life of the people' (CCCCP 1958a, p. 385). Hence, it was inevitable that large-scale People's Communes would develop to combine people's economic, social, and political lives (CCCCP 1958b, p. 520; O'Leary and Watson 1982–1983).

The term 'People's Commune' was coined by Mao Zedong himself, referring to a form of community in which all peasants work and eat together (Bennett et al. 1978). Unleashed in the countryside, the campaign aimed to combine agriculture cooperatives into a vast complex that clustered political, economic, and social functions. Two adjectives provide a vivid illustration—'big' and 'public'. 'Big' referred to the size of the communes. On average, 28.5 agriculture cooperatives were combined into one commune housing approximately 10,000 peasants (Luo 2006, p. 64). The development was rapid. Within less than half a year, by the end of 1958, 120 million rural households, accounting for over 99% of the rural population, had joined a commune organization (CCCCP 1958b, pp. 520–541; Snow 1971). 'Public' referred to the ownership of the means of production. Based on prudential considerations, the authority maintained the collective ownership system in the initial years and began to gradually transform the system to all-people's ownership, that is, public ownership, only after three to six years (CCCCP 1958a, pp. 384–388). However, the final goal of the commune system was to achieve communism, as the Party authority announced (CCCCP 1958a, pp. 385).

As an organization, the commune had multiple functions; of crucial importance were social functions, including social services such as kindergartens, nursing homes, public schools, health centres, and public canteens. Naturally, the commune also had economic functions, including both agricultural and industrial production as well as political and military functions (CCCCP 1958b, pp. 520–541; O'Leary and Watson 1982–1983).

The social functions of the commune were designed to be a model of group living, which was regarded as the key to securing the economic functions of the Commune (Bennett et al. 1978; CCCCP 1958b, p. 520). The characteristics of the 'joint work, joint consumption' style of commune life were clearly illustrated by the organization of the public canteens. One of the purposes of organizing public dining was 'to further emancipate the labour force, especially female workers, and to improve the utility of labour and labour productivity' (Editorial 1958b, p. 450). In principle, private cooking was not allowed after the public canteen was built; exceptions were allowed only in extreme weather, such as severe cold. Typically, one production team or one working unit had one public canteen, and the food was offered free of charge to people working in the unit. Typically, these canteens maintained their farming base for the food supply and were supposed to consider the special dining needs of elderly members, children, breastfeeding women, etc. Therefore, a canteen was much more than just a place offering food. Eating free food together after joint work was regarded as both a form of 'wage' distribution and a style of group living. In such a lifestyle, more hands were liberated from daily housework and therefore could contribute to economic constructs (Luo 2006; O'Leary and Watson 1982–1983).

The role of economic production shouldered by these communes went far beyond agricultural work. Industrial production was another of their major tasks, especially in light industries such as producing farming-related items, including chemical fertilizer, pesticides, and farming implements. This was an expedient arrangement to solve the shortage of light-industrial products that had resulted from the then policy bias towards heavy industries in urban areas. Hence, the People's Communes were encouraged to utilize their particular advantages, develop a suitable industrial production style, and support what had been the steel industry. Additionally, as an integral part of the planned economy, these industrial productions were also supposed to comply with state economic plans (Bennett et al. 1978; CCCCP 1958b, p. 520; CCCCP 1958c, pp. 502–507; Luo 2006; O'Leary and Watson 1982–1983).

This system officially lasted for about two decades. However, in October 1983, the authority announced that it was separating the political function from the communes and constructing township governments as the basic rural political unit, thus repealing the establishment of the commune system.[13]

3.1.3.2 The Great Leap Forward

The term Great Leap Forward (GLF) refers to the political ideal of forwarding economic production, especially industrial production, by leaps and bounds. It first appeared in an editorial of the People's Daily, the mouthpiece of the Party (Editorial 1957, pp. 582–586), and later was officially adopted to describe the economic production goal of China's second Five Year Plan in 1958 (CCCCP 1958d, pp. 370–383; MacFarquhar 1983). The general goal was to build China into a modern industrial country, similar to Western countries, within a few years by using mass mobilization strategies that Mao Zedong had developed during wartime. The general aim was, as Mao claimed, 'to surpass the UK within ten years and within another ten years to surpass the U.S.' (Mao 1958, p. 239).

The most illustrative example of pursuing an unrealistic economic goal was the aim of steel production laid down by the Party for the following years. Also termed Backyard Furnace, this movement was the hallmark of the GLF. It was believed that the output volume of steel was an indicator of industrialization. In other words, the key to reaching the developmental stage of industrialization was to produce more steel. Therefore, the plan was made. According to the national economic plan made by the central authority, the goal of steel production for 1958 was 11 million tons, and that for 1959 was 27–30 million tons. Furthermore, by the end of the second FYP (1962), the aim was to produce 80–100 million tons of steel. However, the actual output of steel in 1957 was merely 5.35 million tons (CCCCP 1958d, pp. 381–383). This meant that the yearly output capacity of steel had to improve 15-fold within five years. Following the announcement of the plan, economic policies tilted heavily towards the steel industry (Mu 2014; Zhang 1999). In 1958 and 1959, throughout China, from urban to rural areas and from northern to southern regions, people threw themselves zealously into producing steel. As the name 'backyard furnace' suggests, ordinary people who possessed no related knowledge participated widely in the campaign. Many of them melted household utensils and tried to manufacture steel in their backyards (Editorial 1958c, pp. 348–351; Editorial 1959, pp. 34–38). The spirit was so high that slogans such as 'The more aggressive we are, the higher the production of the land' were openly published (Editorial 1958d). This movement clearly showed that the central authority was out of touch with reality and revealed

Mao's talent for mass mobilization and the degree of compliance of the people. It was rather ironic to spread propaganda with such an idealistic slogan given that China held materialism as its core ideology.

The movement engulfed China for three years and was not rectified until 1961 (CCCCP 1961, pp. 70–74), and the cost to China went far beyond merely economic terms (Zhou 2012). In those years, society prioritized steel production in an absolute sense, which led to the abandonment of other economic activities and agricultural work. The immediate consequence was the severe grain shortage that threw China into three years of famine (1959–1961), claiming 16–27 million lives in three years (MacFarquhar and Twitchett 1995, p. 598). Furthermore, because Mao was the major advocate of the GLF, both his prestige and his ego were dented, which he could not tolerate. To restore his authority, Mao launched the Great Proletarian Cultural Revolution, a political-ideological social movement aimed at regaining his grip on the Party. This movement swept the country in 1966 and ended only with Mao's death in 1976 (MacFarquhar 1983).

While the decade-long Cultural Revolution threw China into another state of messy chaos soon after the GLF, it was a political movement, and the economic structure was not touched during this period. However, economic performance unavoidably lagged (MacFarquhar and Twitchett 1991, pp. 475–534). Since the end of the socialist transformation in 1956, China's economic system had not undergone any structural changes regardless of the economic and social turmoil that happened afterwards. Until the eve of 1978, the Chinese economy was deeply embedded in a centrally controlled economic system, and the means of production, such as land, implements, and capital, were overwhelmingly publicly owned and at the disposal of the state. This was the political-economic reality when Deng Xiaoping launched the economic reform and opening-up strategy.

3.2 The Law and the Judicial System in the First Thirty Years

3.2.1 Development of the Rule System and Its Characteristics

The first legal modernization movement appeared in China in the late Qing Dynasty when the royal family struggled to maintain their grip on their ruling power. However, before the new laws were put into force, the dynasty sealed its fate with the Wuchang revolt in 1911 (Eto and Schiffrin 1984; Hsu 2000, Chap. 20). Later, after establishing its regime in 1927, the Nanjing Nationalist government (KMT), following the civil law tradition, promulgated six principal legal codes – the Constitution, Civil Code, Criminal Code, Code of Civil Procedure, Code of Criminal Procedure, and Administration laws – and thus laid down a basic formal legal framework for society (Gilpatrick 1950). These laws ruled China for two decades and were not abolished until 1949, when the Communist Party prevailed over the KMT in the Civil War. The abolishment, as asserted by the Party, was due to ideological differences. Socialist China rejected all the laws and regulations of the Nationalist government, as these were capitalist laws that did not suit a socialist state. It was believed that these legal documents promulgated by the capitalist government were prone to protecting the interests of capitalists; thus, they were not in the interests of the people and had to be replaced by socialist legislation (Government Administration Council 1950, p. 393). Thus, together with the Six Codes, all legal documents promulgated by the KMT were abolished on the eve of the establishment of the PRC (Lubman 1999, Chaps. 3 and 4).

However, establishing a complete legal system from scratch is never easy, not to mention that China had only a minimal number of legal experts at the time. As was briefly noted earlier, since the beginning of the twentieth century, China had sent small groups of students to learn from the West, but few of them had studied law (Chen et al. 2007, pp. 188–190). Although China's domestic modern education system had started to emerge in the 1890s,[14] given that China was engaged in years of warfare thereafter and lacked qualified teachers, it would have been reasonable to predict that by 1949, China was incapable of initiating such an undertaking. Thus, by abolishing the established legal system and possessing no legal professionals of its own, the government, in effect, put the whole country into a legal vacuum for a long time.

Moreover, it appears that the newly organized leadership indeed had no intention of building an operational formal legal system, as establishing a legal system did not appear on the political agenda (Bennett 1976).[15] It was not until the late 1970s that China started to carry out this undertaking seriously and systematically. Thus, for the first three decades, China operated without a formal legal framework. Laws were passed sporadically, usually aimed at handling particular issues or in the service of political campaigns. Instead of using formal legal documents, the leaders relied heavily on political propaganda, leaders' speeches, especially those of Mao Zedong, and resolutions of Party conferences to organize and regulate the country and organize economic activities. Thus, during that time, there was no clear boundary between legal documents and political papers.[16]

In those years, China was a 'big' state in an absolute sense, meaning the government relied on substantive rules and directly intervened in as many issues as possible, great and small. The law was one of the tools it employed, an idea explicitly stated by the then State Council: 'the law is the tool that the ruling class used to rule over the ruled and to protect their own class' (Government Administration Council 1950, p. 393). That is, in the newly built country in need of organizing internal and external affairs, while a formal legal system was deemed to be an indispensable institution for these tasks, the laws that appeared in those years showed strong substantive characteristics—almost all were regulative rules for achieving short-term political and economic goals or ad hoc results.

Retrospectively, from 1949 through 1976, laws, in addition to the Constitution, were promulgated mainly to organize and regulate the state, such as organic laws for organizing the People's Court, the State Council, and the Procuratorate as well as public security laws, civil affairs laws on marriage and household registration, military laws, public financial laws on issues such as taxes and public debts, and economic laws such as the bylaws of the agricultural cooperatives. The very absence of all principal codes essential to a modern legal system, such as civil and commercial codes, a criminal code, and procedural laws, indicated that this rule system was not designed for an economy centred on free transactions and private property rights. Although administrative regulations were issued from time to time, most of them were aimed at handling particular issues in a specific period. They were intended not to establish a systematic regulative system but for specific usage. Moreover, as there was no legislation law at the time, legislative power was not clearly divided among different legislative levels, and the hierarchy of different laws was not clear. For instance, the division of labour between the People's Congress and the then State Council constantly overlapped.

To obtain a general idea of the laws enacted during that time, we could take a closer look at the structure and articles of the 1954 Provisional Regulations for Public–Private Joint Industrial Enterprises, the legal document that was designed to regulate China's socialist transformation of national capitalist enterprises and their management afterwards. The whole provision contains only 28 articles to cover topics including shares (Chap. 2), management (Chaps. 3–5), rules of distribution (Chap. 4), and the leadership relationship (Chap. 6). As stated in Article 1, the purpose of formulating the provision was to guide the transformation of private enterprises into joint ventures and thus facilitate the socialist transformation movement. In other words, the rule was made out of consideration of smoothing the path of the political movement, not to assist economic actions that the ventures might have been involved in. Hence, it was much like a set of political commands regarding related issues. For instance, on shares and management issues, private enterprises that were subject to socialist transformation had to accept the government's assessment of their asset values and clear their liabilities, thus confirming each party's shares (Article 5). The principles of fairness were applied to the process of asset assessment (Article 6), although the private party held no bargaining power. The shareholders held limited liability in the joint venture (Article 8). Concerning production and staff management, the provision made it clear that the government would take over the responsibility of daily management of the enterprises (Article 9–10 and 15–16) and the appointment of staff (Article 11). Furthermore, these joint ventures would be led by various levels of the governments of the regions where they were located (Article 23), with governmental departments in charge of affairs related to their functions (Article 24–25).

Hence, the law on public–private ventures was, in essence, a vehicle that the government used to arrange and smooth the socialist political movement. Moreover, the concise and general contents made the rules hardly useful in practice and left much room for discretion in application. Although the State Council later stipulated a few directions to guide the implementation of the provision,[17] only one was about board organization; the rest were all on litigation, interests, or debt-related matters that emerged in the transformation process. No supplementary regulations or directions were issued to guide the application of this law that was too general to be applicable.

In reviewing the laws that emerged in those thirty years, an interesting phenomenon comes to light – a clear watershed dividing China's legislation into two phases: the first eight years from 1949 to 1957 and the later period until 1976. As stated above, the years from 1953 to 1957 were the most successful period in the first three decades of New China, especially in an economic sense. It was the period when the regime started its socialist development after three years of national economic reorganization, and it was also the period when China was implementing its first FYP and the socialist transformation of its three major sectors, in both of which efforts it claimed success. Coincidentally, this was also when China promulgated the most laws and administrative documents compared to other stages. However, from 1958 onwards, China launched the GLF and People's Commune campaigns, which were followed by the subsequent three years of the Great Famine. In the entire eight years following these events, only 40 legal documents emerged despite waves of economic strategies being developed nationwide. The shrinkage of legislation was most striking from 1966 to 1976, when China was in the turmoil of the Cultural Revolution. As a result, the total number of laws passed during that period was four, as the data suggest.[18]

The number of laws will reasonably drop when a regime has finished its fundamental construction of the legal system. Nevertheless, this was not the case in China since its modern legal system was still far from established at that time. As discussed earlier, most laws and administrative documents put into force in the first three decades were aimed at short-term regulation of various kinds of social, political, and economic issues.

Thus far, a few conclusions can be drawn from China's early legislation. First, no clear blueprint for establishing a formal and consistent legal system ever existed in the minds of China's first generation of leaders. Thus, most laws and administrative regulations were promulgated to address immediate issues rather than long-term regulation purposes. Second, features such as vagueness, generality, and thus inapplicability appeared in most regulations that emerged in this period. Hence, considerable leeway existed in implementing those laws, and as a result, political policies constantly intervened. Third, laws were in the service of political and economic goals. Compared to Weber's ideal types of law for economic actions, the characteristics of the law in this period could be categorized as substantively irrational. This is even more vividly demonstrated in the following discussion of the construction of the judicial system.

3.2.2 The Role of the Judicial System and Its Structure

As the law-applying institution, the judicial system was no less important than the law in the book. Whereas the central authority paid rather limited attention to building a complete legal system, the construction of the court system was on the agenda in the beginning years. To introduce the early stage of development of China's judicial system, this section focuses on two aspects: the historical evolution of the court system and the characteristics of the first group of judges in New China.

China's first functional court system in the modern sense was built during the days of the Republic of China (from 1911 through 1949). As the first consolidated government after the overturning of the Qing Dynasty, the then Beiyang government (1912–1927) built a four-level, three-tier court system to implement the law. However, it was not a national court system, and in places where no court existed, cases were tried by local governors (Zhang 1986b, p. 179). In the meantime, the authority also initiated a testing and appointment system for selecting judges (Xu 2000, pp. 107–128; Zhang 2009, pp. 558–563)[19] and held China's first examination for judges in 1916, when 38 were appointed (Li 2017).

The period of the Beiyang government was marred by years of warfare between warlords, with the Nanjing government (KMT) replacing the Beiyang regime in 1928. The Nanjing government thus inherited the judicial system constructed by the Beiyang government (Xu 2000; Zhang 2009, pp. 542–563).[20] The KMT revised the court system into three levels: the local court, the high court, and the supreme court (Tiffert 2016, pp. 114–147). Together with the Six Codes, which the government transplanted from the civil law system, the Republic of China built a modern legal system in the book and in action.

In regions controlled by the Communist Party, a parallel judicial system existed. In 1934, the China Central Soviet regime issued its organic law, which clarified the purpose, rights, and jurisdiction of the regime's supreme court (situated in Ruijin, Jiangxi Province). Local judicial apparatuses were set up at the provincial, county, and district levels. It was a two-tier trial system equipped with a collegial system (with three judges), a judicial challenge system, etc.[21] Whereas the court system had the outward appearance of modern institutional design, the Organic Law of the Chinese Soviet Republic placed it under the leadership of the central executive committee, the administrative organ of the regime; hence, it was not an independent judicial system (Article 34). When recruiting judicial staff, unlike the Nanjing government, which deployed a testing system for selecting judges, the selection criteria for judges in the Soviet regime stressed loyalty to the revolution in addition to basic literacy and analytical capabilities (Lü 2007, pp. 79–80; Tiffert 2016, pp. 114–147). Following the success of the Civil War in 1949, the Soviet judicial system prevailed, and a nationwide judicial system was under construction after 1949.

The laws in the early 1950s laid down the organizational structure of the court system. It first appeared in the Provisional Organic Regulation of the People's Courts of the PRC in 1951, and in 1954, the First Session of the First National People's Congress (NPC) enacted the Organic Law of the People's Courts of the PRC. According to these documents, China's judicial system would be a two-tier trial system with four levels of courts, which would be supplemented by special courts for particular types of cases, such as military courts and transportation courts. This court system structure turned out to fit China's situation quite well and remains in China to this day.

Within the court system, as the 1954 Constitution stipulated, the People's Courts are only subject to the law (Article 78), the lower-level court is subject to the leadership of the higher ones, and the courts are responsible to their respective People's Congress levels, i.e., the legislatures (Article 80). Therefore, institutionally, the courts were (and still are) under the legislatures. Also worth noting is the role of judicial work in this particular period—the major task of judicial work, as elaborated in the Directive for Strengthening People's Judicial Work, issued by the central government after the First National Judicial Conference in 1950, was 'to crush counterrevolutionaries and to protect the people' (Government Administration Council 1950, p. 394). More importantly, after the authority made the first FYP for economic development, Dong Biwu, the first president of the Supreme People's Court, made a speech to motivate judicial workers to engage in it fully, stating that 'the first Five Year Plan … was itself a law. Judicial workers should … fight for the completion of the plan' (Dong 1955, p. 121). However, he admitted that the system still lacked knowledge of how to better serve the economy (Dong 1955, p. 120). Hence, in addition to working for political purposes, the judicial system was also intended to actively serve the economy.

These unique roles assigned to the judicial institution more or less impacted the criteria for recruiting court staff. Party leaders stated explicitly that the judicial work should be in the service of political and economic purposes; hence, to carry out such work, the authority would need a body of staff from politically and ideologically reliable backgrounds. As a result, judicial workers who had formerly been employed by the Nanjing government, approximately 5000 judges, were purged soon after the system started functioning, although some were allowed to be reassigned after they had been reformed through political education (Bennett 1976; Government Administration Council 1950, p. 395). Meanwhile, over 6000 new cadres who had been evaluated as advanced workers during political campaigns were recruited and seated as judges (Xin 2003, p. 16). Supplementing the court staff were workers who had proven reliable in various trades and people with a military background (Government Administration Council 1953, pp. 143–151; He and Lu 1993, p. 131). Thus, the first body of judges in China was established. Although they came from all walks of life, they shared one thing in common—a 'red' political background—and thus were deemed politically reliable and suitable for a judge's job (Xin 2003). The judicial system went through many hard times in subsequent political campaigns, especially during the Anti-Rightist Campaign (MacFarquhar 1960)[22] and the Cultural Revolution, but the basic structure of the judicial system was not touched, and the staff remained.[23]

While only concisely expounded, the above discussion still sheds some light on China's legislative and judicial systems at this point. As the Chinese government had been desperately seeking economic prosperity since the regime was established, it tried numerous approaches, such as copying and revising Soviet models, launching the Great Leap Forward, carrying out the People's Commune, and unleashing the Cultural Revolution. Some of these efforts, such as the first FYP, were successful. Others, such as the GLF, had disastrous consequences. While Chinese society was undergoing an initial transformation under the CCP, establishing a formal and rational legal system and educating real legal experts never seemed to be a priority to China's early leadership. However, in the subsequent chapters, examinations of the following generations of CCP leadership tell another story.

Notes

1. From 1938 to 1949, China's inflation rate climbed to over 200%, and it was tamed only in 1950, when the communist regime undertook strict market control and financial reform. Concerning China's inflation history, see generally Zhang (1986a).
2. After signing the Treaty of Nanjing in 1842 following the First Opium War, China engaged in dozens of unequal treaties with different Western countries before World War II. In most of these treaties, China was forced to cede its consular jurisdictions and territory, cede tariff control, and grant unilateral most-favoured-nation treatment to some countries. From then on, China entered an era of new diplomatic relations.
3. The term 'feudal' was widely used in Chinese writings in reference to institutional structures under imperial rulings. It has some similarities with the Western usage of the term in the economic sense, as the ancient Chinese economy was also based on the relationship between landlord and tenant. However, there was no political or military tie between them, as feudalism as a political system was superseded by the system of prefectures and counties after the Qin Dynasty (221BC). (The feudalist structure remained in some dynasties, such as the Han (202–220 BC) and West Jin (265–316) dynasties.) For China's political system, see Xie (2013).
4. The term 'bureaucratic capitalist' refers to those whose businesses were, wholly or partially, financed by state capital—historically, China had four large bureaucratic capitalist groups (the Chiang, Soong, Kung, and Chen families, named after their surnames) who controlled politics, economics, finance, etc. See Coble (1986). Additionally, the Kuomintang (also known as the Chinese Nationalist Party) was established by Sun Yat-sen in 1894. It formed the Nanjing government under Chiang Kai-shek in 1928 and ruled mainland China until its defeat in the Civil War against the Communist Party and flight to Taiwan in 1949. For the history of the KMT, see Wilbur (1984).
5. For the economic influence of the embargo, see the discussion of China's international trade in chapter five of the present study.
6. According to the statistics on state assets in 1949, the total value of state-owned and public–private joint ownership enterprises amounted to over 19 billion RMB, while the 123,000 national enterprises possessed only two billion. See Dong (1996, p. 29).
7. To name but a few, after the first Opium War, China signed the Treaty of Nanking (1842) and Treaty of Wangxia (1844) with the British Empire and the U.S., respectively. The Treaty of Tientsin (1858) and Treaty of Peking (1860) were signed following the defeat in the second Opium War. In 1895, Japan, via its victory in the First Sino-Japanese War, forced the Guangxu Emperor to sign the Treaty of Maguan (also called the Treaty of Shimonoseki, 1895). Then, in 1901, the Boxer Protocol was signed between China and eleven Western powers following China's failure in its fight against the Eight-Nation Alliance. Many of these treaties included such articles as opening the coastal cities and renegotiating foreign-trade terms, tax terms, and consular jurisdictions.
8. The work of Cheng (1954) thoroughly elaborated the reform process of China's banking system at the time.
9. In addition to the political reason behind the reform, it was due to the low agricultural efficiency caused partly by extremely high land rent, which greatly hindered the economic performance of the agricultural sector.
10. Concerning the steps applied in the land reform, the Land Reform Law provides a detailed description. Also worth notice is that this land reform dealt only with rural land; urban land,

suburban areas, and ethnic minority inhabitant areas were omitted. For a broader perspective on rural China under Mao, see Oi (1989).

11. National capitalists refers to the group of self-reliance entrepreneurs who emerged and developed during the late nineteenth century. Their growth was made possible in that period by industrial technologies coming into China; therefore, most of them engaged in industrial economics. Famous among them were Zhang Jian (1853–1926, textile, oil, and flour industries, education, etc.), the Rong Brothers (1873–1938 and 1875–1952, flour and textile industries), Zhou Xuexi (1866–1947, mineral, textile, and glass industries, etc.). For industrial enterprises in 19th-century China, see Chan (1987). The term 'national' was used to distinguish them from the other two groups of capitalists, bureaucratic capitalists and comprador capitalists, who were native Chinese people who operated businesses by intermediating between foreign enterprises and local markets, see Hao (1980) and Leung (1990).
12. In this article, Mao (1950) explained the reasons for pursuing different strategies towards different classes, and in referring to national capitalists, he said, 'In the future, the national capitalists will be wiped out. But for now, we should unite them and don't push them away' (p. 225) (my translation).
13. For the reform of agriculture after the People's Commune stage, see chapter four of this study. The decomposition of the commune structure was announced via Party and government policy paper CCCCP and the State Council (1983) Guanyu shixing zhengshe fenkai jianli xiangzhegnfu de tongzhi/Circular on separating the government and the commune and building the township government.
14. The earliest attempt to modernize China's education was the self-strengthening movement carried out in the late nineteenth century.
15. The years under Mao's rule were filled with campaigns to suppress counterrevolutionaries (1950–1953, 1955, mainly nationalists), suppress capitalists (the Three-Anti and Five-Anti movements, 1951–1952), and attack intellectuals (the Hundred Flowers Campaign, 1956–1957, and the Anti-rightist movement, 1957–1959) as well as economic movements such as the GLF (1958–1960) and ideological campaigns such as the Socialist Education Movement (1963–1966) and the Cultural Revolution (1966–1976). For a survey of these movements, see Bennett (1976).
16. A close examination of the Selected Key Documents since the Establishment of the PRC (20 volumes) could illustrate this phenomenon. This set of collections incorporated 1232 important documents published or announced between September 1949 and December 1965. Selected socially influential documents include policy papers, editorials, laws, party resolutions, and working reports.
17. From 1956 to 1957, another six directions were stipulated on issues concerning the operation of those joint ventures.
18. A comprehensive database of Chinese laws and regulations in English is available at https://www.lawinfochina.com.
19. The Beiyang government issued the Rules of the Judge Examination and the Rules of Judge Appointment for selecting qualified judicial workers.
20. The Republic of China had two main stages: the Beiyang government, and the Nanjing government. In the first decade after the overturning of the Qing Dynasty, the government attempted to build a modern-style court system. However, the turbulent warring period endangered the operation of the system. The relatively stable period under the rule of the KMT provided an operational environment for the development of the judicial system. For more details, generally see Xu (2000) and Zhang (2009, pp. 542–563).
21. The China Soviet regime established a formal judicial system structure, which operated according to the Organic Law of the Chinese Soviet Republic (issued in February 1934), and laid out the organizational rules for the supreme court, the Provisional Organizations and Judgement Regulations of the Judicial Department, and the Judicial Procedures of the Chinese Soviet Republic.
22. This was an ideological campaign launched from 1957 to 1960, targeting alleged 'rightists'. Most were intellectuals who had criticized the Party during the Hundred Flowers Movement.

MacFarquhar's (1960) work offered good coverage of the fate of Chinese intellectuals under Mao.

23. The authority tried to enhance the ability of these judges with nonlegal backgrounds by offering short-term training, a topic that will be referred to in later discussions of China's legal education.

References

Bennett G (1976) Yundong: mass campaigns in Chinese communist leadership. University of California, Oakland

Bennett G, Kieke K, and Yoffy K (1978) Huadong: the story of a Chinese People's Commune. Westview, Nashville

Bo YB (1952) Zhonghua renmin gongheguo sannian lai de chengjiu/Three years of achievements of the people's republic of China. In: Bo YB (1952) Xinzhongguo de jingji chengjiu 1949–1952 / New China's economic achievements 1949–1952. China Committee for the Promotion of International Trade, Beijing

Bo YB (1953) Guanyu 1953 nian guojia yusuan de baogao/The report of 1953 national budget report. In: CPC Party Literature Research Office (ed) (1991) Jianguo yilai zhongyao wenxian xuanbian juan si/Selected key documents since the establishment of the PRC, vol 4. Party Literature Publishing House, Beijing

Bo YB (1997) Fadong 'wufan,' datui bufa zibenjia de changkuang jingong/Initiating the 'five-anti' movement, fighting back the attack of the illegal capitalists. In: Bo YB (ed) (1997) Ruogan zhongda juece yu shijian de huigu /In retrospect of several major decisions and events. People's Publishing House, Beijing

CCCCP (1951) Zhonggong zhongyan guanyu nongye hezuoshe shengchan huzhuhezuo de jueyi (caoan)/Resolution of the Central Committee of the CPC on agricultural production cooperatives (protocol). In: CPC Party Literature Research Office (ed) (1991) Jianguo yilai zhongyao wenxian xuanbian juan er/Selected key documents since the establishment of the PRC, vol 2. Party Literature Publishing House, Beijing

CCCCP (1958a) Zhongong zhongyang guanyu zai nongcun jianli renmin gongshe wenti de jueyi/ The resolution of the Central Committee of the CCP on constructing People's Commune in rural areas. In: CPC Party Literature Research Office (ed) (1991) Jianguo yilai zhongyao wenxian xuanbian juan shiyi/Selected key documents since the establishment of the PRC, vol 11. Party Literature Publishing House, Beijing

CCCCP (1958b) Guanyu renmin gongshe ruogan wenti de jueyi/Resolutions on several issues of the People's Commune. In: CPC Party Literature Research Office (ed) (1991) Jianguo yilai zhongyao wenxian xuanbian juan shiyi/Selected key documents since the establishment of the PRC, vol 11. Party Literature Publishing House, Beijing

CCCCP (1958c) Guanyu renmin gongshe daban gongye wenti/On running industrial enterprises in the People's Commune. In: CPC Party Literature Research Office (ed) (1991) Jianguo yilai zhongyao wenxian xuanbian juan shiyi/Selected key documents since the establishment of the PRC, vol 11. Party Literature Publishing House, Beijing

CCCCP (1958d) Zhonggongzhongyang guanyu 1959 nian jihua he dierge wunian jihua wenti de jueding/The decisions of the Central Committee of the CCP on the plan of 1959 and the second five-year plan. In: CPC Party Literature Research Office (ed) (1991) Jianguo yilai zhongyao wenxian xuanbian juan shiyi/Selected key documents since the establishment of the PRC, vol 11. Party Literature Publishing House, Beijing

CCCCP (1961) Zhonggong dibajie zhongyang weiyuanhui dijiuci quanti huiyi gongbao/The communique of the 9th meeting of the 8th Central Committee of the CPC. In: CPC Party Literature Research Office (ed) (1991) Jianguo yilai zhongyao wenxian xuanbian juan shisi/

Selected key documents since the establishment of the PRC, vol 14. Party Literature Publishing House, Beijing

Central Finance and Economics Committee (1950) Zhongcaiwei guanyu quanguo jinronghuiyi qingkuang xiang maozhuxi bing zhongyang de zonghe baogao/The general report of the central financial and economic committee to Chairman Mao and the central government. In: CPC Party Literature Research Office (ed) (1991) Jianguo yilai zhongyao wenxian xuanbian juan yi/ Selected key documents since the establishment of the PRC, vol 1. Party Literature Publishing House, Beijing

Chan W (1987) Merchants, mandarins, and modern enterprise in late ch'ing China. Harvard University Press, Cambridge

Chen BD (1964) Zhongguo sida jiazhu/China's big four families. People's Publishing House, Beijing

Chen Y (1949) Yizhi wujia mengzhang/Curbing the soaring prices. In: CPC Party Literature Research Office (ed) (1991) Jianguo yilai zhongyao wenxian xuanbian, juan yi/Selected key documents since the establishment of the PRC, vol 1. Party Literature Publishing House, Beijing

Chen YH, Chen XX and Tian ZP (eds) (2007) Zhongguo jindai jiaoyu shiliao huibian: liuxue jiaoyu/ Collection of historical resources of China's modern history of education: oversees education. Shanghai Educational Publishing House, Shanghai

Cheng CY (1954) Monetary affairs of communist China. Union Research Institute, Hong Kong

Cheng CY (1963) Communist China's economy 1949–1962: structural changes and crisis. Seton Hall University Press, South Orange

Cheng CY (1982) China's economic development: growth and structural change. Westview, Nashville

Clubb OE (1971) China and Russia: the great game. Columbia University Press, New York

Coble PM (1986) The Shanghai capitalists and the nationalist government, 1927–1937, 2nd edn. Harvard University Press, Cambridge

Dong BW (1955) Sifa gongzuo bixu wei jingji jianshe fuwu/Judicial work must be in service of economic construction. In: CPC Party Literature Research Office (ed) (1991) Jianguo yilai zhongyao wenxian xuanbian, juan liu/Selected key documents since the establishment of the PRC, vol 6. Party Literature Publishing House, Beijing

Dong ZK (ed) (1996) 1949–1952 nian Zhongguo Jingji Fenxi/Analysis of China's economy 1949–1952. China Social Science Press, Beijing

Dong ZK and Wu L (eds) (2011) Zhonghua renmin gongheguo jingjishi 1953–1957 shang/Economic history of the People's Republic of China 1953–1957, vol 1. Social Sciences Academic Press (China), Beijing

Eckstein A (1977) China's economic revolution. Cambridge University Press, Cambridge

Editorial (1957) Jianshe shehuizhuyi nongcun de weida gangling/The great program of constructing socialist countryside. In: CPC Party Literature Research Office (ed) (1991) Jianguo yilai zhongyao wenxian xuanbian juan shi/Selected key documents since the establishment of the PRC, vol 10. Party Literature Publishing House, Beijing

Editorial (1958a) Chengfengpolang/Braving the wind and the waves. People's Daily 1 January, p.1

Editorial (1958b) Banhao gonggong shitang/Run well public canteens. In: CPC Party Literature Research Office (ed) (1991) Jianguo yilai zhongyao wenxian xuanbian juan shiyi/Selected key documents since the establishment of the PRC, vol 11. Party Literature Publishing House, Beijing

Editorial (1958c) Tuyang bingju shi jiasu fazhan gangtie gongye de jiejing/Trying both indigenous and imported methods was the shortcut to developing steel industry. In: CPC Party Literature Research Office (ed) (1991) Jianguo yilai zhongyao wenxian xuanbian juan shiyi/Selected key documents since the establishment of the PRC, vol 11. Party Literature Publishing House, Beijing

Editorial (1958d) Renyou duo dadan, diyou duo dachan/The more aggressive we were, the higher production the land. People's Daily 27 August, p. 3

Editorial (1959) Wei 1800 wan dun gang er fengdou/Fighting for the 18 million tons of steel. In: CPC Party Literature Research Office (ed) (1991) Jianguo yilai zhongyao wenxian xuanbian juan shier/Selected key documents since the establishment of the PRC, vol 12. Party Literature Publishing House, Beijing

Ellison HJ (ed) (1982) The Sino-Soviet conflict: a global perspective. University of Washington Press, Seattle

Eto S and Schiffrin H (eds) (1984) The 1911 revolution: interpretive essays. University of Tokyo Press, Tokyo

Fairbank JK (1953) Trade and diplomacy on the China coast: the opening of the treaty ports, 1842–1854. Harvard University Press, Cambridge

Feuerwerker A (1983) Economic trends in the Republic of China, 1912–1949. In: Fairbank JK and Twitchett DC (eds) The Cambridge history of China, vol 12. Cambridge University Press, Cambridge

Friedman E, Pickowicz P, and Selden M (1989) Chinese village, socialist state (Yale University Press, New Haven

Gilpatrick MP (1950) The status of law and lawmaking procedure under the Kuomintang 1925–46. The Far Eastern Quarterly 10(1):38–55

Government Administration Council (1950) Zhengwuyuan guanyu jiaqiang renmin sifa gongzuo de zhishi/Direction of the government administration council on strengthening judicial work. In: CPC Party Literature Research Office (ed) (1991) Jianguo yilai zhongyao wenxian xuanbian juan yi/Selected key documents since the establishment of the PRC, vol 1. Party Literature Publishing House, Beijing

Government Administration Council (1951) Guanyu huafen nongcun jieji chengfen de buchong guiding (caoan)/Supplemented stipulations on division of rural classes (draft). In: CPC Party Literature Research Office (ed) (1991) Jianguo yilai zhongyao wenxian xuanbian juan er/ Selected key documents since the establishment of the PRC, vol 2. Party Literature Publishing House, Beijing

Government Administration Council (1953) Dierjie quanguo sifa huiyi jueyi/Resolution of the second national judicial conference. In: CPC Party Literature Research Office (ed) (1991) Jianguo yilai zhongyao wenxian xuanbian juan si/Selected key documents since the establishment of the PRC, vol 4. Party Literature Publishing House, Beijing

Government Administration Council (1954) Gongsi heying qiye zanxing tiaoli/Provisional regulation on public-private industrial enterprises. In: CPC Party Literature Research Office (ed) (1991) Jianguo yilai zhongyao wenxian xuanbian juan wu/Selected key documents since the establishment of the PRC, vol 5. Party Literature Publishing House, Beijing

Hao Y-P (1980) The comprador in nineteenth-century China: bridge between east and west. Harvard University Press, Cambridge

He LJ and Lu MJ (eds) (1993) Dangdai zhongguo de shenpan gongzuo/Adjudicative work in contemporary China. Contemporary China Publishing House, Beijing

Hsu ICY (2000) The rise of modern China, 6th edn. Oxford University Press, Oxford

Leung Y-S (1990) The shanghai taotai: linkage man in a changing society, 1843–1890. University of Hawaii Press, Honolulu

Li TH (2017) 1916 nian minguo shouci sifaguan kaoshi/1916 the first judge examination of the Republic of China. The Chinese Procurators 6:79–80

Liao HL (2008) Zhongguo nongcun tudi zhidu liushinian: huigu yu zhanwang/Sixty years of China's rural land system: a retrospect and prospect. China Financial & Economic Publishing House, Beijing

Liu SQ (1950) Guanyu tudi gaige wenti de baogao/Report on issues of land reform. In: CPC Party Literature Research Office (ed) (1991) Jianguo yilai zhongyao wenxian xuanbian juan yi/ Selected key documents since the establishment of the PRC, vol 1. Party Literature Publishing House, Beijing

Liu SQ (1953) Guanyu shougongye shengchanhezuoshe wenti/Issues on handicrafts production cooperatives. In: CPC Party Literature Research Office (ed) (1991) Jianguo yilai zhongyao

wenxian xuanbian juan si/Selected key documents since the establishment of the PRC, vol 4. Party Literature Publishing House, Beijing
Liu SQ (1958) Zhongguo gongchandang zhonggongzhongyang weiyuanhui xiang dibajie quanguo daibiao dahui dierci huiyi de gongzuo baogao/The working report of the central committee of the CCP to the second meeting of the 8th NPC. In: CPC Party Literature Research Office (ed) (1991) Jianguo yilai zhongyao wenxian xuanbian juan shiyi/Selected key documents since the establishment of the PRC, vol 11. Party Literature Publishing House, Beijing
Lü F (2007) Zhongguo fayuan wenhua yanjiu/A research on the culture of Chinese court. DPhil thesis. China University of Political Science and Law
Lubman SB (1999) Bird in a cage: legal reform in China after Mao. Stanford University Press, Redwood
Luo PH (2006) Nongcun renmin gongsheshi/The history of people's commune in the countryside. Fujian People's Publishing House, Fuzhou
Lyons TP (1987) Economic integration and planning in Maoist China. Columbia University Press, New York
Ma H and Sun SQ (1981) Zhongguo jingji jiegou wenti yanjiu/A research on China's economic structure. People's Publishing House, Beijing
MacFarquhar R (1960) The hundred flowers campaign and the Chinese intellectuals. Praeger, Westport
MacFarquhar R (1983) The origins of the cultural revolution, vol 2: the great leap forward, 1958–1960. Columbia University Press, New York
MacFarquhar R and Twitchett DC (eds) (1991) Cambridge history of China, vol 15. Cambridge University Press, Cambridge
MacFarquhar R and Twitchett DC (eds) (1995) Cambridge history of China, vol 14. Cambridge University Press, Cambridge
Mao ZD (1950) Buyao simian chuji/Don't make attacks in all directions. In: CPC Party Literature Research Office (ed) (1991) Jianguo yilai zhongyao wenxian xuanbian juan yi/Selected key documents since the establishment of the PRC, vol 1. Party Literature Publishing House, Beijing
Mao ZD (1958) Jieshao yige hezuoshe/Introducing a form of cooperative. In: CPC Party Literature Research Office (ed) (1991) Jianguo yilai zhongyao wenxian xuanbian juan shiyi/Selected key documents since the establishment of the PRC, vol 11. Party Literature Publishing House, Beijing
Myers R (1980) The Chinese economy, past and present. Wadsworth, Belmont
Mu YY (2014) A brief research on backyard furnace campaign in Henan province. Advances in Social Science 3(4):71–79
National People's Congress (1955) Zhonghua renmin gongheguo fazhan guomin jingji de diyige wunianjihua (1953–1957)/The first five-year plan of the national economy of the PRC (1953–1957). In: CPC Party Literature Research Office (ed) (1991) Jianguo yilai zhongyao wenxian xuanbian juan liu/Selected key documents since the establishment of the PRC, vol 6. Party Literature Publishing House, Beijing
Oi JC (1989) State and peasant in contemporary China: the political economy of village government, University of California Press, Oakland
O'Leary G and Watson A (1982–1983) The role of the people's commune in rural development in China. Pacific Affairs 55(4):593–612
Perkins DH (1975) (ed) China's modern economy in historical perspective. Stanford University Press, Redwood
Snow E (1971) China's 70,000 communes. New Republic 164(26):19–21
Shue V (1980) Peasant China in transition: the dynamics of development toward socialism, 1949–1956. University of California Press, Oakland
Standing Committee of the National People's Congress (1955) Nongye shengchan hezuoshe shifangzhangcheng caoan/Protocol regulation on agricultural production cooperatives. In: CPC Party Literature Research Office (ed) (1991) Jianguo yilai zhongyao wenxian xuanbian juan qi/

Selected key documents since the establishment of the PRC, vol 7. Party Literature Publishing House, Beijing
State Council (1956a) Guanyu siying qiye shixing gongsiheying shi dui caichan qingli gujia de jixiang zhuyao wenti de guiding/Stipulations on issues of liquidating private enterprises while enforing public-private cooperation. In: CPC Party Literature Research Office (ed) (1991) Jianguo yilai zhongyao wenxian xuanbian juan ba/Selected key documents since the establishment of the PRC, vol 8. Party Literature Publishing House, Beijing
State Council (1956b) Guanyu zai gongsiheying qiye zhong tuiding dingxi banfa de guiding/Stipulations on measures of practicing fixed rate of interest on capital in public-private joint ventures. In: CPC Party Literature Research Office (ed) (1991) Jianguo yilai zhongyao wenxian xuanbian juanba/Selected key documents since the establishment of the PRC, vol 8. Party Literature Publishing House, Beijing
Teiwes FC (1979) Politics and purges in China: rectification and the decline of party norms, 1950–1965. M. E. Sharpe, New York
Tiffert G (2016) The Chinese judge: from literatus to cadre, 1906–1949. In: Culp RJ, Eddy U., and Yeh WH (eds) (2016) Knowledge acts in modern China: ideas, institutions and identities. University of California, Oakland
Wang YN (1988) Zhongguo dizhu jingji xingtai yu zhongguo guanliao zhengzhi yanjiu /Formation of China's landlord economy and a study on China's bureaucratic politics. In: Wangyanan wenji, vol 4. Fujian Education Press, Fuzhou
Wilbur CM (1984) The nationalist revolution in China, 1923–1928. Cambridge University Press, Cambridge
Wu CM (1955) Diguo zhuyi zai jiuzhongguo de touzi/The investment of imperialist states in old China. People's Publishing House, Beijing
Xi ZX (1992) Guanyu xibei diqu nongye huzhu hezuoshe yundong/On the movement of agricultural mutual-aid cooperation in the northwest region. In: Huang DX, Yu C and Wang XY (eds) Jianguo yilai nongye hezuohua shiliao huibian/Collection of historical resources on agricultural cooperatives since the founding of new China. History of Chinese Communist Party Publishing House, Beijing
Xie BC (2013) Brief history of the official system in China (trans: Chen MR and Wilson AR). Path International, Reading
Xin CY (2003) Chinese courts: history and transition. Law Press China, Beijing
Xu DX and Wu CM (2003) Zhongguo zibenzhuyi fazhanshi disanjuan/The history of development of the Chinese capitalism, vol 3. People's Publishing House, Beijing
Xu XQ (2000) Chinese professionals and the republic state. Cambridge University Press, Cambridge
Xue MQ (1960) Zhongguo guomin jingji de shehui zhuyi gaizao/The socialist transformation of the national economy in China. People's Publishing House, Beijing
Zhang GQ (1986a) Zhongguo tonghuo shi/Inflation history of China (trans: Yang ZX). China Wenshi Press, Beijing
Zhang GF (1986b) Zhongguo minguo fazhi jianshi/A short legal history of the republic of China. Peking University Press, Beijing
Zhang JP (2009) Zhongguo falü de chuantong yu jindai zhuanxing/The tradition and modern transition of Chinese law, 3rd edn. Law Press China, Beijing
Zhang ZH (1999) Rural industrialization in China: from backyard furnaces to township and village enterprises. East Asia: An International Quarterly 17(3):61–87
Zhang ZZ (1993) Lun bupingdeng tiaoyue jian xi zhongwai jiuyuezhang huibiao/A discussion on unequal treaties and an analysis on the collection of old sino-foreign treaties. Modern Chinese History Studies 2:1–20
Zhou EL (1959) Weida de shinian/The great ten years. People's Publishing House, Beijing
Zhou X (2012) The great famine in China, 1958–1962: a documentary history. Yale University Press, New Haven
Zhu D (1953) Ba shougongye zhe zuzhi qilai zou shehuizhuyi daolu/Organizing craftsmen for the socialist path. In: CPC Party Literature Research Office (ed) (1991) Jianguo yilai zhongyao

wenxian xuanbian juan si/Selected key documents since the establishment of the PRC, vol 4. Party Literature Publishing House, Beijing
Zhu D (1957) Fazhan shougongye shengchan, manzu renmin xuyao/Developing craftsmanship, satisfying people's needs. In: Head Office of China Craftsmanship Cooperative (ed) (1958) Shougongye hezuohua hou de zhuyao renwu/The Major Tasks after Handicrafts Collectivization. China Financial & Economic Publishing House, Beijing

Chapter 4
The Paternalistic Role of Law, 1978–1991

Abstract This chapter covers the first decades of China's economic reform initiated by Deng Xiaoping. From 1978 through 1991, the Chinese government liberalized its agricultural sector, opened its borders to foreign investment, and attempted, but failed, to reform its state-owned industrial and commercial sectors. In the meantime, the related rule system was formulated, with characteristics of substantive rules blended with political directives and laws. (4.1) These internal characteristics of the laws are shown via an in-depth analysis of contract laws, and the application of the law, exhibited in case studies, shows a high level of instructive usage of law in adjudication. (4.2) Additionally, China's legal education was undergoing an all-around restoration after having been dismantled during the Cultural Revolution. (4.3) Overall, the Chinese legal system demonstrated a paternalistic role in the economy in this period. (4.4).

4.1 External Functions of the Law

4.1.1 Political Economy from 1978 to 1991

The first decade of China's economic reform featured a struggle to adopt an economic mode, swinging between a centrally planned economy and a market-oriented economy. There was also a political twist that resulted from the unstable economic situations in the early years of the reform—the policy became market-oriented when the economy was gaining pace and shifted to proplanning strategies when it was overheated. The following reviews the overall political economy in this period.

In effect, China's economic adjustments started when Deng Xiaoping assumed real power in 1978. Following the death of Mao in 1976 and after two years of political struggle, Hua Guofeng, Mao's successor, lost control over the Party and was sidelined by the end of 1978 (Vogel 2011, pp. 157–216). In December 1978, the Communist Party of China convened the most significant Party conference in its history, the Third Plenum of the Eleventh Party Congress (hereafter the Third

J. Hu, *The Role of Law in China's Economic Development, 1978–2011*,
https://doi.org/10.1007/978-981-99-9911-8_4

Plenum) (Saich 2004, pp. 57–63). It was a landmark event of the CCP and China. First, this conference altered the whole political atmosphere of the country as it ended the dominant role of political struggle, which had been rampant throughout the last decades of Mao's rule, and brought political attention to economic affairs (Burton 1990, Chap. 1; Li 1998).

Second, the conference marked the beginning of China's economic liberalization, as the Party leadership of Deng was established after it. However, China's economic affairs were in the hands of Chen Yun, a conservative who favoured the planned economy over marketization (Chen 1995; Fewsmith 2011, pp. 468–527; Vogel 2011, pp. 717–722). Hence, it was also an era of continued twists between the two wings of the Party—Deng's market-oriented policy and Chen's planned economic system were political and economic rivals, each competing with and checking the other. At the conclusion of the conference, two political documents were announced: the *Communique* of the conference and Deng's concluding remarks, titled *Emancipating the Mind, Seeking Truth from Facts, Forwarding with Solidarity* (Deng 1978, pp. 140–153). With some overlaps, these two documents laid down the basic political agenda for China's social and economic affairs in the following years.

Deng's concluding remarks set forth the general ideology and mental emancipation of China from the central government to the grassroots, and an idea was sparked by an earlier article titled *Practice Was the Only Criterion to Examine Truth,* authorized by Hu Yaobang, another key figure of the liberal wing (Hu 1978). In this article, Deng emphasized the importance of 'opening the mind', stressing it as an important political issue and thus encouraging Party cadres to be flexible in their future works, a stark reversal of Mao and his successor Hua's ideology of the personality cult—fetters that had chained Chinese people for decades (MacFarquhar 1991, pp. 386–388). The idea of 'seeking truth from facts' was a direct reaction to the working atmosphere of boasting and exaggeration that had prevailed in China during the GLF and had resulted in substantial economic and human disasters. Showing his grasp of China's reality, Deng stressed the importance of adopting a regionally biased economic policy, allowing certain places and groups to prosper first and then achieving common prosperity later (Vogel 2011, pp. 217–248).

In a similar vein, the Communique of the Third Plenum reaccentuated these issues. Regarding the economy, the conference acknowledged that the most damaging defect of the economic system was its overcentralized regulative system. Therefore, it stressed the importance of decentralizing and granting more autonomy to local governments and production units, such as enterprises. Moreover, it claimed that attention should be paid to the functional separation of the Party, government, and enterprises to improve administrative efficiency and motivate all parties to engage in economic construction. By acknowledging the difficulties of fully centralizing the Chinese economy and the importance of decentralization, it proposed a two-line approach to decentralizing China's economy—from the central government to the local governments and from omnipotent government to the separation of political and economic functions in a bid to motivate local governments and the populace (CCCCP 1978, part 4). Furthermore, it stressed the importance of 'constructing the socialist legal system'; by 'institutionalizing and legalizing a democratic system', the Party vowed to achieve the stability and continuity of its institutions and legal system (CCCCP 1978, pp. 1–14). Therefore, the agenda of legislation was being promoted to an important place for the first time since 1949.

Despite stressing the importance of reforming the economy, the authority did not boldly and resolutely convert the economy to a market system. Concern over the relationship between a planned and a market-oriented economy was a key theme engrossing the attention of the Party's major figures (Saich 2004, pp. 64–79; Wu 2005, pp. 57–73). On 3 August 1979, Chen Yun wrote an article titled *The Questions of Plan and Market* in which, while endorsing the place of the market economy and claiming that it was basically harmless, he emphasized the subordinate place of the planned economy (Chen 1979, pp. 62–64). Such a policy was seen in the general strategy of adopting a planned economic strategy for major industries and leaving market rules to small commodities manufactured mainly by small-scale factories and individual businesses (Zhao 1981, pp. 334–336). Such a cautious attitude was also seen in the use of foreign capital for development, and the importance of insisting on a planned economy was reiterated by Chen in the following years (Chen 1980, pp. 523–529; Chen 1982, pp. 426–428).

However, the success of the agricultural reform in the early years of the reform greatly enhanced the confidence of the central government. Thus, in 1984, the authority issued the Decision of Reforming the Economic System, which advocated developing a socialist commodity economy, reforming the price system (albeit still at a moderate level), and developing multiple economic forms (CCCCP 1984a, pp. 47–71; Zhao 1985, pp. 156–177). In this Party document, the vitality of enterprises was centred in the following reform strategies, and it proclaimed the development of a socialist commodity economy with planning (CCCCP 1984a, para. 3–4). The Chinese economy therefore entered its first round of transformation (Deng 1987, pp. 355–362; The Political Bureau of CCCCP 1987, pp. 169–183).

However, inflation soon followed the economic boom in 1988. The central authority concluded that the recent inflation and economic instability had been brought about by the overheated economy and over expanded consumption demands (Vogel 2011, pp. 616–639). Therefore, it accentuated economic policies to suppress social needs and regulate the order of commodity circulation. From this point, the economy entered a period called 'improvement and rectification' (CCCCP 1989, pp. 121–145; Li 1989, pp. 295–306 and 337–340). While the authority had made a conservative turn, it stressed its firm support of forwarding economic reforms and stated that it would adopt a healthier approach by endorsing rectification and reform (Li 1990, pp. 252–262). Then, the economy followed a rather moderate development path until 1992, when President Jiang endorsed Deng's active reform strategy in the second decade of China's economic reform, which is the focus of the next chapter.

In summary, the reform of the economy started with a cautious mix of planned and market strategies. The market strategy gained the upper hand when the agricultural reform achieved impressive success but lost ground to the more conservative planned strategy when overheated development resulted in inflation and economic and social instabilities. Therefore, it was a period of policy swings between proplanning and promarket strategies. Below, the detailed economic policies and the related legal development in this period are examined to understand the peculiar political economy and the law in this stage.

4.1.2 Reform of the Agricultural Sector and Its Rules

The Evolution of the Reform in Agricultural Production

At the outset of the reform, the key means of production in the agricultural sector were tightly gripped by the state via legal institutions and administrative arrangements. According to the Chinese Land Management Law (1986), land in urban areas was wholly owned by the state, and land on the outskirts of cities and in rural areas was under either public or collective ownership (Article 2 and 6). Before the reform, agricultural production had been organized in cooperative production teams, the production units of the People's Commune. However, after the Great Leap Forward, the commune system could not last. The primary reason was the indiscriminate egalitarianism that had eliminated peasants' working incentives and paralyzed the functions of collective work, thus severely reducing agricultural yields to the point where China could barely feed its people (Lin 1990). At this point, the subsistence of the Chinese people was again in danger, and the reforms of the agricultural sector made a breakthrough.

The critical aspect of the reforms in the agricultural sector was the intent to change the relationship between peasants and the land. As discussed above, under the commune system, the land was collectively controlled by each commune; peasants worked for and were paid by the production teams with which they were registered. In this system, the organization of agricultural production detached the farmers from the land by implementing a commune system between them. The actual agricultural yields did not affect the income of the peasants. However, as the system proved to effectively damage productivity, the reform in rural areas unsurprisingly took place first, altering the relationship between the land and the people who worked on it.

As a result, a new system called the Household Responsibility System (HRS) emerged by the end of the 1970s. As the name suggests, this system made the household, instead of the commune's production team, the working unit in agricultural production. Specifically, individual households took responsibility for farming by contracting a certain amount of land from their collectives. Then, within the agreed-upon period of the contracts, these households were obliged to hand in the amount of assigned product to the collectives according to their contracts, after which, if any surplus remained, these households were entitled to dispose of it, meaning they could either retain or sell their extra harvest (Harford 1985, pp. 31–62; Parish 1985).

Whereas the system was put into action only in the late 1970s, it was not new to Chinese society. Similar structures had emerged as early as the 1950s, but at that time, they had not flourished and had been subjected to waves of emerging-suppressing struggle due to concerns about political righteousness (Chen 1993). The main reason behind the suppression was ideological differences. Party leaders at the time deemed the contractual system of production a capitalist mode of economic activity and thus were opposed to it in principle. Therefore, it was eradicated and re-emerged only in November 1978, when the political atmosphere was changing and economic difficulties had accumulated to a perilous point (Lin 1987, 1992).

After its initial endorsement, the authority adjusted several vital facets of the system to improve production. Significant to its function were expanding the range of private ownership of the means of production, which was crucial to enhance motivation. Also subjected to change from time to time was the duration of the land contract, as it was instrumental in maintaining land productivity.

The ownership of the means of production under the HRS was revised and expanded several times, including the right to agricultural products and use-rights to land. The HRS made a substantial change to its predecessor, the production team, by allowing households to engage in agricultural production as a unit. Under the HRS, the collectives contracted out a certain amount of land to individual households for a fixed time. Within this period, in addition to having the right to decide the kinds of agricultural products to grow, most significantly, after producing and delivering the assigned products, peasants could keep their surplus products or sell them at a relatively free market price. Thus, private households gained the right to use the land and keep their surplus products. This change marked the first significant revision of property rights in rural China, but land rights were still severely limited.[1] In 1984, the Party endorsed land transfer between private parties for the first time via a circular (CCCCP 1984b, p. 362) and then legalized it in several acts from 1988 through 2003,[2] which will be discussed in detail later. Hence, after stages of adaptation, as of 2003, rural households involved in the HRS received the right to use and transfer the land they contracted.

In terms of the length of the contract period, initially, households were granted only one to three years of land use rights. Such an arrangement soon proved impractical, as it significantly undermined peasants' enthusiasm for investing in and improving land fertility and productivity. The Party extended the contract term to fifteen years in 1984, and in 1993, it was prolonged to thirty years (Li 1990).[3]

The HRS thrived and prevailed relentlessly within a few years. Officially, it was recognized by the central government in 1982 via an announcement in a political document acknowledging individual households, not collectives, as the basic unit in organizing agricultural production and accounting (CCCCP 1982, p. 362). As the data show, by the end of 1983, 94.5% of households in rural China had left their production teams and converted to this new farming system, and in 1984, 100% of production teams and 98% of rural households were involved in the HRS (Editorial Board of China Agriculture Yearbook 1984, pp. 66–67; Huang et al. 1992, p. 1390; Wu 2005, pp. 108–114). This system was highly successful at the beginning. From 1978 through 1984, the increase in peasants' annual income reached 15.1%, the fastest-growing period in history (Han 2008, p. 34; Perkins 2015, pp. 196–199).

The establishment of the HRS marked the first instance of political ideology yielding to economic reality and the first sign of weakness in the planned economy. It differed from the previous system, the cooperative production team, in a few significant aspects. The idea of a market mechanism started to penetrate Chinese society and led to the first crack in the seemingly seamless planned economic system. As discussed above, under the HRS, the right to the means of production, incomplete rights notwithstanding, began to shift from public to private hands. Notably, use rights and later the right of land transfer were granted to peasant households.

Additionally, households gained a certain amount of autonomy regarding agricultural production. For instance, they gained autonomy to decide the kind of crops they wanted to grow. Second, their rights to surplus agricultural products were recognized. This meant that after delivering the assigned amounts of products to the government, households have the autonomy to dispose of their surplus if any remains. These changes marked the first emergence of the capitalist mode of production in China.

The 'Rule' System of the Agricultural Sector

While the actual change to agricultural production took place in 1978, the HRS was a bottom-up initiative that had not been purposefully designed by the central government. Therefore, it initially operated outside the state regulating system, as there existed neither political nor legal documents acknowledging its official status. As a result, it received attention from the central government only after it had achieved some success.

In September 1980, the Central Committee of the CCP issued a paper on agricultural production that claimed the necessity of regulating the HRS on the policy level and allowed poor and remote areas to adopt such a system while blocking other regions from engaging in it (CCCCP 1980, p. 469). From 1982 through 1986, the central government and the Party announced a series of Number One documents at the beginning of each year to guide work in rural areas, signalling an undoubted emphasis on the agricultural system in the years of the commencement of the reform era.[4] These Party and administrative papers and directives thus constituted the regulatory framework for adjusting agricultural production in the following years.

The Number One document of the Party in 1982 acknowledged the HRS as a part of the socialist economy, granting it confirmed political status for performance for the first time (CCCCP 1982). In 1983, in addition to endorsing the HRS, the Party announced the reform of the People's Commune system to establish township governments, separating the economic function from the administrative organ. However, after a few years of implementation, it was proven that the rather crude regulation of the HRS required some subtle refinements. For instance, due to the nature of agricultural production, the length of land-lease contracts needed to be clarified and institutionalized. Therefore, in 1984, the Party prolonged the period of the land-lease contract to encourage peasants to invest in the land and improve land productivity (CCCCP 1984b).

From 1985 onwards, in addition to stressing agricultural production in various Party documents, some regional legal documents emerged as supplements to political documents in regulating the operation of the HRS. In response to the Agriculture Ministry, the State Council stressed the importance of legalizing land contracts, and by 1992, 24 out of 34 provinces had issued local laws regulating land contracts (State Council 1992). However, it was only in 2003, after the National People's Congress promulgated the Law of the People's Republic of China on the Contracting of Rural Land, that the HRS started to operate within a formal legal framework.

Overall, the regulation of the HRS passed through three major stages, from running purely under political regulation to a mix of political and local legislation and finally to receiving the support of national-level formal law. This changing structure of the regulation mode showed the gradual concession of the government, on both the political and legal fronts, to the economic reality of the time. From being a subject of politically disapproval to winning recognition in the Constitution and other department laws, the HRS won legitimacy through its economic performance. On the other hand, it exemplified the force of economic growth in driving political concessions, which would be more vivid in the other sectors that we will discuss in the following. Nevertheless, at this point, it would be fair to say that the rules for the HRS were a latecomer whose presence was allowed because of actual needs; that is, the changing social realities led to the existence of such legal responses.

4.1.3 Reform of the Industrial and Commercial Sector and Its Rules

Currently, the Chinese industrial and commercial sector comprises various types of economic entities. It includes state-owned enterprises, collective enterprises, share-cooperative enterprises, joint enterprises, limited liability corporations, limited shareholding corporations, private enterprises, and individual businesses. It evolved into the current structure after rounds of ownership reforms that spanned over two decades.

Before the economic reform took place, the entire Chinese economy was publicly owned, centrally organized, and deeply embedded in and intertwined with the bureaucratic system. This economic structure was brought about by the socialist transformation that happened in the mid-1950s. During that period, the Chinese government initiated the ownership transformation movement of all industries to build a socialist planned economy. Upon the completion of this movement, Chinese economic entities were either state-owned or under collective ownership (SOEs); the private economy had therefore been eradicated. Moreover, these entities were organized and operated according to economic production plans made by the state, which meant their productive activities had to strictly adhere to state orders. Their management and staff had been closely intertwined with the government since the socialist transformation.

As mentioned above, the economic situation was rather desperate after years of social and political turmoil. Hence, after 1978, a series of reforms were implemented, and the Chinese industrial sector gradually changed from uniform public ownership into a complex entity in which multiple types of ownership structures coexist. Broadly speaking, two primary waves brought the industrial sector to its current state. The first involves the rise of township and village enterprises, the early-stage reform of SOEs, and the emergence of individual businesses, which took place in the 1980s.

The second surge embraced the massive scale of corporatization and privatization reform of SOEs and the formation of China's private enterprises during the 1990s, which will be discussed in the next chapter.

4.1.3.1 The Rise of Township and Village Enterprises

Township and village enterprises (hereafter TVEs) were the first rising force in China's industrial sector. The term 'TVEs' suggests location rather than ownership structure. In other words, these were rurally located enterprises, including both collectively owned and private businesses. They started to emerge in the early 1980s and maintained momentum for a decade, with their growth climaxing in the mid-1990s (Huang 2008, Chap. 2). By 1996, over 23 million TVEs were dispersed throughout China, employing approximately 135 million workers (Huang 2008, p. 79).

Origin and Causes of the Rise of TVEs

The predecessors of TVEs were communes and brigade enterprises,[6] which can be traced back to the early stage of the People's Commune period, roughly around 1958. As mentioned previously, the People's Commune system also engaged in industrial production as a complex incorporating social, political, and economic functions. Its production teams or brigades usually ran these communal industrial enterprises, producing products to facilitate agricultural production (Perkins 2015, pp. 175–187). Therefore, their functions were restricted mainly to producing fertilizer, manufacturing and fixing farming tools and processing agriculture products. In 1958, over six million such enterprises were operating within the People's Commune system nationwide, contributing 5.8% (approximately 6.25 billion *yuan*) of the gross industrial output (Luo 2016, p. 436).

However, this situation did not last and declined immediately in 1959. The primary reason was the extreme economic difficulties caused by the Great Leap Forward (Lardy 1987, pp. 360–397), which left the government no option but to concentrate as many resources, including raw materials and labour, as possible on agricultural production. A cap of no more than 2% of the total labour force of the brigades for local enterprises was dictated via several regulations.[7] By 1965, only 12,000 communal enterprises were still in operation, generating approximately 530 million *yuan* in industrial output (Luo 2016, pp. 438–439).

The turbulent period of the Cultural Revolution saw a slight increase in both the number of enterprises and their output (Perkins 2015, pp. 137–206). This was largely due to the increasing awareness of the importance of implementing mechanical farming. The government wanted technical advancement to help improve agriculture yields, and the employment cap on communal enterprises was therefore lifted. At the end of 1976, as the Cultural Revolution was drawing to a close, over one million communal enterprises across the country were producing approximately 25 billion *yuan* of industrial output (Ma 1991, pp. 47 and 56). These enterprises thus laid the foundation of and were the predecessors of China's rural enterprises.

Regarding communal and brigade enterprises providing a basis for the rise of TVEs, several other factors are worth mentioning. For example, the availability of the rural labour force, the expanding savings of rural residents, and the freeing of the entrepreneurial spirit, along with the loosened ideological grip, may all have played crucial roles in the emergence of TVEs (Du 1990). The first two factors partly resulted from China's agricultural reform, and the third was due to the changing political atmosphere.

Before the take-off of the TVEs, rural China possessed a sizable surplus labour force. Many reasons can be suggested for this phenomenon. First, the rapid growth of the population in the preceding decades had resulted in decreased per capita arable land. For example, from 1952 through 1977, the Chinese rural population saw rapid growth of as much as 55.6%, while the per capita arable land declined from 3.29 to 1.85 mu (Du 1990, p. 49).[8] The growing birth rate added to the decreasing availability of arable land generated the 'rural reserve army' for emerging TVEs. Second, after the application of the HRS in rural areas,[9] agricultural productivity was significantly improved (Lin 1988), and therefore, less labour was needed for farming activities.

In the meantime, the success of the HRS greatly improved the income of rural Chinese people. Moreover, with swelling savings accounts, the consumption incentives of the population were simultaneously released, which prepared an emerging market for consumer goods. Additionally, private investment in rural industry became possible as farmers became more affluent, and they were therefore capable of providing additional financial support for some start-up TVEs (Du 1990, pp. 51–55).

Finally, the released spirit of rural entrepreneurship, although it appears to have been a less tangible factor, was extremely important to the rise of TVEs. With the opening of the market and the loosening of political control over rural enterprises, the long-suppressed innovation spirit of rural entrepreneurs exploded (Huang 2008). In the early 1980s, the rural industrial sector, based on the foundation of its predecessor and benefiting from the HRS reform, possessed a sufficient rural labour force, expanded financial resources, and an emerging consumer market that enabled it to take off.

Characteristics of TVEs

The operating systems of TVEs were a mixture of improved autonomy over external economic activities and still greatly constrained internal corporate governance. On the one hand, the TVEs gained a certain degree of autonomy for their production and financial control compared to their predecessors. Nevertheless, their management and personnel arrangements were still tightly controlled by local governments (Wong 1988, pp. 17–24).

Before the reform, these communal and brigade enterprises, despite using the term 'enterprise', were not even remotely close to the modern concept. Instead, they were merely production units of rural governments (Wu 2005, pp. 96–104). That is, they possessed no autonomy regarding the procurement, management, and distribution of their profit and products. These critical elements of production were all in the hands of local governments.

A stark example is that these communal enterprises had to follow the so-called three-local principle doctrine, which meant the purchasing of raw materials, the production processes, and the selling of their products all had to be done within the local regions where the enterprises were located. In addition, as the communal enterprises were in the service of agricultural production, they had to follow government instructions on both the category and the quantity of products they produced. For instance, they had to engage in the production of farming tools, pesticides, and other farming inputs (Bennett et al. 1978; Luo 2016). No autonomy was granted for production decisions. In other words, local governments decided the production targets, and the communal enterprises fulfilled them. Therefore, strictly following the state plans, these communal enterprises were operating to satisfy particular government orders rather than for the market.

However, these restrictions no longer applied to TVEs after the reform commenced. The three-local principle was lifted, and their products were no longer strictly tied to farming activities. The release of control over production oriented the TVEs towards market-responsive development. The structure of the products became more diversified as a result.[10] Also changed was the peculiar wage system. As TVEs started to possess independent financial control of themselves, they could pay wages directly to workers, who were formerly paid by the production teams where they originated according to the work points they earned (Wong 1988, p. 19).

Nevertheless, the liberation was limited to the production section and some financial issues. The original employment and management structures remained untouched. The top managers of these enterprises were still incumbents in local government, and the workforce had to be recruited from the local population; only a few exceptions were allowed for specific reasons. The reserve personnel structure immediately indicated that the actual control of these enterprises was still in the hands of local governments.

The Rise of TVEs and Their Legal Structure

The evolution of the TVEs consisted of two stages. The first was the boom period, ranging from the beginning of the reform to the mid-1990s. Afterwards, it came to a halt due to policy shifts and was subjected to ownership reconstruction in the late 1990s. In the following discussion, the economic performance of the TVEs is put in the context of a legal framework to examine the characteristics of the laws that supported the evolution of the TVEs.

Since 1981, the Chinese State Council and the CCCCP have issued a series of liberal-oriented policy documents to adjust rural economic activities, sending clear signals of political prioritization of developing the rural economy and thus significantly propelling rural industries.[11] In addition to policy papers, the State Council has stipulated a few regulations to institutionalize the operations of TVEs. Among them, of importance were rules for income tax,[12] distribution of profits,[13] production quality controls,[14] and general rules for the organization of rural enterprises.[15] However, a closer review of these regulations reveals that they were aimed at specific regulation outcomes rather than establishing a uniform legal framework for TVEs.

Nevertheless, TVEs achieved rapid growth during this period (Huang 2008, Chaps. 2 and 3).[16] From 1978 through 1996, their GDP value added experienced a leap forwards, jumping from less than 6% in 1978 to 26% in 1996; their annual employment growth rate was 9% during this period, and the total amount of labourers working in TVEs increased from 28 million in 1978 to 135 million in 1996 (Naughton 2007, pp. 274 and 286).

After the early 1990s, the political atmosphere was changing, and economic policies started to favour urban areas in the wake of the Tiananmen massacre; as a result, to support the construction of the urban sector, the central government taxed rural regions (Huang 2008). From then on, the economic performance of TVEs showed a declining trend. As a result, in 1994, the number of private TVEs and the number of their employees fell by 21.5% and 10.8%, respectively (Huang 2008, p. 129). In 1996, when TVEs were in decline, the legislature issued the Law of the PRC on Township Enterprises, the first legislation to set formal rules for TVEs.

The above discussion underlines two aspects: the changing structure and economic performance of TVEs and their related legal structure. First, as the data reveal, TVEs rose regardless of the informal legal infrastructure but entered a stalemate even though the legal institutions of China were improved in the 1990s. The turning point was the shifting political bias, which favoured rural areas in the 1980s and shifted focus to urban regions in the 1990s. Second, the deadlock of TVEs was broken only in the late 1990s, when they were subjected to ownership restructuring along with SOEs.

4.1.3.2 Traditional Chinese SOEs and Their Early-Stage Reforms

In 1978, over 83,700 state-owned industrial enterprises were operating across China, contributing nearly 80% of the gross industrial output value (State Statistics Bureau 1985, pp. 305–306). These SOEs were the products of China's early socialist transformation movement that had been completed at the end of 1956. On the verge of the reform years, except for a small portion that was collectively owned, the state controlled the vast majority of the national economy. This social and historical background implies some distinct socialist characteristics of these SOEs.

The Chinese name for an SOE is *danwei*, or 'working unit'. This term possesses much stronger connotations than the word 'company' or 'corporation'. Generally, these traditional SOEs had a highly bureaucratic managerial structure and were burdened with multiple social responsibilities along with their production functions. Operating within the planned economic system, similar to the former communal and brigade enterprises, the traditional SOEs had no autonomy in production, management, investment, hiring, etc. Instead, these functions were controlled by different governmental branches (Wu 2005, pp. 139–153). For instance, the planning commission and the economic commission administered production and investment, the Party organizational department and the human resources department of the government handled the appointment of chief executives of SOEs, and the labour department managed the allocation of the labour force. Therefore, as production units directly run by government entities, traditional SOEs were, in effect, run by multiple branches of the government.

Moreover, traditional SOEs carried heavy social burdens. They were not merely economic units but also had social functions. In addition to paying salaries, most importantly, they were in charge of providing a wide range of social benefits and security for their employees. Social services such as education, public health, housing, subsistence, and child and elder care were all the responsibility of the SOEs (Naughton 2007, p. 116; Wu 2005, Chap. 4). Indeed, SOEs by then were anything but corporations in the modern sense.

Before launching the large-scale corporatization and privatization reform, the government tried several adjustments without touching on the ownership structure. From 1978 through 1992, the government first pursued the strategy of 'expanding enterprise autonomy', and when the outcome proved unsatisfactory, the 'enterprise contracting system' tactic followed (Zhang and Yuan 2008, pp. 14–47). The initial diagnosis of the Chinese government regarding its state sector was that the over-centralized control of SOEs had crippled their development. Thus, the 'power delegating and profit-sharing' strategy was adopted. After trying some pilot programmes (Wu 2005, p. 145),[17] in July 1979, the State Council issued five documents to extend the strategy nationwide.[18] By this approach, the SOEs were granted some autonomy of operation and management and were allowed to retain part of their profits. By the end of 1980, over 6600 large and medium-sized SOEs were making such adjustments, accounting for 70% of the total profit of the SOE sector (Wu 2005, p.145).

Nevertheless, the economic performance of these SOEs did not show any improvement. Therefore, from 1981 on, the strategy shifted to the 'enterprise contracting system', similar to the system developed by and successfully operating in the agricultural sector. The 'enterprise contracting system' allowed SOEs to sell their products after meeting the assigned production goal in the hope of providing incentives. By the end of 1989, almost all SOEs had adopted this system (Chen 2008). In 1992, the State Council issued the Regulations on Transforming the Management Mechanism of State-owned Industrial Enterprises to further expand the managerial and operating autonomy of SOEs.

The reforms in this period can be characterized as adjustments within the institutional structure. Neither granting autonomy to SOEs nor contracting out the enterprises had touched on the core features of traditional SOEs. They were still operating in a planned economy with opaque protection of property rights and were protected by the 'soft budget constraint'.[19] In fifteen years of trial and error, despite the ongoing adjustments, the financial performance of SOEs declined. The GDP profit percentage of industrial SOEs decreased from 14% in 1978 to approximately 2% in 1992 (Naughton 2007, p. 305). A more thorough reform of SOEs would take place a few years later, as will be discussed in the next chapter.

4.1.3.3 The Rise of Individual Business and Its Rules

At present, China's private sector consists of various types of businesses. For example, there are private limited liability companies, private shareholding limited companies, private sole proprietorship enterprises, private partnership enterprises, and individual businesses. In general, the formation of the private sector consisted of two major steps—the rise of individual businesses in the 1980s and the shaping of private enterprises during the 1990s. One way to track the process is to review the amendments of Article 11 of the Constitution, which concerns the legal status of China's private sector. These amendments vividly exemplify the changing political attitude and the growing legal support for the private sector, which contributed to the enlargement of the private sector over the years.

As discussed, the socialist transformation wiped out the whole private sector, and the Chinese private economy operated on a minimal scale and was of no importance to the economy at the beginning of the reform years. Nevertheless, along with the loosening of political control and completion of legal support, the scale of private business increased incrementally and soared after each constitutional amendment.

The first emerging component of the private economy was the so-called individual business (*getihu*), which was a direct reaction to the aftermath of the Cultural Revolution (Xue 1984, pp. 216–235).[20] In 1981, the State Council stipulated the Policies Regarding the Urban Non-Agriculture Individual Businesses to regulate the operations of individual businesses. Individual businesses are economic entities that are privately owned and have fewer than eight employees.[21] In 1982, China released the current version of its Constitution, and Article 11 reads, 'The individual economy of urban and rural working people, operating within the limits prescribed by law, is a complement to the socialist public economy'. It therefore laid the legal foundation for the first appearance of the private economy. Immediately thereafter, the State Council issued a series of related regulations to guide individual businesses—among them were Provisions on Cooperation between Urban Labours (1983), Provisions on Rural Individual Businesses (1984), Provisional Regulations on Urban–rural Individual Businesses (1987)—in the hope of providing a comprehensive legal network for their operations.

According to statistical data, from 1982 through 1988, the gross industrial output value of urban and rural individual businesses followed a steady uprising trend, jumping from 340 million *yuan* in 1982 to 79 billion *yuan* in 1988 (State Statistics Bureau 1990, p. 414). With this increase in economic performance, individual businesses demonstrated their importance to the economy by generating a large number of jobs. In 1978, individual businesses in urban areas hired only approximately 150,000 workers (State Statistics Bureau 1986, p. 124); however, the number of employees had jumped to 4.5 million by 1985 (Lardy 2014, p. 83; State Statistics Bureau 1986, p. 124). As the size of individual businesses continued to expand, the eight-employee cap became a fetter restricting growth. As a result, more leeway was desired. Against this backdrop, from 1988 onwards, Article 11 of the Constitution has been amended repeatedly, signalling an ever-loosening grip on the private economy and thereby paving the way for the growth of private enterprises (*siying qiye*) over the next decade.

4.1.4 Reform of the International Investment System and Its Rules

Because China was a developing country seeking capital and technology, one of the economic strategies for opening up was to attract foreign investment. Broadly speaking, there have been three major phases of foreign investment inflow into China since 1980, and each of them corresponds to a particular period of policy and legal framework adjustment. As UN data show,from 1980 through 1991, when China operated a planned economy with open-door policies, the initial FDIs in China appeared to be steady but modest, reaching only $3.4 billion as of 1990. The second stage saw a sharp increase in inwards capital flow, from $4.3 billion in 1991 to $45.6 billion in 1998, and this abrupt surge corresponded to Deng Xiaoping's Southern Tour, which marked the market-oriented turn of China's economy. The third phase of the FDI boom arrived when China joined the WTO in 2001, and since then, FDI inflow has grown steadily, reaching $139 billion by the end of 2018.[22] This post-WTO period paralleled China's substantial effort to standardize its administration and legal system, which is one of the focuses of the next chapter.

This section explores the institutional changes that brought waves of FDI inflow after 1978. In summary, the basic framework for attracting foreign capital had three major components. The first was related to policy arrangements, such as setting up numerous special economic zones, offering preferential taxes for foreign enterprises, granting some local governments greater autonomy to reduce red tape, granting economic privileges for foreign investments, and purposefully constructing foreigner-friendly or more Western-style infrastructures to attract foreign businesses. Second, a raft of laws and regulations was promulgated for foreign businesses. They were specifically designed for different forms of foreign investment, and by doing so, China successfully countered a certain anxiety about its socialist political environment among foreign investors. Third, in addition to constructing a domestic legal infrastructure for FDIs, China also actively wove an international legal network to ensure that foreign investors felt secure. For example, it concluded BITs with over a hundred countries and ratified the ICSID convention.

4.1.4.1 Setting up Special Economic Zones and Beyond

The immediate political strategy that the Chinese government followed to open its doors was to carve out several cities and designate them as Special Economic Zones (SEZs) where local authorities were granted autonomy concerning foreign investment policies to a certain extent. China intended to attract foreign capital to these selected regions and concentrate it there; the basic rationale was to experiment with economic strategies in a few insignificant coastal cities. If this arrangement worked, it would then be applied to other regions (Deng 1985, p. 133; Deng 1987, p. 239; Deng 1991, p. 366).[23] This opening-up policy unfolded incrementally and has lasted for decades. With its growing success, the central government became more confident, and thus, numerous cities and regions joined the programme (Falkenheim 1986; Jao and Leung 1986). Eventually, cities and regions along the coastline and many inland regions opened up one after another, weaving a nationwide network of selected areas for foreign investment.

This trial-and-error process started in 1980, when China carefully selected Shenzhen, Zhuhai, Shantou, and Xiamen as SEZs. Except for Xiamen, they are located in Guangdong Province, which borders Hong Kong (Vogel 1989, Chap. 4). In contrast, Xiamen is situated in the southern coastal province of Fujian and is home to many overseas Chinese specializing in business (Deng 1991, p. 366). As SEZs, these cities were allowed to offer special economic policies to attract foreign capital. For instance, the Regulations of SEZs of Guangdong Province, stipulated by the local legislature of Guangdong Province, listed preferential measures for foreign investment[24] that included land use rights, tax exemptions for importing equipment and raw materials, preferential tax rates for corporate income taxes, and so on (Article 12–18).

In 1984, Deng visited Shenzhen, Zhuhai, and Xiamen and was impressed by the rapid development of these cities; therefore, he decided to extend the strategy to another fourteen coastal port cities (Deng 1977, p. 51).[25] A year later, three southern areas, the Yangtze River Delta, the Pearl River Delta, and the Xiamen-Zhangzhou-Quanzhou Triangle in southern Fujian, were demarcated as open regions. Soon afterwards, in 1988, two northern coastal regions, the Liaodong Peninsula and the Shandong Peninsula, were designated open economic areas, and in the same year, all of Hainan Province was designated an SEZ (Vogel 1989, pp. 275–312). This stage ended when Pudong (a district of Shanghai) was assigned as the New Zone in 1990. Therefore, in the first decade of opening up, China opened almost all of its major waterfront cities and regions, from southern coastal areas to the northern region.

Since Deng Xiaoping's Southern Tour in 1992, China has deepened its opening-up policy and opened its inland regions on a large scale. From 1992 onwards, China successively unlocked 13 inland border cities, 18 inland capital cities, and 8 cities along the Yangtze River. By 2000, Beijing had woven a web of open regions covering coastal and inland areas. This network possessed 5 SEZs (Shenzhen, Zhuhai, Shantou, Xiamen, and Hainan), 54 special zones for economic and technological development, 53 specialized zones for the high-tech industry, and 15 bonded zones (Naughton 2018, pp. 428–429). The speed of mapping out different types of zones accelerated in the following years, and the number of open zones currently amounts to over two thousand, covering basically all major cities in every province (National Development and Reform Commission et al. 2018).[26] In 2010, two cities in Xinjiang Province, Kashgar and Khorgas, joined the SEZs.

From carefully selecting the first four SEZs to mapping out different types of zones throughout the whole nation, the initially unique characteristics of these areas are no longer distinctive. Nevertheless, it is worth sketching these characteristics to gain perspective. Whereas the names and purposes of these areas vary, they share similarities in terms of economic policies.[27] In general, the local authorities in charge of these zones possessed certain privileges regarding fiscal policies and administrations and special legislative powers over economic affairs. For example, in terms of fiscal autonomy, the most common policies were to offer tax holidays, such as exempting newly established foreign enterprises from income taxes for three years. Moreover, in terms of administration, these regions were less bureaucratic in dealing with foreigner-involved affairs. Therefore, foreign investors found themselves facing less red tape in conducting businesses, which has arguably been crucial to China's success in attracting FDI (Sachdev 2006). While possessing certain privileges in making economic policies, such power appeared to be no longer unique, as these privileges became available in a vast network throughout the country. As a result, the geographic significance of these areas became less relevant to China's massive inflow of FDI, especially in later stages. Thus, the more substantial reason for the flooding in of foreign capital may have a bearing on the design of the legal framework for foreign investment.

4.1.4.2 The Domestic Legal Structure for Foreign Investment

China's domestic legal system for foreign investment consists of three tiers: the Constitution,[28] national laws enacted by the NPC or its Standing Committee, and administrative regulations and rules enacted by the State Council and its ministries (mainly the MOFCOM[29]). Alternatively, the Chinese legal system of foreign investment could be projected as three building blocks, two domestic laws plus one international law, with each block serving particular regulative purposes. In block one, there were three national laws to settle the legitimate forms of foreign investment, namely, the Law of the PRC on Chinese-Foreign Equity Joint Ventures (1979), the Law of the PRC on Wholly Foreign-Owned Enterprises (1986), and the Law of the PRC on Chinese-Foreign Contractual Joint Ventures (1988). Together with them were several laws concerning particular areas involving foreign interests, such as contracts and taxes.[30] This batch of legal documents served as the bedrock for foreign investment.

The second block of laws focused on more specific issues concerning foreign investment and therefore served as an extended legal guide for investors. Mostly, they were departmental rules stipulated by the MOFCOM. Overall, they can be classified in four types. First, a raft of regulations was issued to facilitate the implementation of the three laws for foreign enterprises mentioned above, as is illustrated below. Second, there were rules to provide instruction for particular modes of cooperation, such as the Notice on Some Issues of Utilizing Foreign Investment in the form of BOT (1995) and the Provisions on Merger and Acquisition of Domestic Enterprises by Foreign Investors (2003). Third, there were rules concerning particular types of companies and management issues of foreign-invested enterprises, to name but a few, the Provisional Regulations on the Establishment of Stock Companies with Foreign Investment (1995), the Provisions on Holding Companies with Foreign Investment (1995), the Regulations on Modifications of Shares with Foreign Investment (1997), and the Regulations on Merger and Separation of Enterprises with Foreign Investment (1999). Finally, there was a group of documents that dealt with particular business areas when foreign capital was involved, such as the Regulations on the Exploration of Offshore (1982)/Onshore (1993) Petroleum Resources in Cooperation with Foreign Enterprises, the Regulations on the Commerce with Foreign Fund (2004), and the Regulations on Leasing Business with Foreign Fund (2005).

Additionally, to steer the orientation of foreign investment, in 1995, the State Council issued the Guidance on the Direction of Foreign Investment and the Guiding Catalogue of Industries for Foreign Investment. This document is to be updated every few years. The catalogue classifies all categories of foreign investment in four groups, namely, encouraged, restricted, prohibited, and permitted. Foreign investment classified as permitted is allowed by default, and the remaining categories are all defined with detailed lists of specifications.

Foreign Investment Laws as a Temporary 'Legal Enclave'

As mentioned above, China designed and legalized three forms of enterprises exclusively for foreign investment and supplemented them with a set of administrative regulations to smooth the implementation of these laws and guide foreign investment in general. Together, this precisely fabricated legal network for foreign investment effectively formed a 'legal enclave' that was exclusively in the service of businesses with foreign elements. Moreover, these laws formed enterprises with foreign capital into a privileged group that possessed rights unavailable to their Chinese competitors. The following section first probes the details of these laws and then examines the legal privileges they granted by comparing them with the rights of domestic enterprises.

From 1979 through 1988, China promulgated three legal forms of enterprise tailored solely for foreign capital: the equity joint venture (EJV), the cooperative joint venture (CJV), and the wholly foreign-owned enterprise (WFE).[31] Accordingly, their legal rights and obligations were written in a set of laws and regulations. The first law for foreign ventures was the Law of the PRC on Chinese-Foreign Equity Joint Ventures, stipulated in 1979, which was complemented by a raft of administrative regulations for its implementation, such as the Regulations for the Implementation of the Law of the PRC on Joint Ventures Using Chinese and Foreign Investment. Then, in 1986, the Chinese government gave a green light to wholly foreign-owned businesses, and the Law of the PRC on Wholly Foreign-Owned Enterprises came into force in the same year.[32] In a similar vein, a number of regulations to assist its operation were put into effect in the following years. Among them were the Detailed Rules for the Implementation of the Law of the PRC on Wholly Foreign-Owned Enterprises in China and An Explanation of Several Terms Used in the Detailed Rules for the Implementation of the Law of the PRC on Sole Foreign Investment Enterprises. Soon afterwards, in 1988, the third legal form of foreign investment was designed, and then came the Law of the PRC on Chinese-Foreign Contractual Joint Ventures. Likewise, it has a string of supplementary rules, such as the Detailed Rules for the Implementation of the Law of the PRC on Sino-Foreign Joint Cooperative Ventures.

The timeline of the three laws shows that the Chinese government spent ten years introducing the three forms of enterprises for foreign capital, from the first introduction of EJVs in 1979 to granting the operation of CJVs in 1988. It is thus intriguing to speculate that while China was desperately in need of cash and advanced technology to accelerate its modernization, as a socialist and planned economy, the government was cautious about the inflow of foreign capital. Therefore, instead of hesitantly completing the whole strategy for foreign capital all at once, the Chinese government chose to allow foreign investment step by step. Such deliberation was also expressed in granting the rights and duties of these foreign enterprises.

All three legal documents announced that the state protected the legal rights and profits of foreign enterprises according to law[33] and granted them tax preferences.[34] However, the legal status of enterprises varied under the three documents. Only EJVs were mandated to be set up as legal persons with limited liability,[35] and the other two types of enterprises could gain legal person status only when certain conditions were met.[36] The management of joint ventures (both EJVs and CJVs) was split between the two parties, with the Chinese Party assuming the dominant role.[37] The distribution of the net profits and risks of joint ventures was to correspond to each party's share[38] or according to their additional agreements.[39]

While the government did not incorporate the production of foreign enterprises into its economic plans, it mandated that foreign investors had to report their production and operation plans to Chinese officials, and purchases of raw materials or other means of production should be conducted primarily in the Chinese market.[40] The ventures were allowed to transfer their net profits abroad if they were to be dissolved or suspended, and the income of foreign employees was allowed to be transferred abroad after they paid income tax.[41] When arguments arose between parties that the board of directors could not solve, each party in these ventures had the legal right to file arguments either for Chinese arbitration or for another form of agreed-upon arbitration.[42]

In comparison with the laws for SOEs, which were issued in the same period,[43] foreign enterprises, regardless of the form they took, possessed certain freedoms and privileges. The most visible and crucial were the freedom to operate outside the planned economy, as they were obliged only to report. In contrast, the Law of the PRC on Industrial Enterprises Owned by the Whole People (WPE) explicitly stipulated that the basic responsibility of SOEs was to respond to the state plan and market needs.[44] Another significant aspect was freedom of employment. None of the three laws for foreign enterprises curtailed the liberty of enterprises regarding employment,[45] while the heads of SOEs were appointed by the government.[46]

In addition to the three laws for foreign enterprises, there were separate laws for general economic activities that involved foreign interests. Among them, the laws on contracts and taxes were crucial. While China did not promulgate its Contract Law until 1999, it issued the Law of the PRC on Economic Contracts Involving Foreign Interest (expired), which particularly served foreign investors, as early as 1985. This legal document guided foreign contractual activities for fifteen years until the uniform contract law replaced it in 1999. Also directly related to foreign investment was the income tax law of foreign enterprises, which thus far has been through three stages of transformation. In 1980, China stipulated two separate income tax laws for two different types of foreign enterprises.[47] These laws were merged into the Income Tax Law of the PRC for Enterprises with Foreign Investment and Foreign Enterprises in 1991, paralleling the domestic tax law system. The dual-track tax system was at last abolished and replaced by a unified income tax law system for all types of enterprises in 2008, the Enterprises Income Tax Law of the PRC.

Therefore, during the first decade of reform, when China operated a planned economy, foreign capital in China was allowed a certain degree of liberty in both production and employment. This deliberately tailored legal structure, plus tax preferences and explicit legal protections of rights and profit, appeared attractive to foreign investors who were eager to acquire shares in the Chinese market. In essence, the Chinese government carved out a 'legal enclave' that possessed capitalist characteristics from its domestic socialist legal system.[48] However, this distinctive legal environment for capitalist businesses evolved as China's economic situation changed. The general approach, as discussed above, was initially to promulgate laws exclusively for foreign investment and later to either merge them, as in the tax laws and the three laws for foreign enterprises that were merged into the Foreign Investment Law (January 2020), or replace them with uniform laws that were universally applicable to all participants, as in the enactment of the uniform Contract Law.

In summary, while foreign capital received extensive legal privileges, these were special rights that were subjected to adjustments according to the changing political-economic environment. At any rate, the domestic legal system constituted only one piece of the puzzle. To form an integrated picture of the entire legal system for foreign investment, it is necessary to examine international laws concerning investment.

4.1.4.3 International Legal Framework for Foreign Investment

If the above two types of domestic law constituted two blocks for foreign investment, the international legal network for investment was the third block designed to attract and guide foreign capital. Since 1982, when China concluded its first bilateral investment treaty (hereafter BIT) with Sweden, it had been actively forming such bilateral frameworks with many countries, hoping the agreements would assure foreign investors of China's favourable legal environment for investment. As of 2015, China had concluded a total of 145 BITs,[49] of which 107 are currently still in force.[50] Additionally, China signed and ratified the ICSID convention in the early 1990s, which thereafter significantly shaped the articles of dispute settlement in China's later BITs.

The international law system is essential to foreign investment because it usually allows investors to circumvent the local court system and file disputes, if they occur, with the international tribunal directly. Moreover, such a mechanism can, to the extent possible, guarantee investors impartial resolution by removing the sovereign shield that host countries often use in the face of an international trial. Therefore, the evolution of the article on investor-state disputes in Chinese BITs demonstrates how and to what extent China protected foreign investment at the international level.

To date, China has had three versions of Model BITs that were announced in 1984, 1989, and 1997 (Gallagher and Shan 2009, pp. 427–437).[51] While the actual BITs that China signed may deviate from the models, depending on the results of different bilateral negotiations, the ongoing evolution of the Model BITs still sheds light on the general legal features of China's investment treaties. All three Chinese Model BITs are concise, each consisting of 13 articles. Taking the current version as an example, the contents include a preamble, definitions, substantive articles referring to the complete process of investment, issues such as the promotion and protection of investment, treatment of investment, expropriation, compensation for damages and losses, transfer, subrogation, a settlement mechanism for disputes between the states and disputes between investors and the state, and procedural provisions for issues such as applications, consultations, entry into force, duration, and termination.

While the main structures of the three Model BITs are similar, some articles have been substantively revised, implying the changing attitude of the Chinese government towards certain issues. Among them, revisions of Article 9 of the three Model BITs, which stipulates the resolution mechanism of investor-state disputes, stand out as crucial to investors, as this article impacts the power balance between the sovereign state and private parties. However, the stance of China on this issue appears to have been overly cautious. To a great extent, this is because China, as a developing country with a painful memory of its recent war history, has been sensitive to sovereignty issues (Chen and Gu 2013; Zeng 2014; Zeng 2016).[52]

Therefore, in the first Model BIT (1984), Article 9 states that the jurisdiction over disputes between an investor and the host state belongs to the local court of the host country, with the only exception being disputes over the amount of compensation for expropriation, which, according to the article, can be submitted to an ad hoc arbitral tribunal if they cannot be solved within six months through negotiations. This arrangement of investor-state dispute resolution remained intact in the second Model BIT, which was put into force around 1989.

In February 1990, China signed the ICSID Convention and later ratified it in January 1993, which resulted in a major shift in its stance on jurisdiction issues. Upon ratifying the convention, China notified the ICSID that it would only consider submitting 'disputes over compensation resulting from expropriation and nationalization to the Center' (Gallagher and Shan 2009, p. 551). Despite this reservation, the third Chinese Model BIT (constructed around 1997) expresses a more receptive attitude to the centre. Article 9 of the third Model BIT accords investors the choice of submitting any legal dispute to either the local court or the ICSID. Two crucial aspects of this article stand out. The first is that the scope of the ICSID jurisdiction has been expanded to all types of legal disputes, regardless of the statement China had made upon ratifying the treaty; the second is that investors can directly refer to the ICSID for dispute resolution, which guarantees a greater likelihood of impartial trial for foreign investors. One speculation concerning this change is China's growing ODIs since the late 1990s, which could be one of the triggers for it changing its stance on the issue of ICSID jurisdiction (Davies 2009; Gallagher 2015, pp. 180–214).

However, as mentioned above, the contents of signed BITs are usually based on case-by-case negotiations. In terms of jurisdiction, while the early versions of the Chinese Model BITs did not mention the ICSID, the reference to the centre in the signed BITs existed before China ratified the convention, such as those with Spain and Greece in 1992 (Spain BIT Article 9 (2); Greece BIT Article 10(4)). Nevertheless, a direct reference to the ICSID appeared only when China ratified the treaty in 1993, and since then, the number of BITs that include the ICSID jurisdiction has increased. As of 2015, according to the UNCTAD database, 47 BITs included such articles, accounting for approximately half of them.[53]

From cautiously claiming jurisdiction to providing open access to the ICSID, China's stance on foreign investment and international judicial was changing alongside its growing economic power. After it had successfully attracted large amounts of foreign investment and as its outwards direct investments started to surge, China's attitude towards international rules also altered.

In addition to articles of dispute settlement, other aspects equally merit notice. For instance, the article about the standard of compensation for expropriation also underwent constant revision (Thompson 1979; Zeng 2006).[54] The 1984 Model BIT proclaimed that compensation 'shall be equivalent to the value of the expropriated investment at the time when expropriation is proclaimed' (Article 4). This was altered in the 1989 Model BIT to proclaim that compensation 'shall be calculated based on the market value' of the expropriated investment (Article 4). However, after China acceded to the ICSID, the standard of compensation was readjusted to the one in the first model, as Article 4 of the current Model BIT reads, 'The compensation ... shall be equivalent to the value of the expropriated investments immediately before the expropriation is taken or the impending expropriation becomes public knowledge, whichever is earlier'. The back-and-forth over the compensation standard clearly implies China's deep concern and wariness about open access to an international tribunal.

4.2 Internal Characteristics of the Law

4.2.1 Characteristics of the Economic Relationship

Economic relationships are a subcategory of social relationships. They are, as Weber (1978) noted, situations in which two or more parties engage in conduct oriented towards each other, and in a given social and economic environment, such conduct is, to a certain extent, determinable and predictable (pp. 26–28). The examination of economic relationships in this section focuses on three specific aspects, namely, the parties, the freedom to form an economic relationship, and the categories of economic relationships that are formed. These three elements are crucial for revealing the characteristics of the economic relationship, as they underline and reveal the norms or maxims that guide economic conduct in a given society. In other words, the nature of the participants, such as public, private, or foreign capital, and their autonomy in conducting economic activities shape economic relationships in general.

First, the entitlement of agents to form economic relationships indicates that they possess a legitimate status to engage in economic transactions. An economic right that seems natural in most free economies was rather complicated in China's case. As mentioned above, China, in its beginning years of reform, adopted a planned economic system with public ownership in virtually all possible economic sectors. That is, in those years, the majority of economic transactions occurred within state sectors, with only some individual businesses operating on the periphery of the economy. On the other hand, because China was a nation in need of capital, foreign investment was allowed and encouraged on certain conditions. Therefore, in the 1980s, the parties to economic relationships were limited to different state entities, entities of foreign origin, and individuals.

Second, as a planned economy, the state mostly monopolized the autonomy to form economic relationships. The typical economic relationships were formed between the state and the industrial and commercial sectors, with the former placing production orders with financial backing from the treasury and the latter fulfilling the orders. This was the typical relationship between the state and its many SOEs and virtually the relationship between different state sectors. In the industrial and commercial sectors, the reduced economic autonomy was embodied in spheres such as internal enterprise regulation, autonomy of employment, and autonomy of quantities, qualities, and categories of production. While the pain of low economic efficiency under such a mode was less acute in the industrial sector, in the beginning, inadequate production in the agricultural sector inflicted such pain almost immediately. In response, some adjustments to the autonomy of agriculture were allowed after the HRS was adopted; viz., the peasants were allowed to retain their surplus products after meeting their assigned production targets, and gradually, the transfer of land use rights was allowed, adding more flexibility for rural households. In contrast, foreign enterprises were granted more leeway in internal management, as they retained the right to employment and predominantly the orientation of production.

Third, in an economy where private capital, the supposedly most dynamic participant, was heavily regulated, the types of economic activity were naturally of limited scope. The most significant economic activity in this period was industrial production under state orders. The state contract, or public-public economic relationship, was the dominant form that channelled capital flow and navigated the economy in this period. In the state-run economy, access to finance was guaranteed by state banks, which minimized the social and economic need for the financial relationship. The state provided means of production, and therefore, the wide range of contract freedom was not significant. The state allocated the labour force and managed industrial production. Hence, employment was immobile, and there was no room for the formation of a labour market. In a similar vein, while foreign enterprises were given much more leeway in management and production, the scope of their economic activities was delimited by the mechanism of the planned economy, leaving legal guidance focused largely on technical contracts.

4.2.2 *Formation of the Rules—A Case Study of Contract Laws*

Whereas the previous section illustrated the legal network of economic relationships in each sector with a broad brush, this section zooms in on the law-making effort by closely examining the system of contract laws operating in this period. The contract as an instrument for formulating economic relationships plays an indispensable role in an economy, making the system of rules, especially those concerning the formation and enforcement of contracts, crucial. The following discussion sketches the image of the primitive legal environment for the freedom of transactions in the Chinese economy in the 1980s. In general, it focuses on two aspects. First, it provides a general overview of the legal system that governed different types of contractual behaviour. Second, three types of contractual rules that were significant to agricultural production, the industrial and commercial sectors, and foreign investment, viz., rules of land use contracts, general economic contracts with a focus on purchase and sale contracts, and contracts involving foreign interests, are put under the spotlight to reveal their external functions through internal characteristics.

As mentioned above, a uniform contract law guiding all kinds of contractual behaviour was promulgated as late as 1999. Before that, contractual activities were governed by different laws and rules, with many kinds of contracts having their own specific rules. Furthermore, these rules did not emerge simultaneously, and the first to be issued was the Economic Contract Law of the PRC in 1981. Subsequently, the Law of the PRC on Economic Contracts Involving Foreign Interest (1985) and the Law of the PRC on Technology Contracts (1987) were issued. Together, the three specialized contract laws worked to guide all types of contracts formed in China until the legislation of the uniform *Contract Law* a decade later.

4.2.2.1 Rural Land Contractual Relationships

As mentioned, the most significant economic achievement in the 1980s was the reform of the land contracting system. However, the formal law regulating contractual land relationships was promulgated in 2003, almost 25 years after the system was actually in operation. From 1978 through 1981, the initial years after the HRS emerged, no legal documents and no policy paper guided possible conduct under the system. The almost laissez-faire state of rural contractual relations received policy-level concern soon after the system demonstrated its economic value. In the following decades, the contractual relationships between rural households and their collectives were guided primarily by broad-brush policy papers and some regions with local regulations (State Council 1992) as well as judicial opinions in hearings on disputes over rural contracting (Supreme People's Court 1986; Supreme People's Court 1999).

Despite the demonstrated economic significance of the HRS and the Party's concern, formulating an applicable legal system remained on the agenda for years. In its place, the central authority relied heavily on issuing policy papers to coordinate related issues and actions. Nationwide, important policies concerning land contracts included the following. In 1982, the CCCCP stated, 'Production teams shall take care of the work of concluding contracts, … to confirm the rights and duties of both parties with contracts. … the conclusion of the contract shall be based on democratic negotiations and shall be abided by once the contract is concluded' (CCCCP 1982, p. 362). In 1983, the Party announced, '[We] shall establish and complete the contracting system' (CCCCP 1983, p. 231). A similar slogan style of Party policies for land contracts reappeared in the following years (CCCCP 1991, p. 278; CCCCP and State Council 1990, p. 685). In the 1990s, the central government stepped up. In 1992, the State Council issued an opinion asserting that 'to stabilize the HRS on a long-term basis and perfect it in the meanwhile, [we] shall bring it in line with the rule of law' (State Council 1992). Soon afterwards, in 1995, the State Council announced the importance of defending the integrity of the contract agreement and noted that any behaviour that infringed on rural households' legal rights would be investigated according to the law (State Council 1995, p. 329).

On the surface, these guidelines appeared to be nationally applicable, given that they were issued by the central authority. However, these policies and governmental opinions appeared to be too general to be applicable in reality, which undoubtedly left a great deal of discretion to local officials. A nationwide uniform implementation of a land contract system was hardly imaginable given the degree of abstractness of these rules. As a result, the management and regulation of the system were region-specific. Furthermore, such diversified practices led to difficulties in keeping judicial rulings uniform, an issue that is examined in detail in the following section.

4.2.2.2 Economic Contracts in General

In the industrial and commercial sectors, the rule system was somewhat different. As mentioned, the Economic Contract Law was the first to be promulgated among all legal documents for contractual conduct. In addition to promptly promulgated this law, the central authority reified a list of substantive rules for different contracts. This section first provides an overview of the Economic Contract Law and then examines the Regulations of Purchases and Sales Contracts as a lens through which to learn the format of the rules governing contractual behaviours in the 1980s.

The Economic Contract Law, according to its articles, was promulgated, among other reasons, to protect the development of a socialist market economy and socioeconomic order (Article 1). While the law did not state that it was formulated according to legal norms, the formation of economic contracts should follow the law and administrative regulations (Article 4).

The main body of the law consisted of both general rules for all economic contracts and specific rules for particular types of contracts. The structure of the law conformed to the sequence of concluding a contract, from rules for establishing and enforcing contracts to rules for the modification and rescission of economic contracts. Additionally, there were articles for liability issues once contracts were breached and dispute settlement mechanisms. In addition to general terms regulating a contract from its birth to its death, the law named ten categories of contracts and prescribed specific rules for their conclusion and performance (Article 17–26) as well as liability issued for each party once a breach occurred (Article 38–47).[55] The ten types of contracts, although broad, were all of economic interest. Three were of financial concern, such as contracts for the lease of property, loan contracts, and property insurance contracts; five that directly concerned economic transactions were purchases and sales contracts, contracts for construction projects, processing contracts, contracts for the transportation of goods, and warehousing contracts. The remaining two were public utility contracts and contracts for scientific and technological cooperation, which were later promulgated as a separate law, the Law of the PRC on Technology Contracts (1987). Among these types of contracts, four were further facilitated by administrative regulations issued by the State Council, including the Implementing Regulations of Road/Waterway Transport of Goods, Rules of Sales Contract for Agricultural Products/Mineral Products, Rules for Loan Contract, Rules for Processing Contracts, and Enforcement Regulations of Warehousing Contracts. In total, eight legal documents were issued to regulate different kinds of economic contracts.

The multilevel legal system structure for contracts can be illustrated by taking the Regulations of Purchases and Sales Contracts as an example. In concluding a sale contract, the parties would find that there were two to three tiers of rules, depending on the subject matter of their contract. First, their contractual behaviour should conform to the general terms of the Economic Contracts Law that were applicable to all kinds of economic contracts, such as rules of legitimate format, performances, and possible obligations. Second, as a sales contract, in addition to the general terms, the parties would find their contractual behaviours under the regulation of Article 17 for conclusion and performance and Article 38 in case of breach of contract; both were stipulated expressly for purchase and sales contracts. Third, for buying and selling particular goods, i.e., agricultural products, industrial and mineral products, the parties had to consult the two administrative regulations issued for particular use for these types of contracts. A similar structure was used for other categories of contracts, such as Transportation Contracts, Loan Contracts, and Warehousing Contracts. Hence, in the field of contractual relationships, the most common type of economic conduct, China constructed a three-level legal system consisting of general terms for universal application to all contracts and particular articles and lower-level rules for particular types of contracts.

While the system appears to have been relatively reasonable for use, it must be reiterated that in the 1980s, China had a planned economy, which meant the laws played the role of bringing economic transactions into line with governmental economic plans and therefore eliminated the freedom of both parties involved. Again, in the case of contractual behaviours, although the rules for such actions appear general and universally applicable, freedom in terms of the subject matter of a contract—quantity, quality, price, etc.—in principle had to conform to state plans and was therefore non-negotiable between parties (Economic Contract Law, Article 17).

4.2.2.3 Economic Contracts with Foreign Interests

In the 1980s, China was still sensitive to ideological righteousness, and interactions involving foreign parties had to be dealt with discreetly to avoid unwanted political consequences. This caution also applied to economic interactions when China opened its doors to foreign direct investment. Furthermore, the Economic Contracts Involving Foreign Interest contained stipulations for such particular purposes. This law regulated contractual relations between Chinese enterprises or other economic organizations and foreign enterprises, organizations, or individuals (Article 2). Chinese individuals were not allowed to form economic relationships with foreign parties. In Articles 4 through 6, the law stated that to guarantee formality and conformity with international standards, the conclusion of contracts should conform to Chinese laws; the laws for contractual arguments could be Chinese laws, international treaties, or international customs, depending on the concrete situation. These articles clarified that the rules governing contractual behaviour between Chinese and foreign parties were legal rules of either domestic or international origin.

In terms of application, the composition of the rules was of a more general style than the style governing domestic contractual behaviour. On the one hand, the law consisted of general rules regarding formal requirements for legitimate contracts, such as the forms of contract and the terms that should be incorporated into a contract (Chap. 2); the performance of contracts and liability for breach of a contract (Chap. 3); the assignment (Chap. 4), modification, rescission, and termination (Chap. 5) of contracts; and ways of settling possible disputes (Chap. 6). On the other hand, substantive rules for particular types of contracts that appeared in the law for domestic economic contracts were not incorporated. Therefore, a total of 43 articles guided the general process of contractual actions from the legitimate format of the contract to the enforcement of the contract and possible dispute resolutions, covering all stages of contractual transactions, and could be universally applied to all economic contracts insofar as they were concluded between legitimate parties. Hence, the form and the level of generality of the law guaranteed its broad applicability.

In total, during the first decade of the reform, the legislature and the State Council issued thirteen laws and regulations on contracts. The three laws on contracts all stated that the formulation of contracts should follow related laws and administrative rules.[56] The remaining regulations all started with a statement that the promulgation of the regulation was in accordance with higher-level laws. Therefore, the rule system for contracts was formal in the sense that only laws provided guidance for contracting conduct. Moreover, these laws were composed of general rules that were universally applicable to cases falling into their category. Thus, to a certain extent, the laws for contractual behaviour were also rational, at least outwardly.

4.2.3 Application of the Rules

Whereas the law on the books in the 1980s presented itself as formalistic on the surface, these black-letter laws are only one piece of the puzzle for understanding the Chinese legal system. How the law operated through the economic lives of many Chinese entities makes it indispensable to formulate the image of the law in question. The case studies presented below (and the related sections in Chaps. 5 and 6) are intended to fulfil this purpose. Hence, to view how the above-discussed contract laws were applied in guiding economic behaviour and resolving economic disputes, we shift our attention to selected judicial cases.[57]

In December 1982, a collective located in Shanxi Province contracted a piece of an apple orchard to four individual contractors for five years, with a negotiated annual price of 1512 *yuan*. In the first year, the orchard was poorly managed, and economic losses followed, which resulted in the three contractors dropping out. Then, Mr. Wang individually contracted the land on the condition that he would be allowed to contract the land for ten years at the previously negotiated fixed price—1512 *yuan* per year for ten years. In November 1983, the collective and Wang formally signed the contract for the next five years. However, in the following years, the market price of fruit rose, and the profit of Wang's orchard also rose, which disturbed the members of the collective. In October 1987, without reaching a mutual agreement with Wang, the collective unilaterally terminated its contract and contracted the orchard to another party. Wang sued the collective in court (Supreme People's Court 1990) (hereafter Case A).

By referring to Article 6 of the Economic Contract Law,[58] the Court ruled that 'the contract concluded between the two parties was legally valid and should be protect by the law'. Hence, the unilateral termination of the contract by the collective had breached its obligation under the contract. The change in the market price of the fruit or the changed profits of the contractor, the Court argued, could be addressed by renegotiating the contracted price. In other words, the Court held that the termination of the contract was unnecessary as long as the changed external factor could be rectified by altering the content of the contract. Based on the above rationale, the Court acknowledged the validity of the contract. However, it ruled that the contents of the contract should be substantively changed by doubling the contracted price of the orchard, regardless of whether the plaintiff or the defendant had made such a claim.

In the same period, a gas company located in Wuhan signed two contracts with an instrumentation company regarding transferring assembling skills and selling gas metres. They concluded a contract agreeing that the instrumentation company was obliged to deliver, in two years (1988–1989), 70,000 instruments at a fixed price of 57.3 *yuan* each. However, by mid-1989, due to the rising price of the raw materials, the instrumentation company argued that the cost of the instruments had risen to 79.22 *yuan* each and the governmental guiding price was 83 *yuan*; therefore, it wanted to renegotiate the price and raise it to 75.5 *yuan* each. This request was denied by the gas company, which required the implementation of the original price (Supreme People's Court 1996) (hereafter Case B).

The case went through two instances. The first instance court, the Wuhan Intermediate People's Court, ruled in favour of the gas company. The Court argued that the contract signed by the two parties was 'based on equality and mutual benefit, … the content of the contract did not violate related policies. The contract was valid and should be protected by the law'. Therefore, the Court argued that the changing market price of raw materials should not constitute a legitimate reason for changing the agreed-upon contract price. Hence, the instrumentation company should be bound by the original contract. The judgement adopted a formal application of the law and dismissed the external factors, which the instrumentation company found unfair. Therefore, it appealed to the High Court.

In contrast to the strict formal application of the law, the High Court took into consideration the external factor—the changing market price of raw materials—and the legal principle of fairness. The Court argued that 'in implementing the contract, situations beyond the predication and precaution of the parties occurred, viz. the state price of raw aluminium, the key material of the subject matter of the contract, rose from between 4400 and 4600 *yuan* to 16,000 *yuan*, … it would be unfair to ask the instrumentation company to deliver the instrumentation at the original negotiated price'. Therefore, the Court argued that the good-faith principle of the General Principles of the Civil Code (Article 4) and paragraph 1 of Article 27 of the Economic Contract Law should be applied.

The critical aspect of the two cases was the influence of external nonlegal factors on legal decisions. In both cases, a change in the overall economic situation or the price of particular materials became the key factor in contractual disputes. The reasoning process of the courts in weighing these elements while making legal decisions reveals the characteristics of law finding in legal practice. Moreover, the above briefly introduced reasoning of the courts indicates that the two cases resulted in two different kinds of rulings in similar situations. While the market price change was not unusual, especially in a transforming economy, given that the terms of such contracts usually span many years, it was not a legitimate excuse for changing the terms of the contract.

In Case A, the Court dismissed the market price change as a legitimate reason for one party to terminate the original contract. Here, the Court adopted strict formal reasoning and endorsed upholding a legally concluded contract. However, while the Court confirmed the legal status of the contract, it did consider that the original contents of the contract should be altered. In this case, whereas the Court dismissed the substantive factors in acknowledging the legal validity of the contract, these factors in reality impacted the ruling in a material sense—the Court ruled that the price of the orchard contract should be doubled, regardless of the fact that the original contract price had been negotiated by the two parties and neither party had appealed the Court to adjust the price. While the exact reason was not explained, considering that the case was caused by the rising profits of the orchard, it is reasonable to speculate that the Court was taking an active role in achieving a rule of equity. In other words, the Court exercised considerable discretion in reaching this particular judgement by incorporating the changed price situation at that time into its consideration.

A similar formal application of the law was embodied in the judgement of the first instance court of Case B, which dismissed the change in the cost of materials and ruled that the terms of the original contract should be honoured. The High Court, however, weighed external factors in making its legal decision. By referring to general and abstract legal principles,[59] rather than concrete rules, the appeals court considered that the continuing implementation of the original contract in a changing economic environment would be unfair to one of the parties. Hence, the strict formal application of specific rules should give way to legal principles for a higher value, which was, in this case, fairness. This ruling shows that particular and nonlegal elements, such as the changing economic environment, could sway the Court's decisions on law finding, forcing the Court to discard the formal application of the law and resort to more general legal principles to achieve the intended result. The ultimate purpose of such flexible application of the law, as the Court implied, was to pursue social fairness—a social and economic value outside the law per se.

4.3 The Restoration of Legal Education

In 1949, the communist regime inherited an education system with 205 universities and 117,000 enrolled students from the KTM government (Editorial of China Education Yearbook 1984, p. 79). 53 law departments offered legal studies, with a teaching body of 542 law teachers (Editorial of China Education Yearbook 1984, p. 265; Zeng 2012, p. 399). At the time the PRC was established, China had the 'Six Codes' that had been promulgated by the Nationalist government in the 1920s. Due to ideological differences, the Communist Party deemed these codes capitalist laws that were opposed to the interests of the proletariat and therefore should be abolished. The law professionals applying and teaching these 'Six Codes' should be subjected to reeducation to learn the theories of Marxism and Leninism and Mao Zedong's thoughts (CCCCP 1992, pp. 150–153). Against this ideological background, the central government initiated a nationwide reconstruction of colleges and universities in the early 1950s, intending to build a Soviet-style socialist education system (Editorial of China Education Yearbook 1984, p. 80).

The Soviet education system accentuated levels of expertise rather than breadth of knowledge. The construction of universities, therefore, favoured specialized schools and discouraged comprehensive universities. As a result, universities covering broad disciplines in China were reduced, and it became vital to build engineering and science departments, with much less heed paid to social sciences and humanities (Editorial of China Education Yearbook 1984, p. 80). The entire programme of reorganizing universities was rather far-reaching. For example, the China Political Science and Law University was formed by the law department of the then Peking University and the political and sociology departments of the then Tsinghua University, Yenching University, and Furen University. The East China Political Science and Law University was established by merging the law schools and political science and sociology departments of Fudan University, Dongwu University, St. John's University, Xiamen University, and Nanjing University.[60] Upon the conclusion of the reforms, four law departments[61] and four specialized law schools existed in China. In the first decade after the establishment of the PRC, over 13,000 undergraduate and postgraduate students received legal degrees (Li and Mo 2014, p. 19).

The newly resumed legal education, as mentioned, was based on the Soviet model. To smooth the construction of the ensuing Soviet-style legal education, the central government sent students and teachers to the Soviet Union to study its laws and legal systems and hired Soviet experts as consultants or instructors (Huo and Wang 2009, p. 13). According to some studies, during that period, approximately 80 students were sent to the Soviet Union to study its laws (Huo and Wang 2009, p. 13; Li 1988, p. 99), and Soviet laws and teaching materials were translated and introduced into China. It is estimated that approximately 165 different types of Soviet legal materials, such as codes, monographs, and textbooks, were introduced in the early 1950s (Zeng 2012, p. 401). This worship of the Soviet legal system came to an end when the two countries split in 1960, which also marked the end of China's early attempts to reform its legal education system.

After the late 1950s, China threw itself into waves of political movements, and intellectuals were subjected to frequent criticism as a form of class struggle. The political turbulence to climaxed when the Cultural Revolution broke out in 1966, bringing legal education to a halt. By 1971, except for the law departments of Peking University and Jilin University, which still existed in an administrative sense, all law schools in the country had been closed (Editorial of China Education Yearbook 1984, pp. 82–83; Huo and Wang 2009, p. 16). Professors and educators, especially those who had studied overseas, were criticized as capitalists and subjected to political persecution (Editorial of China Education Yearbook 1984, p. 82). Some committed suicide as their humiliation escalated; others were sent to rural areas for re-education by working as manual labourers (Ji 2016). In this period, China's legal education was completely uprooted, damaging legal institutions and faculties. This situation ended only with the closure of the Cultural Revolution in 1976.

4.3.1 The Institutional Structure of Legal Education

Following the end of the Cultural Revolution, the issue of reopening law schools appeared on the political agenda. In the 1978 national judicial conferences, the idea of 'reestablishing law schools, educating judicial experts' was announced (Jiang et al. 2008). In the following years, the central government pointed out that law schools and law departments that had been closed in the past should reopen as soon as possible; liberal arts universities with sufficient resources should build law departments or add law majors; and provincial governments should build law schools and schools for cadres in judicial and police departments step by step (CCCCP 1979).

With law schools closed, teachers persecuted, and books damaged, China's legal education had to restart from scratch in the aftermath of the Cultural Revolution. However, along with restoring the national examination system of higher education, university legal education was officially brought back in 1979. As reported, from 1949 through 1966, the year before the Cultural Revolution, approximately 19,000 students had received formal legal education from either universities or political-legal institutes (Editorial of China Education Yearbook 1984, p. 265).[62] In 1981, China had a total of 1141 law teachers and 9944 law students enrolled in different law schools (Editorial of China Education Yearbook 1984, p. 269). Those once closed law schools began to reopen. The first group included Peking University, Jilin University, Renmin University, and the five specialized law schools. By 1983, approximately 36 universities were offering legal education (Zeng 2012, pp. 405–406).

As a newly reinstituted field of study, China's legal education, in the first decade, unfolded in a multilevel manner, aiming to train different types of legal professionals for different roles. In general, there were two forms of legal education: the formal study of law hosted by universities, junior colleges, research institutes, etc., which usually spanned two to four years and aimed to train newly admitted university students who had no previous legal knowledge, and vocational training, which was mainly short-term on-the-job training for incumbents such as judges and judicial workers in governmental offices.

Formal legal education took place in the law departments of universities and political-legal institutes and the legal branches of research institutes. Currently, these formal legal educational institutions no longer differentiate themselves in terms of their training targets, but in the 1980s, each was focused on training a specific type of legal professional—lawyers, cadres, or academics.

Among them, university law departments may have been the least purposive 'training centre' of legal professionals. As a result, law students, having received up to four years of formal legal training, might have ended up in different legal careers (Han and Kanter 1984, pp. 543 and 563–565). Admission to a university law school, after being restored in 1977, was a merit-based system, with students admitted according to their performance in *gaokao*, the Chinese university entrance examination.[63] Admissions were low in number in the early years. Taking Peking University as an example, only 182 and 230 students were enrolled as law undergraduates in 1979 and 1980, respectively, and approximately 40 were enrolled in postgraduate study (Editorial of China Education Yearbook 1984, p. 966).[64] The entire law faculty of Peking University numbered approximately 70 at that time (Gelatt and Snyder 1980, pp. 44–45).

Following Peking University, law departments sprang up nationwide within a few years. The majority of them are currently the cluster of 985/211 institutes, the top tier of Chinese universities, including, to name but a few, Renmin University, Xiamen University, Wuhan University, Nanjing University, and Fudan University (Gelatt and Snyder 1980, p. 48). From a geographical perspective, the first group of law schools was more or less evenly scattered through all provinces of the mainland. In 1987, China's law schools educated a body of students with over 12,639 law graduates, and 1294 were certified as legal postgraduates (Ji 2005, p. 20).

In addition to university law schools, by mergers and adjustments among the departments of a group of universities, within the five years from 1979 through 1984, China constructed five specialized institutions focusing on law and political science and placed them in each geographic region of the territory—the China University of Political Science and Law (Beijing), the East China University of Political Science and Law (Shanghai), the Zhongnan University of Economics and Law (Wuhan), the Southwest University of Political Science and Law (Chongqing), and the Northwest University of Political Science and Law (Xi'an) (Han and Kanter 1984, p. 557).

At present, these specialized universities are less special in that they also offer a wide range of courses that are no longer limited to law and politics, and their students enjoy the same career choices as graduates from comprehensive universities. In the 1980s, however, they were institutions with particular tasks—to train legal workers for China's judicial systems, namely, judges, procurators, and legal officials of governmental bureaus (Han and Kanter 1984, pp. 563–565). With particular career orientations, the curricula in these institutions were slightly different from those in university law schools, which are examined in the next section.

In addition to the above two types of higher education for law, since 1978, China has also restored its research institutes, which offer graduate study in law. The law institutes under the Chinese Academy of Social Science and the Shanghai Academy of Social Sciences were among these institutes. Restored in October 1978, the Shanghai Academy of Social Sciences Institute of Law resumed its graduate programme in 1979, and in 1988, 30 graduates were enrolled (Shanghai Academy of Social Sciences Institute of Law n.d.).

Overall, China's formal legal education, at both the undergraduate and postgraduate levels, was conducted by these higher-level institutions. The law departments and specialized universities that emerged or reorganized in those years no doubt were among the most prestigious in China then, as they are now, and the forms of legal education and the substantive aspects of legal studies established in these institutes would have a lasting impact on generations of legal professionals to come.

In addition to formal legal education, some training schools also offered part-time, short-term studies of law, mainly for incumbents, such as judges, procurators, and judicial workers in governmental branches. However, this month-long training was conducted primarily in cadre training schools and training centres for judges.[65] While this on-the-job training had nothing to do with systemic legal study, it was of particular importance to China in the 1980s, as by then, China was in need of enough personnel to preside in the once repealed national judicial system, and its law schools had just reopened and had yet to train enough law graduates. As a result, courts, procurators, police, and legal advisory offices had to rely heavily on these short-term training programmes. As a result, cadres usually attended these schools for one to six months and intensively studied certain introductory legal courses for practical use (Gelatt and Snyder 1980, p. 54; Han and Kanter 1984, p. 565).

While law received close attention from the authority, the enrolment of law majors was low compared with other majors. For example, in 1978, students enrolled in political science and law accounted for only 0.2% of the student body (Editorial of China Education Yearbook 1984, p. 967). While the ratio increased throughout the decade, by 1991, there were still merely 2% of university students in the related field (Ying 2008, p. 117).

4.3.2 Curriculum Structure and Teaching Materials

The curriculum of law education, to a great extent, was the critical environment that assumed a dominant role in socializing China's early group of legal professionals. The general aim of this section is to examine the level of uniformity of China's early legal education, as a uniform formal legal education is crucial to forming the mode of legal thought and thus the emergence of group awareness and the self-reproduction of legal professionals (Boudieu and Passeron 1977). Some elements are indispensable to achieve a certain level of uniformity of legal education. Among them are a similar structure of legal courses and standard textbooks, especially for law beginners. As the discussion below reveals, law schools offered a rather similar curriculum structure but used various types of teaching materials, mostly compiled by individual teachers, which was an issue that the Chinese authority would solve in the coming decades.

4.3.2.1 Curriculum Structures

In general, the curricula of legal higher education share a common structure, which guarantees that university law students receive similarly structured legal knowledge in their initial years of legal study.

In 1978, the Education Ministry issued a teaching plan for law majors of university law departments for consideration. It was later endorsed by the Ministry of Justice as a suggested outline for the group of specialized institutions. The mandated legal courses included general theory of law, the Constitution, history of the Chinese legal system, history of foreign legal systems, civil law, marriage law, general theory of economic law, civil litigation law, criminal law, criminal litigation law, the science of evidence, the science of criminal investigation, forensic medicine, writing judicial documents, international law, and private international law (Editorial of China Education Yearbook 1984, pp. 269–270). The general idea was to keep law programmes intact and not break into separate law departments in the initial academic years; from the third year on, students were offered a choice of elective courses. Although political courses were emphasized, both the general theory of political science and the history of the Communist Party were compulsory courses (Editorial of China Education Yearbook 1984, pp. 269–270).

While the five specialized political and law institutions had to follow a strict curriculum structure and accentuate exposure to political lessons, the course structure of the law departments of universities enjoyed a certain leeway depending on their available resources and teaching body (Han and Kanter 1984, p. 561). In standard courses and specialized classes, it was mandatory for students to take courses such as English, Marxist philosophy and political economy, Mao's ideology, and Deng Xiaoping's theory (Han and Kanter 1984, p. 561).

The law major was typically set up as a general discipline, and specialized legal study was not common and had low enrolment. The most common specialty area was economic law, which was understandable given that China had just announced its economic reform plan. For an overview of the detailed course framework, the study plans of Peking and Wuhan Universities, two influential comprehensive universities located in two centres of the country, are informative in providing a general idea of legal training in the early years.

Decades into the Sino-Soviet split, the Chinese education system still bore imprints of the Soviet-style educational mode, with specific emphasis on specialized study (Lofstedt 1980; Whyte 1974). In the case of legal education, specialized legal studies prevailed in undergraduate education. For instance, the law department of Peking University offered three fields of legal education: law,[66] public international law, and economic law (Gelatt and Synder 1980, p. 46). Four years of general law major study offered a broad range of legal courses without specialization, including general introductory courses about Chinese legal history, jurisprudence, criminal law, civil law, procedural laws, constitutional law, foreign legal history, history of foreign legal thought, marriage law, economic law, and public and private international law (Gelatt and Synder 1980, p. 45).

However, unlike Western-style legal education, which structures specialized legal study at a more advanced graduate stage, Peking University also provided specialized law majors such as public international law and economic law at the undergraduate level (Gelatt and Synder 1980, p. 46). Hence, for students who chose the international law major, obligatory classes in addition to the abovementioned general classes included comparative constitutional law, the history of international relationships, the history of China's foreign relations, international organizations, and international economic law (Editorial of China Education Yearbook 1984, pp. 269–270). Students who took an interest in economic law received specialized classes on the general theory of economic law, the laws of the People's Commune, the law of industrial enterprises, commercial law, fiscal and financial law, labour law, natural resources law, judicial and arbitration law, foreign civil law, international trade law, and international investment law (Editorial of China Education Yearbook 1984, pp. 269–270). Students in all majors were required to complete a thesis in order to graduate.

The courses offered by Wuhan University were in a similar framework. Akin to Peking University, the law school of Wuhan University provided a general law major and an international law major. Students in the general law major would receive basic legal courses such as constitutional law, civil and economic law, and criminal law, with a total of 42 courses (24 obligatory and 18 electives). Students interested in international law also had to take courses such as public/private international law, international economic law, and international relations (Han and Kanter 1984, pp. 558–559).

4.3.2.2 Teaching Materials

As mentioned earlier, the shelves of law departments did not survive the Cultural Revolution, as law books and references were raided and destroyed during those years, and new publications were put on hold (Cohen 1970, pp. 20–49). Therefore, the aftermath of the revolution left Chinese legal libraries with stark shortages, which forced law education to resume in parallel with an effort to refill the bookshelves, especially in the beginning years. As a result, law faculties eventually relied on teaching materials that were edited and compiled by their own teachers, with no standard and formalized textbook available (Gelatt and Snyder 1980, p. 46; Han and Kanter 1984, p. 562).

In 1979, a National Program for the Study of Law was announced that would span eight years. Among its commitments, an effort was made to produce a range of law materials, including textbooks, monographs, and reference materials (Macdonald 1980). In 1980, in a joint effort of the Ministry of Justice and the Ministry of Education, law faculties from several universities were organized to compile approximately thirty items of teaching materials that were published in subsequent years. The collection covered all major topics in the legal field, from the general theory of law and legal history to specialized legal fields (Han and Kanter 1984, pp. 562–563).

In the meantime, an effort to translate foreign legal materials was underway in a bid to introduce broad coverage of legal topics to the Chinese legal community (Gelatt and Snyder 1980, pp. 46–47). A coordinated effort on this front also included academic journals featuring translations of articles, laws, and legal developments in foreign countries, such as the bimonthly Peking University Law Journal (*zhongwai faxue*) produced by the law faculty of Peking University (Han and Kanter 1984, p. 565).

4.3.3 The Teaching Body and Pedagogic Features

In addition to a uniform legal structure and teaching materials, law teachers, like those directly channelling legal knowledge, are an indispensable element in forming legal thought or thinking styles. Therefore, their training and qualifications would significantly impact the quality and formation of China's future lawyers. Additionally, their training background would influence the way they educated the next generation (Kraus 1989, pp. 121–125).

In China, the law was an emerging discipline that was unfamiliar to ordinary Chinese people. Moreover, the history of early years of legal education suggests that the number of qualified law professionals was minimal compared to those in other fields of study (Hsiao 1932; Pepper 1987, pp. 189–191; Second Historical Archives of China 2010, pp. 334–335).[67] Worse still, political movements such as the Anti-Rightist Campaign in the 1950s and the Cultural Revolution from 1966 through 1976 had effectively wiped out the prime years of China's already small number of intellectuals, including law professionals (Herman 1982, p. 795). The extreme shortage of law teachers nationwide was observed on the eve of the resumption of formal legal education (Editorial of China Education Yearbook 1986, pp. 120–122),[68] and to resolve the rather urgent issue, the Ministry of Justice and other legal institutions organized short-term training classes for law teachers with the aim of mitigating the extreme scarcity of faculty members (Editorial of China Education Yearbook 1986, pp. 120–122). The situations in prestigious universities was slightly better. For example, the law faculty at Peking University had approximately 70 teachers, 20 of whom were full professors (Bryant 1980, p. 667), and Wuhan University had over 50 law teachers and researchers following its restoration (Han and Kanter 1984, p. 558).

With law educators diversified in both quality and quantity, it was hardly possible to maintain national legal education at a comparable level across institutions. In other words, it is reasonable to speculate that the law graduates trained in the first decades after the reopening of law schools may have developed somewhat divergent structures and levels of legal knowledge.

While the teaching body might have been divergent in terms of quality, it was less so with respect to training background, as the majority had been educated in a spoon-fed manner, meaning the teaching method they applied was rather uniform in style. Moreover, while still rudimentary in the 1980s, China's legal system nevertheless followed the civil law tradition, consisting of written codes rather than precedent cases. The structure of the legal system, in turn, made the continental training tradition the preferred teaching method. To a great extent, China's law teaching was conducted primarily in the form of lecturing with an emphasis on memorizing black-letter laws.[69]

Other styles of teaching, such as seminars and case discussions, were limited (Gelatt and Snyder 1980, p. 47). There may have been many reasons for this. First, the ratio of faculty to students also determined the size of the classroom, which made focused discussion more difficult and individual supervision a daunting task. Second, the Chinese learning atmosphere granted teachers the authority of final say and the singular status of having the correct answer to any legal issue, which made any open discussion of cases or legal issues difficult, and challenges of teachers by students were almost non-existent. Third, as the teachers themselves had been educated mainly by lecturing, it was natural for them to continue that training style in the classroom.

4.3.4 Evaluation System

This section investigates the changing criteria for people to enter the legal profession. It is a critical lens through which to view the quality levels of China's legal professionals at the beginning stage of their career and therefore a starting point for understanding the characteristics of the group and China's judicial system.

In the 1980s, entry into the legal profession was rather chaotic. Lawyers and judges had different selection systems. Moreover, no national uniform examination was applied to either group. By reviewing the elements of China's early qualification systems for lawyers and judges, this section unveils the general situation of law professionals in the 1980s.

From 1978 through 1992, there were two stages of certifying lawyers in practice, with 1986 as a watershed year—before 1986, each province had the jurisdiction to conduct evaluations and issuing lawyers' certificates (Article 9). By 1986, before the first national bar exam took place, 14,500 people had qualified as professional lawyers (Gan 1987, p. 892). From 1986 through 1992, the Chinese authority was in an experimental stage of holding national-level bar exams.

According to the Regulation of Lawyers of the PRC, which entered into force in January 1982, eligible educational backgrounds for applying for lawyer qualifications included (1) graduates of higher education law programmes plus more than two years of law-related work, (2) those with legal training plus practical experience as judges or procurators, and (3) those with higher education plus over three years of economic or technology working experience and some legal knowledge (Article 8(1) (2) (3)). In 1986, approximately 29,000 people registered for the exam, and 1134 passed (Gao and Jiang 2020, p. 73). From 1986 through 1992, the state held four lawyer qualification exams every two years. The first national bar exam was open only to people working in the judicial and administrative systems. The central government was in a trial-and-error stage regarding the form of the bar exam, which resulted in different types of exams being designed and administered in such a short period (Hua 1993).

For instance, the structure of the 1986 examination suggested an emphasis on testing memory ability.[70] The examination consisted of four written sections—paper one, criminal law and criminal procedural law; paper two, civil law, marriage law, and inheritance law; paper three, civil procedural law and economic law; paper four, lawyers' regulatory regime, basic knowledge of the law, and constitutional law. Although each of these sections had a considerable number of fill-in-the-blank and short-answer questions (together, they amounted to 153 points out of 400), both types of questions require memorizing hard facts and knowledge points rather than the ability of case analysis. The 1992 bar exam eliminated this testing style but added political knowledge, such as questions referring to Marxism-Leninism (Hua 1993). From 1993 onwards, the State Council normalized the bar exam as an annual event open to all participants with the required educational background.

At this stage, the bar exam was only for lawyers' credentials. For judges and prosecutors, there was no standard examination system. In 1979, China issued its first Organic Law of the People's Court, which stated that all levels of judges, except assistant judges, should be appointed by the Standing Committees of local People's Congresses (Article 35). This law was slightly revised in 1983, and an item reading 'judges of People's Courts shall possess legal knowledge' (Article 34 (2)) was added. While a unified examination system was lacking, the state did set up two training centres for incumbents: the National Spare-Time University of Court Cadres in 1985 and the Training Centre of Senior Judges in 1988. They merged into the National Judge College in 1997 (National Judge College 2022). These training centres proved to be indispensable in the 1980s for the rapid training of China's judges.

With such divergent selection procedures and standards for different legal careers, it is reasonable to speculate that China's legal professionals in the 1980s had diverse legal knowledge and skill levels, as there was an absence of a nationally unified system to create a uniform measurement for career entrance.

4.4 The Paternalistic Role of Law and the Planned Economy

The role of law in a given economy has inextricable links to the characteristics of the legal education that a given society provides. China, however, on the eve of economic reform, had closed its law schools and destroyed legal materials throughout the Cultural Revolution and needed to rebuild the whole education system for legal study from scratch.

The educational institution built in this period was a multilevel system. The general idea of legal education was to purposively train different types of legal expertise for different roles and thus design the education system with divergent types of institutions training specific legal professionals with an orientation towards specific careers. For instance, the five specialized law and political science universities trained public legal workers and provided vocational training for incumbents. Likewise, the teaching materials used in this period were not formalized. As the many bookshelves of law departments had been emptied during the Cultural Revolution, for many years, law departments relied on their own teachers to produce and edit teaching materials, and this group of people was few in number and varied in qualifications in those days.

Whereas the teaching materials lacked uniform standards, the legal curricula offered in this period showed a uniform tendency with an emphasis on practical application of the law. This was particularly telling given that some major law departments offered specialized studies on economic law and international law in response to social and economic needs. Another embodiment of the overall situation of legal education was the early bar exam's low degree of difficulty, which suggests that legal study, as a whole, was in a primitive stage.

Hence, the legal education restored in those years had multiple forms in terms of educational institutions and learning materials and was uninformed about the social and economic utility of the law. These features would be obvious in the internal characteristics of the law that appeared in the 1980s and their external functions.

As the legal system had to be built from scratch, it is informative to examine what social spheres received legal attention in the beginning. In the economic sphere, it appears that the central authority prioritized foreign enterprises and state capital and omitted private economic relationships, although the Constitution had lifted institutional restrictions on private ownership in 1988. As a result, legislative priority was given to foreign and state-owned enterprises, various types of contractual behaviours, and intellectual property. The laws that emerged in this period were few in number and substantive in character, an inevitable result given the greatly constrained human resources in the legal field.

The limited amount of legislation indicates that the state had to rely on other means to regulate the country. Therefore, the state substantively intervened in economic regulations. The most common instruments employed by the state were administrative directions, departmental regulations, and resolutions passed by the Central Committee of the Party. Together with national laws, these instruments constituted a unique rule system for the economy at that time. However, this relatively diversified rule system suggests that many rules were oriented towards substantive and specific issues, and many others were simply too general to be applicable. For instance, the authority promulgated three separate contract laws for different types of contracts and lower-level regulations for more specific categories of contracts, Party resolutions were constantly referred to in regard to carrying out agricultural reforms, and numerous departmental decisions were issued for instruction in specific affairs. This hybrid system indicates the potential for clashes between different types of rules. Moreover, in the judicial field,[71] judges even actively converted advice that was not requested into binding legal judgements to correct economic inequality, an abuse of discretion for substantive results.

Overall, the focus of the first batch of legislation indicates that legislative activities were highly selective and the rules tended to regulate all kinds of social and economic affairs, great and small. It is a peculiar phenomenon that was rooted in the political economy of the 1980s—a unique period when the economy has just emerged from decades of economic disasters and political turmoil. In those years, the path towards prosperity was unsettled among the top leaders, who frequently switched between planned and market economic strategies. These social and economic backgrounds, in turn, left their footprints in the legal field.

For example, the bottom-up agricultural reform in China at the end of the 1970s forced the authority to respond by issuing torrents of precisely targeted administrative regulations. Additionally, because of the need for foreign capital to drive economic growth, a series of laws and rules for foreign capital were purposefully and meticulously constructed by the central authority, incorporating both international treaties and specific domestic laws for particular types of foreign entities and for contractual behaviours related to foreign interests. Furthermore, as the economy was dominated by public ownership, laws regarding the private sector were neglected, as they were of no use at the time, and only a handful of administrative rules were enacted to regulate emerging individual businesses.

In summary, as the economy had yet to embrace market rules and planned economy strategies were dominant, the rule system kept a tight grip on the economic sphere, especially on areas being reformed. Such strict control of the law could be seen in the highly selective targets of legislation, the specific timelines of laws related to economic reforms, and the rather substantive nature of the laws and rules. These characteristics of the law equipped the state with the power to steer the economy towards its planned results and therefore consolidated the designed economic order. Additionally, such strong intervention of the state in the economy demonstrated that the authority had spent much care and thought on reforming and navigating the economy via these substantive laws—a show of the paternalistic role of the law in constructing the planned economy with particular results in mind.

Notes

1. Land in China was and is either state owned or collectively owned. The object of land transactions in China is a fixed period of land use rights, usually ranging from forty to seventy years. Landownership is reserved for the state or collectives and is not transactional in any circumstances. See Land Management Law of the PRC Article 2, 6, and 7. Hence, though the HRS gradually granted peasants ownership of agricultural products and means of production, the full right to land is not possible.
2. Article 2 of the 1988 Constitutional Amendment, Article 13 of the Agricultural Law (1993), and generally the Rural Land Contract Law (2003).
3. The detailed provisions are more complicated, as the length of the land period differs according to the physical situation of the land. For instance, the contract period is thirty years for arable lands and fifty years for barren or mountainous lands.
4. The so-called Number One Documents are Party policy papers that signalled the priorities of the party in the coming year. The name signalled the sequence of a paper as well as the significance of the issue covered by the paper.
5. Individual economy refers to China's small-scale businesses that employed fewer than eight people. Because individual businesses were private in nature, the state had difficulty legitimizing them because of ideological concerns. Hence, the Constitution was revised several times to legalize individual businesses and later larger-scale private economic activities. For a more detailed discussion, see the section below.
6. As the People's Commune drew to a close, the commune became the township, and brigades were renamed villages. Thus, the names of these commune enterprises also changed. The term TVEs first appeared in a policy document called Guanyu kaichuang sheduiqiye xinjümian de baogao/Report on Creating A New Situation for Commune and Brigade Enterprises on 1 March 1984. In the second paragraph of the document, TVEs were officially defined: 'TVEs include enterprises sponsored by townships and villages, the alliance enterprises (*lianying qiye*) formed by peasants, other alliance enterprises and individual enterprises'.
7. Working Rules on the People's Commune in Rural Areas 1961, and the Amendments to the Working Rules on the People's Commune in Rural Areas, 1962.
8. *Mu* is a unit of area commonly used in China, with 1 mu equalling 0.067 hectares.
9. The development of the household responsibility system is introduced in a previous section of the chapter. Therefore, issues related to the HRS, such as agricultural productivity and the increasing income of the rural population, are not discussed in this section.
10. Regarding the changing structure of TVE products over the years, see the statistical data of production that are available in various versions of the TVE section of Zhongguo nongye tongji ziliao/The Materials of Agriculture Statistics of China and Zhongguo jingji nianjian/ The Economic Yearbook of China.
11. After 1984, a series of No.1 documents were released by the Central Committee of the Chinese Communist Party, emphasizing a strong political preference for developing rural areas. Along with these policy papers, administrative-level regulations flooded in over the following years. A detailed list of these documents is available at http://www.gov.cn/zhengce/gongbao/guowuyuan1954-1999.htm. Accessed 28 September 2021
12. Provisional Regulations on Income Tax of Collective Enterprises (1985)
13. Provisional Regulations on Bonus Allocation of Collective Enterprises (1985)
14. Regulations on the Qualities of Industrial Products of the TVEs (1987)
15. Provisions on Collective Enterprises in Villages (1990)

16. In his study of China's policy shift between the 1980s and the 1990s, Yasheng Huang (2008) interpreted the rapid growth seen in the rural industrial sector as related to the relatively liberal policies and property rights securities of the 1980s as well as the entrepreneurial spirit that was released in rural areas.
17. According to Wu (2005), in 1978, six SOEs located in Sichuan Province were selected to experiment with the strategy.
18. The five documents are the Several Provisions on Expanding the Autonomy of Operation and Management of the State-run Industrial Enterprises, Several Provisions on Profit Retention of the State-run Enterprises, Provisional Regulations on Fixed Asset Tax of the State-run Industrial Enterprises, Provisional Regulations on Improving the Fixed Asset Depreciation Rate and Cost of the State-run Industrial Enterprises, and Provisional Regulations on Enforcing Acquisition of All Circulating Funds Through Credit to the State-run Industrial Enterprises.
19. The notion of 'soft budget constraint' is defined by Maskin (1996) as follows: '[it] arises whenever a funding source finds it impossible to keep an enterprise to a fixed budget, i.e., whenever the enterprise can extract ex post a bigger subsidy or loan than would have been considered efficient ex-ante' (p. 125). See Maskin E (1996) Theories of the Soft Budget-Constraint. Japan and the World Economy 8(2):125–133.
20. Xue (1984) suggests that during the Cultural Revolution (1966–1976), numerous educated young people were sent to the countryside to learn from the masses. As the revolution drew to a close, they returned to cities and faced severe employment difficulties. Thus, they were encouraged to start their own businesses.
21. This claim was made by a Chinese economist named Zili Lin. In his study of Marx's doctrine, he argued that hiring fewer than eight workers did not constitute exploitation and would not clash with socialist ideology.
22. Data concerning China's foreign investment were gathered from the database of the United Nations Conference on Trade and Development. Available at https://unctadstat.unctad.org/wds/TableViewer/tableView.aspx. Accessed 5 June 2020
23. Deng Xiaoping's writings also show that Shanghai was too important for China to fail, whereas Shenzhen was merely a small fishing village that the government could afford to lose if things went wrong. Therefore, he chose Shenzhen rather than Shanghai in the first batch of experimental SEZs. The rationale behind the SEZ ideas is evident in Deng's many articles in Deng Xiaoping Wenxuan.
24. Some of these measures have separate rules to detail more specific regulations, such as the Regulations for the Control of the Accounting of Foreign-Related Enterprises in SEZs in Guangdong Province (effective in 1986, expired in 1995) and the Regulation on Land Administration in SEZs of Guangdong Province (effective in 1991, expired in 1999).
25. The fourteen coastal cities are Dalian, Qinhuangdao, Tianjin, Yantai, Qingdao, Lianyungang, Nantong, Shanghai, Ningbo, Wenzhou, Fuzhou, Guangzhou, Zhanjiang, and Beihai.
26. According to a survey conducted in 2018, there are a total of 2683 open areas nationwide. Among them, there are 218 national and 2056 provincial-level economic and technology open zones and 168 national-level high-tech zones. For details, see National Development and Reform Commission, Catalogue of Approved Developmental Zones in China (No.4 2018).
27. The names used for different areas include SEZs, open cities, open economic zones, developing zones, high-tech zones, and new zones.
28. Article 18 of the Constitution reads, 'The People's Republic of China permits foreign enterprises, other foreign economic organizations, and individual foreigners to invest in China … Their lawful rights and interests are protected by the law of the People's Republic of China'.
29. The name of the Ministry of Commerce (MOFCOM) was adopted in 2003; before that, its official name was the Ministry of Foreign Trade and Economic Cooperation (MOFTEC). As the study covers both periods, both names appear in the text in relation to the events concerned.
30. These three laws were replaced by the Foreign Investment Law of the PRC in January 2020.
31. According to the newly enacted Foreign Investment Law, the legal form of foreign-funded enterprises must follow the related articles in the Company Law and Partnership Enterprises Law (Article 31).

32. It was amended and the name changed to Law of the PRC on Foreign-Funded Enterprises in 2000.
33. Article 2 of Law of the PRC on Chinese-Foreign Equity Joint Ventures (hereafter Law on EJV), Article 3 of Law of the PRC on Chinese-Foreign Contractual Joint Ventures (hereafter Law on CJV), and Article 4 of Law of the PRC on Wholly Foreign-Owned Enterprises (hereafter Law on WFE).
34. Law on EJV, Article 7 (the tax preference for EJVs was only granted when they possessed world-level advanced technology), Law on CJV, Article 21, and Law on WFE, Article 17.
35. Law on EJV, Article 4.
36. Law on CJV, Article 2, Law on WFE, Article 8.
37. Law on EJV, Article 6, Law on CJV, Article 12.
38. Law on EJV, Article 7.
39. Law on CJV, Article 22.
40. Law on EJV, Article 9, Law on CJV, Article 19, and Law on WFE, Article 11 and 15.
41. Law on EJV, Article 10 and 11, Law on CJV, Article 23, and Law on WFE, Article 19.
42. Law on EJV, Article 14, Law on CJV, Article 26.
43. Law of the PRC on Industrial Enterprises Owned by the Whole People was promulgated in 1988.
44. Article 3, 22, and 35 of Law of the PRC on Industrial Enterprises Owned by the Whole People (hereafter Law on WPE).
45. As an exception, joint ventures are required to hire a certain number of Chinese employees.
46. Law on WPE, Article 44.
47. The two laws are the Income Tax Law of the PRC concerning Chinese-Foreign Equity Joint Ventures and the Income Tax Law of the PRC for Foreign Enterprises.
48. Among them, laws significant to the economy were the Bankruptcy Law (1986), the Labour Law (1994), the Labour Contract Law (2007), and the Property Law (2007). These laws all universally applied to the whole economy.
49. Among the 145 BITs, 18 were terminated for resignature and 20 were signed but are not yet in force.
50. The detailed list is available at https://investmentpolicy.unctad.org/international-investment-agreements/countries/42/china. Accessed 28 September 2021.
51. The English version of the first Chinese Model BIT is available at the UNCTAD International Investment Agreement (IIA). Professor Shan Wenhua translated the second version of the Model BIT, and the English version of the current Model BIT is provided by the Directorate-General of Treaty and Law of the MOFCOM. Both texts can be found in Gallagher and Shan (2009).
52. Regarding BIT negotiations, many Chinese international law scholars, such as Chen and Gu (2013) and Zeng (2014 and 2016), emphasized that the current international economic order does not favour developing countries' interests, and therefore, articles in BITs should be carefully designed to protect China's interests. This view could shed lights on the frequent back-and-forth over certain BIT articles.
53. Also worth mentioning is that a number of BITs that concluded after 1993 did not include open access to an international tribunal, such as the Qatar BIT signed in April 1999. Case numbers are calculated according to the list provided by UNCTAD. Available at https://investmentpolicy.unctad.org/international-investment-agreements/countries/42/China. Accessed 5 June 2020.
54. Historically, China had expropriated foreign companies without paying compensation, which resulted in a dramatic shrinkage in FDI over the following years. Hence, concerns about economic interests as well as China's economic sovereignty over expropriation underpinned the later struggle over the standard of compensation, and the principle of appropriate compensation was deemed to be in favour of developing countries' interests.
55. The rules regulating the ten contract types were substantive and specific, though varied in level of detail. For instance, Article 17 for sales contracts incorporated four items covering rules for quantity standards, product and packaging quality, pricing, and contract period. Nevertheless,

rules for loan contracts (Article 24) were succinctly summarized: 'Article 24: Loan contracts shall be concluded in accordance with the credit plan approved by the state and the relevant provisions. The contract shall expressly provide the amount of the loan, the use, the term, the interest rate, the procedures for settling accounts, the liability for breach of contract and other similar terms. The interest rate on loans shall be set by the state and controlled by the People's Bank of China'.

56. Article 4 of the Economic Contract Law, Article 4 of the Economic Contracts Law involving Foreign Interest, Article 3 of the Law on Technology Contracts.
57. The cases discussed in this section are by no means intended to present empirical evidence of any sort. That said, given that these cases are published in the Communique of the Supreme People's Court, the legal analysis and judgements therein represented offer a glimpse of the official legal rationale and stance on similar circumstances.
58. Article 6 of the Economic Contract Law reads, 'As soon as an economic contract is established per the law, it shall have legally binding force, and the parties must fully perform their obligations as stipulated in the contract. Neither Party may unilaterally modify or rescind the contract'.
59. Article 4 of the General Principles of the Civil Law: 'In civil activities, the principles of voluntariness, fairness, making compensation for equal value, honesty and credibility shall be observed'.
60. The East China Political Science and Law University was abolished and merged with Fudan Law School in 1958 and was subsequently subjected to several rounds of repeal and reestablishment until 1979, when the current East China Political Science and Law University was established.
61. The four law departments were at Renmin University, Wuhan University, Jilin University, and Xibei University. The Northwest Political Science and Law University was constructed in 1958, later than the other four.
62. Data were estimated by the number of law students enrolled during this period.
63. In Mao's era, admission to higher education was based on students' political background. Thus, priority was given to students from revolutionary backgrounds, peasants, and proletariats, and students from so-called capitalist families were excluded from access. See generally the introduction to China's early judicial system in chapter three of the study.
64. Nationwide, there were 3315 enrolled law students in 1979 and 6029 in 1980. While the number was still very small, growth was taking place in these years.
65. Both types of training schools were set up for judicial officials with political rank who had no formal legal education but worked in the judicial system. Additionally, these schools existed at both central and local levels to cater to people of different ranks and regions.
66. The law major refers to general legal studies, covering balanced legal courses without a specific course focus to distinguish it from specialized legal studies.
67. In the period of the Republic of China, the nation had built an education system that revolved around the Western curriculum, from elementary school through universities, with subjects including science, geography, history, politics, and law. According to a scholarly survey conducted in 1932, over half of the students enrolled in full-degree university programmes studied law, politics, and literature. Hence, one could reasonably speculate that law students educated under the Kuomintang government may have been a component of the teaching body. From 1912 through 1937, there were a total of 32,713 college-level law graduates, amounting to one-third of total college graduates.
68. According to the China Education Yearbook 1982–1984, in 1981, China had a total of only 1077 law teachers nationwide. The legal education system planned to cultivate 35,000 law students from 1983 through 1990.
69. The emphasis on reciting specific rules and legal propositions is exemplified in the style of the bar exam at that time, as is illustrated in the next section.
70. While there was no explicit policy indicating that it was a closed-book exam, the later style of bar exams suggests that it is reasonable to believe that students were not allowed to use codes or other law books. Additionally, types of questions such as filling-in-the-blank and

short-answer questions would be meaningless if students were allowed to consult law books in the exam.

71. This refers to the case study in Sect. 4.2.3. Although it was a single case judgement, given that it was the model case selected by the Communique of the Supreme People's Court, this parental style of judgement could be regarded as having the acknowledgement and endorsement of high-level judicial officials.

References

Bennett G, Kieke K, and Yoffy K (1978) Huadong: the story of a Chinese People's Commune. Westview, Nashville

Bourdieu P and Passeron J-c (1977) Reproduction in education, society and culture. Sage, Thousand Oask

Bryant CA (1980) China: A personal note. Florida Bar Journal 54(10):672–678

Burton C (1990) Political and social change in China since 1978. Greenwood Press, Westport

CCCCP (1978) Shiyijie sanzhong quanhui gongbao/Communique of third plenum of the eleventh party congress. In: CPC Party Literature Research Office (ed) (1982) Sanzhong quanhui yilai zhongyao wenxian xuanbian, shang/Selected key documents since the Third Plenum, vol 1. Central Party Literature Press, Beijing

CCCCP (1979) Guanyu baozheng xingfa xingshi susongfa qieshishishi de zhishi/Directions on guaranteeing the implementation of the criminal law and the criminal procedure law

CCCCP (1980) Guanyu jinyibu jiaqiang he wanshan nongye shengchan zerenzhi de jigen wenti/ Issues on further reinforce and complete the responsibility system of agricultural production. In: CPC Party Literature Research Office (ed) (1982) Sanzhong quanhui yilai zhongyao wenxian xuanbian, shang/Selected key documents since the 3rd Plenary Session, vol 1. Central Party Literature Press, Beijing

CCCCP (1982) Quanguo nongcuo gongzuo huiyi yijiao/Conference summary of national rural work. In: CPC Party Literature Research Office (ed) (1982) Sanzhong quanhui yilai zhongyao wenxian xuanbian, xia/Selected key documents since the 3rd Plenary Session, vol 2. Central Party Literature Press, Beijing

CCCCP (1983) Danqian nongcun jingji zhengce de ruogan wenti/Several issues on the current rural economic policy. In: CPC Party Literature Research Office (ed) (1986) Shierda yilai zhongyao wenxian xuanbian, shang/Selected key documents since the 12th National Congress of the CCP, vol 1. Central Party Literature Press, Beijing

CCCCP (1984a) Guanyu jingji tizhi gaige de jueding/Resolution on the reform of the economic system. In: CPC Party Literature Research Office (ed) (1986) Shierda yilai zhongyao wenxian xuanbian, zhong/Selected key documents since the 12th National Congress of the CCP, vol 2. Central Party Literature Press, Beijing

CCCCP (1984b) Guanyu 1984 nian nongcun gongzuo de tongzhi/Concerning the 1984 Rural Work. In: CPC Party Literature Research Office (ed) (1986) Shierda yilai zhongyao wenxian xuanbian, shang/Selected key documents since the 12th National Congress of the CCP, vol 1. Central Party Literature Press, Beijing

CCCCP (1989) Guanyu jinyibu zhili zhengdun he shenhua gaige de jueding (zhaiyao)/Decisions on rectifying and furthering the reform (digest). In: CPC Party Literature Research Office (ed) (1991) Shisanda yilai zhongyao wenxian xuanbian, zhong/Selected key documents since the 13th National Congress of the CCP, vol 2. Central Party Literature Press, Beijing

CCCCP (1991) Guanyu jinyibu jiaqiang nongye he nongcun gongzuo de jueding/Decisions on further reinforcing agricultural and rural work. In: CPC Party Literature Research Office (ed) (1993) Shisanda yilai zhongyao wenxian xuanbian, xia/Selected key documents since the 13th National Congress of the CCP, vol 3. Central Party Literature Press, Beijing

CCCCP (1992) Guanyu feichu guomindang liufaquanshu he queding jiefangqu sifa yuanze de zhishi/Directions on abolishing the Six Code of the KMT and confirming judicial principles of the liberated areas. In: Central Archives (ed) (1998) Zhonggong zhongyang wenjian xuanji, di 18 ce/Collected papers of the Central Committee of the CCP, vol 18. CCP Central Party School Press, Beijing

CCCCP and State Council (1990) Guanyu 1991 nian nongye he nongcun gongzuo de tongzhi/ Circular on 1991 agricultural and rural work. In: CPC Party Literature Research Office (ed) (1991) Shisanda yilai zhongyao wenxian xuanbian, zhong/Selected key documents since the 13th National Congress of the CCP, vol 2. Central Party Literature Press, Beijing

Chen XW (1993) Zhongguo nongcun gaige: huigu yu zhanwang/China rural reform: review and prospect. Tianjin People's Publishing House, Tianjin

Chen Y (1979) Jihua yu shichang wenti/Issues on planning and marketing. In: CPC Party Literature Research Office (ed) (1982) Sanzhong quanhui yilai zhongyao wenxian xuanbian, shang/ Selected key documents since the 3rd Plenary Session, vol 1. Central Party Literature Press, Beijing

Chen Y (1980) Jingji xingshi yu jingyan jiaoxun/The economic situation and experiences and lessons. In: CPC Party Literature Research Office (ed) Sanzhong quanhui yilai zhongyao wenxian xuanbian, shang/Selected key documents since the 3rd Plenary Session, vol 1. Central Party Literature Press, Beijing

Chen Y (1982) Jiaqiang jihua jingji/Strengthening the planned economy. In: CPC Party Literature Research Office (ed) (1982) Sanzhong quanhui yilai zhongyao wenxian xuanbian, xia/Selected key documents since the 3rd Plenary Session, vol 2. Central Party Literature Press, Beijing

Chen Y (1995) Chenyun wenxuan disanjuan/The selected works of Chen Yun, vol 3. People's Publishing House, Beijing

Chen JG (ed) (2008) Zhongguo qiye gaigefazhan sanshinian/Thirty years reform and development of China's enterprises. China Financial and Economical Publishing House, Beijing

Chen A and Gu EN (2013) "Nanbei maodun shijiao" yingdang "bingqi" ma?: Jujiao "Zhong-Jia 2012 BIT"/Should the perspective of South-North contradictions be abandoned?: focusing on the 2012 Sino-Canada BIT. 35 Modern Law Science 35(2):135–148

Cohen JA (ed) (1970) Contemporary Chinese law: research problems and perspectives. Harvard University Press, Cambridge

Davies K (2009) While global FDI falls, China's outward FDI doubles. Transnational Corporations Review 1(2):20–23

Deng XP (1977) Guanyu kexue he jiaoyu gongzuo de jidian yijian/Opinions on science and education work. In: Deng Xiaoping (1993) Deng Xiaoping wenxuan dierjuan/The selected works of Deng Xiaoping, vol 2. People's Publishing House, Beijing

Deng XP (1978) Jiefang sixiang, shishiqiushi, tuanjieyizhi xiangqiankan/Emancipating the mind, seeking truth from facts, forwarding with solidarity. In: Deng Xiaoping (1993) Deng Xiaoping wenxuan dierjuan/The selected works of Deng Xiaoping, vol 2. People's Publishing House, Beijing

Deng XP (1985) Tequ jingji yao cong neixiang zhuandao waixiang/The economy of the special zones should turn from internal to external-oriented. In: Deng Xiaoping (1993) Deng Xiaoping wenxuan disanjuan/The selected works of Deng Xiaoping, vol 3. People's Publishing House, Beijing

Deng XP (1987) Gaige de buzi yao kuai yixie/Accelerating the reforming pace. In: Deng Xiaoping (1993) Deng Xiaoping wenxuan disanjuan/The selected works of Deng Xiaoping, vol 3. People's Publishing House, Beijing

Deng XP (1991) Shica Shanghai shi de tanhua/Talks during the inspection in Shanghai. In: Deng Xiaoping wenxuan disanjuan/The selected works of Deng Xiaoping, vol 3. People's Publishing House, Beijing

Du HY (1990) Causes of rapid rural industrial development. In: Byrd WA and Lin QS (eds) China's rural industrial: structure, development, and reform. Oxford University Press, Oxford

Editorial Board of China Agriculture Yearbook (1984) Zhongguo nongye nianjian 1984/China agriculture yearbook 1984. Agricultural Publishing House, Beijing

Editorial of China Education Yearbook (1984) Zhongguo jiaoyu Nnanjian 1949-1981/China education yearbook 1949-1981. Encyclopaedia of China Publishing House, Beijing

Editorial of China Education Yearbook (1986) Zhongguo jiaoyu nianjian 1982-1984/China education yearbook 1982-1984. Hunan Education Publishing House, Hunan

Falkenheim VC (1986) China's special economic zones. In: U.S. Congress, Joint Economic Committee, China's economy looks towards the year 2000. U.S. Government Publishing Office, Washington, DC

Fewsmith J (2011) Reaction, resurgence, and succession: Chinese politics since Tiananmen. In: MacFarquhar R (ed) The politics of China: sixty years of the People's Republic of China, 3rd edn. Cambridge University Press, Cambridge

Gallagher N (2015) China's BIT's and arbitration practice: progress and problems. In: Shan WH and Su JY (eds) China and international investment law: twenty years of ICSID membership. Brill Nijhoff, Leiden

Gallagher N and Shan WH (2009) Chinese investment treaties: policies and practice. Oxford University Press, Oxford

Gan ZD (ed) (1987) Zhongguo falü nianjian 1987/China yearbook of law 1987. Law Publishing House, Beijing

Gao YF and Jiang W (2020) Falü zhiye zige kaoshi gaige de huigu yu sikao/Review and reflection on the reform of Bar Exam. Public Security Science Journal—Journal of Zhejiang Police College 3:72–78

Gelatt TA and Snyder FE (1980) Legal education in China: Training for a new era. China Law Reporter 1(2):41–60

Han J (2008) Zhongguo jingji gaige 30 nian: nongcun jingji juan 1978–2008/China's 30 years of economic reform: rural economy volume 1978–2008. Chongqing University Press, Chongqing

Han DP and Kanter S (1984) Legal education in China. American Journal of Comparative Law 32(3):543–582

Harford K (1985) Socialist agriculture is dead; long live socialist agriculture!: organizational transformations in rural China. In: Perry EJ and Wong C (eds) The political economy of reform in post-Mao China. Harvard University Press, Cambridge

Herman RA (1982) The education of China's lawyers. Albany Law Review 46(3):789-804

Hsiao T E (1932) The history of modern education in China. Peking University Press, Peiping

Hu FM (1978) Practice was the only criterion to examine the truth. Guangming Daily 11 May, p. 1

Hua L (ed) (1993) Quanguo lüshi zige tongkao shiti ji daan huibian (1986-1992)/The collection of the papers and answers of the national lawyers' qualification test (1986-1992). Qunzhong Publishing House, Beijing

Huang YS (2008) Capitalism with Chinese characteristics: entrepreneurship and the state. Cambridge University Press, Cambridge

Huang DX, Yu C, and Wang XY (eds) (1992) Jianguoyilai nongye hezuohua shiliao huibian/ Collection of historical materials of agricultural cooperation since the establishment of the country. Chinese Communist Party History Publishing House, Beijing

Huo XD and Wang J (2009) Liushinian faxue jiaoyu de shijian yu tansuo/Sixty years of practice and exploration in legal education. Paper presented at the Seminar in the Theory of New China's Development of Rule of Law and the Study of the Law, Chinese Academy of Social Science, Beijing, 24–25 October 2009

Jao YC and Leung CK (eds) (1986) China's special economic zones: policies, problems, and prospects. Oxford University Press, Oxford

Ji WD (2005) Legal education in China: a great leap forward of professionalism. Kobe University Law Review 39:1–22

Ji XL (2016) The cowshed: memories of the Chinese Cultural Revolution (trans: Zha JY and Jiang CX). New York Review Books, New York

Jiang AJ, Liu XG, and Zhao L (2008) Faxuejiaoyu 30 nian pandian/The inventory of 30 years of legal education. Legal Daily 31 August, p. 6
Kraus J (1989) Legal education in the People's Republic of China. Suffolk Transnational Law Journal 13(1):75–134
Lardy NR (1987) The Chinese economy under stress, 1958-1965. In: MacFarquhar R and Fairbank JK (eds) The Cambridge History of China, vol 14. Cambridge University Press, Cambridge
Lardy NR (2014) Market over Mao: the rise of private business in China. PIIE Press, Washington DC
Li FJ (1988) Gaodeng xuexiao faxue jiaoyu gaikuang/General situation of legal education in universities. In: Zhognguo falü nianjian 1988/China yearbook of law 1988. Law Press China, Beijing
Li P (1989) Ba wending gaige fazhan tongyi qilai/Unifying stability, reform, and development. In: CPC Party Literature Research Office (ed) (1991) Shisanda yilai zhongyao wenxian xuanbian/ Selected key documents since the 13th National Congress of the CCP, vol 1. Central Party Literature Press, Beijing
Li P (1990) Gaige kaifang yao yanzhe jiankang de guidao qianjin/Reform and opening-up should forward through a healthy path. In: CPC Party Literature Research Office (ed) (1991) Shisanda yilai zhongyao wenxian xuanbian/Selected key documents since the 13th National Congress of the CCP, vol 2. Central Party Literature Press, Beijing
Li DS (1998) Weida de zhuanzhe, lishi de biran: Huiyi shiyijie sanzhong quanhui de zhaokai/A great turning point, the inevitability of history: recollections of the opening of the Third Plenary Session of the Eleventh Central Committee. In: Guangyuan Yu et al. Gaibian Zhongguo mingyun de 41 tian: Zhongyang gongzuo huiyi, shiyijie sanzhong quanhui qinliji/The forty-one days that changed the fate of China: a record of my experience at the central work conference of the Third Plenary Session of the Eleventh Central Committee. Haitian Press, Shenzhen
Li L and Mo JH (2014) Zhongguo falü zhidu/Legal institutions of China. China Social Science Press, Beijing
Lin JYF (1987) The household responsibility system reform in China: a peasant's institutional choice. Centre Discussion Paper No.526 Yale University, New Haven. Available at http://hdl.handle.net/10419/160449. Accessed 18 Sept 2021
Lin JYF (1988) The household responsibility system in China's agricultural reform: A theoretical and empirical study. Economic Development and Cultural Change 36(3):199-224
Lin JYF (1990) Collectivization and China's agricultural crisis in 1959-1961. Journal of Political Economy 98(6):1228–1252
Lin JYF (1992) Rural reforms and agricultural growth in China. The American Economic Review 82(1):34-51
Lofstedt J-i (1980) Chinese educational policy: changes and contradictions, 1949-79. Almqvist & Wiksell, Stockholm
Luo PH (2016) Nongcun renmin gongsheshi/The history of the People's Commune in the rural area. The People's Press, Beijing
Ma JS (1991) Dangdai zhongguo de xiangzhen qiye/The township and village enterprises in modern China. Contemporary China Publishing House, Beijing
Macdonald R S J (1980) Legal education in China today. Dalhousie Law Journal 6(2):313–337
MacFarquhar R (1991) The succession to Mao and the end of Maoism. In: MacFarquhar R and Fairbank JK (eds) The Cambridge history of China, vol 15. Cambridge University Press, Cambridge
National Development and Reform Commission et al. (2018) Catalogue of Approved Developmental Zones in China
National Judges College (2022) Brief introduction of the national judge college. Available at http://njc.gjfgxy.cn/article/index/id/MygtMTBINCAOAAA.shtml. Accessed 10 Mar 2023
Naughton B (2007) The Chinese economy: transition and growth. MIT Press, Cambridge
Naughton B (2018) The Chinese economy: adaption and growth, 2nd edn. The MIT Press, Cambridge

Parish WL (ed) (1985) Chinese rural development: the great transformation. Routledge, London
Pepper S (1987) Education for the new order. In: MacFarquhar R and Fairbank JK (eds) Cambridge history of China, vol 14. Cambridge University Press, Cambridge
Perkins DH (2015) The economic transformation of China. World Scientific, Singapore
Sachdev R (2006) Comparing the legal foundations of foreign direct investment in India and China: law and the rule of law in the Indian foreign direct investment context. Columbia Business Law Review 1:167–214
Saich T (2004) Governance and politics of China, 2nd edn. Palgrave Macmillan, London
Second Historical Archives of China (2010) Zhonghua mingguo shi dangan ziliao huibian diwuji diyibian jiaoyu yi/Collection of archives and sources of the history of the republic of China: volume 5 part I education I. Phoenix Publishing & Media, Nanjing
Shanghai Academy of Social Sciences Institute of Law (n.d.) The History of the Shanghai Academy of Social Sciences Institute of Law. Available at https://ilaw.sass.org.cn/2521/list.htm. Accessed 19 September 2021
State Council (1992) Guowuuan guanyu zhuanpi nongyebu guanyu jiaqiang nongye chengbao hetong guanli yijian de tongzhi/Circular of the State Council approved agriculture ministry on reinforcing the regulation of agriculture contracts. Available at http://www.gov.cn/zhengce/content/2016-10/20/content_5122199.htm. Accessed 14 Feb 2023
State Council (1995) Guanyu wending he wanshan tudi chengbao guanxi de yijian/Opinions on stabilizing and completing the relationship of land contracts. In: CPC Party Literature Research Office (ed) (1997) Shisida yilai zhongyao wenxian xuanbian/Selected key documents since the 14th National Congress of the CCP, vol 2. Central Party Literature Press, Beijing
State Statistics Bureau (1985) Zhongguo tongji nianjian/Statistic Yearbook of China. China Statistics Press, Beijing
State Statistics Bureau (1986) Zhongguo tongji nianjian/Statistic Yearbook of China. China Statistics Press, Beijing
State Statistics Bureau (1990) Zhongguo tongji nianjian/Statistic Yearbook of China. China Statistics Press, Beijing
Supreme People's Court (1986) Guanyu shenli nongcun chengbao hetong jiufen anjian ruogan wenti de yijian/Opinions on issues concerning the trial of rural contracts cases. Communique of the Supreme People's Court 3. Available at http://gongbao.court.gov.cn/Details/7d1673d00ed2ba4d674568b64f6c20.html?sw=. Accessed 28 Sept 2021
Supreme People's Court (1990) Wang zhoucun, Ren guixia su qinglong cun qizu guoyuan chengbao hetong jiufen an/Zhoucun wang and guixia ren sue qinglong village over orchard contract. Communique of the Supreme People's Court 3. Available at http://gongbao.court.gov.cn/Details/e896cc505a242cbc8c184cc6f2db1a.html. Accessed 28 Sept 2021
Supreme People's Court (1996) Wuhan meiqi gongsi su chognqing jiance yibiao chang meiqibiao zhuangpeixian jishu zhuanrang hetong, meiqibiao sanjian gouxiao hetong/Wuhan Gas Co. sues Chongqing Instrumentation Factory over technology transfer contract and sales contract. Communique of the Supreme People's Court 2. Available at http://gongbao.court.gov.cn/Details/d1eb75db7b0335b0785fa489580cbc.html. Accessed 28 Sept 2021
Supreme People's Court (1999) Guanyu Shenli nongye chengbao hetong jiufen anjian ruogan wenti de guiding/Stipulations on issues concerning the trial of agricultural contracts cases. Communique of the Supreme People's Court 4. Available at http://gongbao.court.gov.cn/Details/f9f1aec4aef2a72877ded28d9836c7.html?sw=. Accessed 28 Sept 2021
The Political Bureau of the CCCCP (1987) Ba nongcun gaige yinxiang shenru/Deepening the rural reform. In: CPC Party Literature Research Office (ed) (1988) Shierda yilai zhongyao wenxian xuanbian / Selected key documents since the 12th National Congress of the CCP, vol 3. Central Party Literature Press, Beijing
Thompson TN (1979) China's nationalization of foreign firms: the policies of hostage taking 1949–57. Occasional Papers, Reprints Series in Contemporary Asian Studies 27(6). Available at https://core.ac.uk/reader/56353790. Accessed 21 Sept 2021

Vogel EF (1989) One step ahead in China: Guangdong under reform. Harvard University Press, Cambridge
Vogel EF (2011) Deng Xiaoping and the transformation of China. Harvard University Press, Cambridge
Weber M (1978) Economy and society: an outline of interpretive sociology (eds: Roth G and Wittich C). University of California Press, Oakland
Whyte MK (1974) Educational reform: China in the 1970's and Russia in the 1920's. Comparative Education Review 18(1):112–128
Wong CPW (1988) Interpreting rural industrial growth in the post-Mao period. Modern China 14(1):3–30
Wu JL (2005) Understanding and interpreting Chinese economic reform, Thomson/South-Western, Singapore
Xue MQ (1984) Xue Muqiao jingji hunwen xuan/Selected economic papers. People's Publishing House, Beijing
Ying WJ (ed) (2008) Zhongguo gaodeng jiaoyu gaige yu fazhan 30 nian (1978–2008)/30 years of reform and development of China's higher education (1978–2008). Shanghai University of Finance and Economics Press, Shanghai
Zeng HQ (2006) Waizi zhengshou jiqi buchang biaozhun: Lishi de fenye yu xianshi de tiaozhan/The expropriations of foreign investment and the standards of compensation: historical division and practical challenge. In: Chen A (ed) Journal of international economic, vol 13. Peking University Press, Beijing
Zeng XY (2012) Lüxue yu faxue: zhongguo falv jiaoyu yu faxue xueshu de chuangtong jiqi xiandai fazhan/The science of law and legal study: the tradition and modern development of China's legal education and legal academia. China Renmin University Press, Beijing
Zeng HQ (2014) Balance, sustainable development, and integration: innovative path for BIT practice. Journal of International Economic Law 17(2):299–332
Zeng HQ (2016) Lun shuangbian touzi tiaoyue fangben de yanjin yu zhongguo de duice/On the evolution of bilateral investment treaty models and China's response. Chinese Review of International Law 4:60–79
Zhang WK and Yuan DM (2008) Zhongguo jingji gaige 30 nian, guoyou qiyejuan/China's thirty years of economic reform: the state-owned enterprises. Chongqing University Press, Chongqing
Zhao ZY (1981) Dangqian de jingji xingshi he jinhou jingji jianshe de fangzhen/The Current economic situation and the following policies on economic construction. In: CPC Party Literature Research Office (ed) Sanzhong quanhui yilai zhongyao wenxian xuanbian/Selected key documents since the 3rd Plenary Session, vol 2. Central Party Literature Press, Beijing
Zhao ZY (1985) Dangqian jingji xingshi he jingji tizhi gaige/The current economic situation and the reform of the economic system. In: CPC Party Literature Research Office (ed) Shierda yilai zhongyao wenxian xuanbian/Selected key documents since the 12th National Congress of the CCP, vol 2. Central Party Literature Press, Beijing

Chapter 5
The Facilitative Role of Law, 1992–2001

Abstract This chapter shifts to the years when China undertook its most aggressive market reform of the economy, approximately from 1992 through 2001. During this period, the central government fundamentally restructured state-owned enterprises, reshaped the banking system, rebuilt the capital market, and liberated the foreign trade system in preparation for joining the WTO in 2001. (5.1) Simultaneously, the government engaged in formalizing the legal system, which is illustrated through a review of company law transformation and the application of the law in practice. (5.2) In addition, the group of legal professionals was expanding, and the quality of legal education was improving, backed by the enhanced career threshold. (5.3) As a whole, the role of law appeared to facilitate the full-fledged market economy. (5.4).

5.1 External Functions of the Law

5.1.1 Political Economy from 1992 to 2001

As the reform approached its second decade, the Chinese authorities made an effort to move towards a market economy at full speed. Economic strategies for this period were embodied in the political document announced in the Third Plenary of the Fourteenth Party Conference in 1993 (CCCCP 1993, pp. 452–476). This year was a turning point as Deng officially stepped down as China's paramount leader and Jiang Zemin, who had been hand-picked by Deng, started to assume power. As Deng's successor, the Jiang administration duly unfolded Deng's vision of economic reform (Kuhn 2004, Chaps. 12–13). The general idea for economic development during this stage was to 'speed up reform and opening-up'. With strong backing from Deng and the declining conservative faction, the Jiang administration, unlike the previous generation of Party leadership, did not face substantial power checks within the Party—internal political hindrances disappeared, and the economy gathered momentum.

On a macrolevel, the overall mechanism of the economy was set to transformation. Inheriting a heavily planned economic system with a few spheres opened

J. Hu, *The Role of Law in China's Economic Development, 1978–2011*,
https://doi.org/10.1007/978-981-99-9911-8_5

up, the Jiang administration pushed for structural change in the economic system. It announced that to build a socialist market economy, the traditional idea of the planned economy should be transformed, or, to use Deng's term (1978), 'emancipating the mind'. The general guideline was to minimize the role of the state in economic life, transforming it from directly intervening in economic production to focusing on macrolevel governing and granting more autonomy to enterprises. Under this agenda, a series of macrolevel changes took place over the next decade (CCCCP 1993, para. 3, 19, and 21).Of particular importance were the transformation of state-owned enterprises (SOEs), the liberation of the price system and foreign trade institutions, and the reformulation of the financial system.

Specifically, the reform of SOEs transformed the old management style of China's SOEs, which had featured an all-around role of the state. More precisely, it structurally transformed these omnipotent state enterprises into modern corporations and thus significantly curtailed the state's role in China's industrial and commercial sector (CCCCP 1993, para. 4–9). Three key points were highlighted by the then premier Zhu Rongji—separating governmental functions from SOEs, completing the management system of SOEs, and completing the social security system (Zhu 1994, pp. 75–81). The political focus on reforming SOEs continued throughout the decade (CCCCP 1999, pp. 163–184; Jiang 1995, pp. 367–380; Wu 1995, pp. 493–498). Moreover, in response to serious social consequences of the massive layoffs that followed SOE reform, the issue of building a social security system appeared on the authority's agenda (CCCCP and State Council 2002, pp. 743–755; Zhu 1997, pp. 245–252; Zhu 2000a, pp. 369–387).

Due to the earlier national planning system, China's state banks were heavily intertwined with its SOEs, and the reform of SOEs therefore could not succeed if the financial sector was left untouched. As a result, the reform of the financial sector took place hand in hand with that of the SOEs. The goal of reconstructing the financial system was to transform it from a money bag for SOEs to a competitive and well-regulated financial market (State Council 1993, pp. 517–527). These goals were broken down to redefining the central bank's functions, separating policy banks from commercial banks, and reforming the old currency system. However, whereas the system has been structurally reformed, unlike the SOEs, China's financial system is still heavily state-controlled.

In addition, the foreign trade system was one of the targets in this decade. Following the currency reform announced in 1993, the authority further liberated the operational mechanism of foreign trade companies (State Council 1994, pp. 557–563). In the meantime, to cultivate and develop a market system, the central authority initiated price reform—liberating the price system by gradually substituting governmental pricing guides with market price and developing the labour market, real estate market, technology, and information market (CCCCP 1993, para. 10–13). In 2000, before the closing era of the Jiang government, the authority launched initiatives to develop the backwards western regions of the country to address regional inequities (Zhu 2000b, pp. 270–282).

On another front, the Party stressed the necessity of building up the legal system in its political agenda. As a result, various Party documents formulated legal directions to guide the relationship between the law and economic activities. For instance, in 1992, the central authority advocated having the law support the economy. According to this, the starting point and ends of political and legal work were 'to emancipate and enhance productivity, to better serve economic constructions' (CCCCP and the Political Bureau 1992, pp. 590–599; Li 1995, pp. 578–583). Therefore, the legal framework for the socialist market economy was deemed urgent, especially laws regulating major market actors, adjusting their relationships, and improving collaborative economic development (Qiao 1993, pp. 291–297). As a result, legislation on the market economic system accelerated after 1995 (Qiao 1996, pp. 686–691), and legislative work accepted the leadership of the Party, was guided by Jiang's political ideas,[1] and was in service of reform, development, social stability (Li 2000, pp. 536–547). The general political idea of the role of law in the economy is best illustrated by the following lines in the concluding document of the Party conference:

> [L]egislation shall embody the spirit of the reform and guarantee the process of the reform … strengthen the leadership of the Party on legislation, completing, improving, and accelerating the process of legislation, and thus to provide legal regulations for [China's] socialist market economy (CCCCP 1993, para. 45).

With such a legal idea in view, in 1997, President Jiang announced the 'rule of law' as the hallmark of his governing style (Li 1998, pp. 226–232). The overall idea of the law was to build a socialist legal system to facilitate the construction of a market economy. Hence, the authority should build the legal system alongside economic transformations and translate policies into related laws to achieve this goal (Lubman 1999, pp. 102–138).

In short, this decade was the most significant period of China's economic reform. The leadership touched on SOEs, the financial system, and the foreign trade mechanism and brought China into the WTO before Jiang stepped down. Most crucially, the construction of the legal system for related economic sectors was purposively accelerated due to the direct attention of the authority (Lubman 1999, p. 124).[2] Having laid out the political ideas for the economy and the law in general, the next section examines the detailed economic reforms under these guidelines and the accompanying legal system.

5.1.2 Reform of the Industrial and Commercial Sector and Its Rules

5.1.2.1 SOE Reform—Corporatization and Privatization

The far-reaching SOE reform of corporatization and privatization was the second round of reforming China's state-owned enterprises and was intended to break the economic stagnation.[3] This reform aimed to reconstruct China's public sector, namely, SOEs and the collectively owned TVEs (Huang 2008, p. 77).[4] The significance of this reform was that it touched the most significant portion of China's economy, covering all the lifelines of the national economy and sweeping throughout the country. As the previous chapter has provided an overview of the characteristics of traditional Chinese SOEs and the early adjustments that the government tried and failed to accomplish, this chapter turns to the much more thorough structural reforms of the SOEs, which finally broke the fetters that had chained the economy for decades.

With ever-worsening SOE financial performance since the early 1990s, further reform was urgently needed. Therefore, in 1993, the Company Law was promulgated and legally prepared the second stage of the reform. The strategy of this reform was 'grasping the big and letting go of the small', or corporatizing large and high-performing SOEs and privatizing or bankrupting small and medium-sized SOEs. Notably, the 'corporatization' process referred only to the changing operation structure, as these SOEs were still state-owned, while 'privatization' touched on the ownership structure.

Whereas these SOEs were all state-owned, in effect, there were two types regarding the right of control: centrally controlled SOEs and those within the purview of local governments. In general, industries concerned with the economy, such as energy, telecommunications, transportation, and heavy industries, were regulated directly by the central government. In contrast, less essential enterprises, such as small goods manufacturers, retail shops, household appliance factories, and services industries such as restaurants and tourism, were overseen by local governments, either provincial or municipal. The government plan was, on the one hand, for those less essential industries, to either let them go private or go bankrupt if the price of saving them was too high, and on the other hand, to enforce a thorough restructuring plan on industries connected to the lifeline of the national economy.

The privatization of small and medium-sized SOEs climaxed in 1995. By the end of 1996, more than half of the small SOEs had gone private or bankrupt, laying off millions of workers (Song 2015, p. 88). From the mid-1990s through 2004, the total number of SOEs shrank from 120,000 to 31,750 (Naughton 2007, pp. 274 and 313). Some were privatized, and some were shut down or restructured. The process of privatization was, however, unfortunately opaque. As most small and medium-sized SOEs were under the control of local governments, there was little documentation of the process and concrete arrangement of how these enterprises were privatized. It is reasonable to speculate that shares in many SOEs were sold to insiders at a bargain price, contributing to the formation of the Chinese style of crony capitalism (Pei 2016).

The restructuring of those critical industries entailed several crucial adjustments. First, a new type of business model, 'business group' (*qiye jituan*), was created. The strategy was to encompass a single industry in one business group and within the group to set up several enterprises to run similar businesses or the same business and thus compete with each other. For instance, the China National Aviation Holding Corporation Limited, also known as Air China Group, was set up in 2002. It was formed by merging the China National Aviation Corporation (Group) Limited, Air China, and China Southwest Airlines. This structure guaranteed that the state could control large industries; meanwhile, the competing parallel enterprises ensured business vitality.

Second, along with these parallel enterprises, two-tier subsidiaries were generally set up within the group. The first-tier subsidiaries were those wholly or primarily owned by the group. Mostly, they were public companies that issued less than 20% of their shares; thus, the state still retained control rights after their listing. In most cases, among these subsidiaries, one was a financial company that provided the business group with in-group financial support. For instance, Petro China, which was listed on the Shanghai, Hong Kong, and New York Stock Exchanges, was set up as a subsidiary under the China National Petroleum Corporation (CNPC), and the CNPC Capital Company Limited was the financial corporation within the group. The second-tier subsidiaries were primarily joint ventures operating peripheral activities such as restaurants and travel services.

Third, at the ministry level, a governmental agency named the State-owned Assets Supervision and Administration Commission (hereafter SASAC) was established in 2003. Additionally, local SASACs were set up by provincial and city governments to oversee SOEs within their regions. These SASACs acted as government shareholders and monitor these state-controlled nonfinancial business groups. To name a few of their responsibilities, they were in charge of appointing senior managers and holding them accountable for allocated financial targets, improving the aggregate value of state assets, and gradually reducing the number of centrally controlled business groups to less than a hundred.

After this reform program, the numbers of both SOEs and their employees were slashed. The total number of SOEs plummeted from 262,000 in 1997 to 111,000 in 2008, and the number of 'business groups', according to the name list provided by the SASAC, has decreased to only 96 currently.[5] The number of employees dropped to 64 million in 2008 from 113 million in 1995, accounting for only 20% of total urban employment compared to 60% in 1995 (Kroeber 2008, p. 98). Figure 5.1 illustrates the changing performance of SOEs over the years.

More or less concurrently, the Chinese government made an effort to expand its legal system. Since the early 1990s, the pace of legislation had accelerated. Laws crucial to economic transactions, competition, financial regulations, etc. were promulgated, for instance, the Company Law, the uniform Contract Law, the Guarantee Law, the Commercial Banks Law, and the Insurance Law. Around 2000, the basic legal framework for economic activities was constructed, and after that, the readjusted economic structure was able to operate within an established formal legal framework.

5.1.2.2 The Emergence of Private Enterprises and Their Rules

In chapter four, this study introduced the emergence of the individual economy (*getihu*) and its legal status granted by the Constitution. Following the progress of opening up, the growing private economy faced institutional constraints in the form of individual economies. The expansion of the private economy was deemed essential

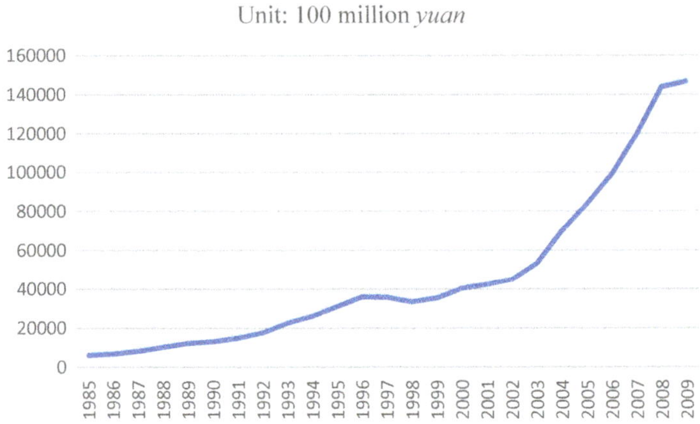

Fig. 5.1 Gross industrial output values of SOEs, 1985–2009 (Generated by data collected from various versions of the Statistical Yearbooks of China)

to China's economic development; hence, the law had to compromise, and first and foremost was the need to lift constitutional constraints on the private economy (CCCCP 1988, p. 360).[6] In 1988, the CCCCP proposed to the Standing Committee of the NPC that the legal status of the private economy be recognized (CCCCP 1988, pp. 350–360).[7] Thereafter, the NPC passed the 1988 constitutional amendment, Article 11, which reads, 'the State permits the private sector of the economy to exist and develop within limits prescribed by law. The private sector of the economy is a complement to the socialist public economy'. In the same year, the State Council stipulated the Provisional Regulations on Private Enterprises (1988). By then, private enterprises had received the green light for operation, and in the ensuing years, laws related to enterprises and their activities emerged one after another.[8] Thus, by the end of the 1990s, the private sector could operate in a more or less established legal framework.

Along with the completion of the legal framework, the share of the private sector grew. The registered number of private enterprises was only 90,600 in 1989, but it soared to 1,508,900 in 1999; the gross industrial output value in 1999 was nearly 80 times that in 1989 (Zhang and Yuan 2008, pp. 58–59). Additionally, the percentage of total employment of urban registered private and individual businesses rose from 3.9% in 1990 to 14.7% in 2000 (Lardy 2014, p. 83).

Deng's opening-up economic strategy, under the endorsement of the Jiang administration, gained momentum throughout the 1990s. In the fifteenth Party Congress, President Jiang (1997) announced that China should 'hold high the great banner of Deng Xiaoping Theory'; that China was in the primary stage of socialism and therefore all forms of ownership conducive to development should be adopted; and that the nonpublic economy was a significant component of the socialist market economy (pp. 1–44). Soon after, the NPC passed constitutional amendments (1999) that, among other changes, revised Article 6 by confirming China's 'primary stage of socialism' and the legal status of 'diverse forms of ownership' and revised Article 11, which reads, 'The nonpublic sectors of the economy such as the individual and private sectors of the economy, operating within the limits prescribed by law, constitute an important component of the socialist market economy'.[9] In 2004, Article 11 was again modified to read, 'The state protects the lawful rights and interests of the non-public sectors of the economy, including individual and private sectors of the economy. The State encourages, supports and guides the development of the non-public sectors of the economy, and exercises supervision and control over the non-public sectors according to law'. In the meantime, the legal framework for economic activities was under ongoing construction. Laws and regulations critical to the economy's legal environment, such as the Law on Individual Proprietorship Enterprises and Contract Law (1999) and Law on the Promotion of Small and Medium-sized Enterprises (2003), were issued along with the evolution of the Constitution.

A brief review of the changing legal environment of the private sector indicates that there was growing support from and release of control by the state as of 1988. As a result, the Constitution went from permitting the existence and development of the private economy to recognizing it as an essential component of the socialist market economy. Finally, in 2004, the Constitution claimed that the state encourages and supports the development of the nonpublic sector. This increasing constitutional support for the private sector was then echoed by establishing the legal framework for private economic activities over the following years. Thus, by 2010, the Chinese government had primarily constructed the legal system for its economy.

The closure of the legal gap for economic activities echoed the growth of the private sector. Since 2000, the private sector has shown vitality and performed in a stable yet growing state. By 2010, over 8.5 million registered private enterprises and 34.5 million individual businesses were operating across the country, hiring 94.2 million and 70.1 million workers, respectively (Lardy 2014, p. 70). In combination, they accounted for over 30% of total employment in 2010 (Lardy 2014, p.83).

5.1.3 Reform of the Financial Sector and Its Rules

The reform of the financial sector, while less thorough than that of enterprises, was crucial in that the demand for financial vehicles would be much more diversified in a market-oriented economy than in a planned economy. Deeply embedded in a planned economic system, China's financial system at the outset was monopolized by the state and dominated by the banking system and provided a limited range of financial services. This state had to change if the economic efficiency of the financial system was to be achieved.

During the first decade of the reform years, the central government largely left the financial sector untouched. Although some minor changes were made in the banking system, they were confined to the internal division of labour among different governmental branches. In other words, the ownership of China's banking sector was still closely held by the state, and there was no capital market in the 1980s. This situation changed in the second decade of reform when China's financial system underwent a momentous transformation.

The banking sector evolved from a monobanking system to the current diverse and complex banking network. Various forms of nonbank financial institutions were established to fulfil different types of financing purposes. The Chinese capital market, which emerged from scratch, currently incorporates a sizable bond market and a multilayered structure of stock exchanges. Profound changes in structure notwithstanding, the Chinese government, to a great extent, did not intervene in the ownership structure of its financial system, which currently is still mainly the playground of state capital. It has been argued that the financial system is therefore China's least reformed sector (Lardy 1998).

The most significant part of China's financial system is the banking sector, dominated by state-owned and party-controlled commercial banks. However, the capital market, which is approximately half the size of the banking sector, was also packed with state capital. Specifically, the bond market was filled with governmental bonds, and the stock market, especially the two Main Boards, was primarily occupied by SOEs. Therefore, while China put much effort into restructuring its financial system over the years, this system was still only moderately diversified, with private money stuck at the periphery.

The following first elaborates on the present composition of China's banking system and its evolving history and then examines the governance model of state-owned banks. The third part illustrates the infrastructure of the capital market that China has built over the years. Then, the study shifts attention to China's rising curb market, a peculiar phenomenon resulting mainly from China's underdeveloped financial market. The last section then places the financial system's legal infrastructure in perspective with a general introduction to and spotlight on certain critical legal institutions.

5.1.3.1 Transformation of the Banking Sector

Since the reform was unveiled, China's banking sector has been fundamentally restructured. From 1979 through 2010, the Chinese government transformed its monobanking system into a sophisticated compound system. The current banking system in China consists of three major components: the Central Bank (called the People's Bank of China; hereafter PBC) and three policy banks as financial instruments of the central government; a vast network of commercial banks, which again can be divided into three tiers according to their sizes; and an array of nonbank financial institutions.

Central Bank and Policy Banks

From the late 1950s through 1978, the PBC was the only bank operating in the country. The creation of this monobanking system resulted from the so-called socialist transformation campaign during the mid-1950s,[10] when all private money institutions and banks were subjected to ownership reconstruction and then merged into the then PBC. While it was nominally called the Central Bank during the prereform era, the PBC was omnipotent, functioning as both a central and commercial bank. Consequently, the PBC dominated four-fifths of the country's financial resources (Lardy 1998, p. 249), with over 15,000 affiliates spread all over the nation before the transformation was set in motion (Byrd 1983, p. 10).

As the reform unfolded, China's financial system changed from a monobanking system to a system of multiple commercial banks juxtaposed with the PBC (Lardy 1998, pp. 15–18).[11] The reform started by splitting off some branches of the PBC and the Ministry of Finance (MOF) and converting them to independent commercial banks so that the PBC could morph into an actual central bank. Hence, several subsidiaries of the PBC and MOF were strategically carved out and shaped into four large state-owned commercial banks (this was the origin of the 'big four'), each tasked with a specific function. This divorcing process took a couple of years to accomplish. The first stage took place in 1979, when the government set up three specialized banks: the Agricultural Bank of China (ABC) to support agricultural development, the Bank of China (BOC) to handle foreign exchange business, and the People's Construction Bank of China (CCB) to focus on fixed-assets investment. In 1984, the Industrial and Commercial Bank of China (ICBC) was established to take over the savings and loan business from the PBC. Finally, after five years of adjustments, the PBC shook off its commercial functions and was ready for its role as an actual central bank (Wu 2005, pp. 217–220).

In 1994, China set up three policy banks, which, like the PBC, were all subordinated to the State Council. The China Development Bank is responsible for financing large-scale governmental projects; historical projects include the Three Gorges Dam and the Shanghai Pudong International Airport. In 2008, it was transformed into the China Development Bank Corporation and began to operate as a development finance institution. The Export–Import Bank of China focuses on financing foreign trade, international investment and cooperation, and the 'going global' strategy. It has an extensive business scope, including export credit, import credit, loans for offshore contracts, and special loans designated by the State Council. By the end of 2018, its total assets amounted to RMB 4.19 trillion (The Export–Import Bank of China 2018, p. 7). On the other hand, the China Agricultural Development Bank concentrates exclusively on the so-called three rural issues, namely, the issues of agriculture, rural areas, and farmers. Therefore, its business scope is mainly providing loans for purchasing agricultural essentials, constructing rural and agricultural infrastructure, and supporting agricultural enterprises. Together, the three policy banks' total assets accounted for 10.11% of market value as of 2017 (The China Banking Regulatory Commission 2018, p. 184).

Formation of the 'Big Five' Commercial Banks

The 'big five' represents the largest group in China's banking system, with 36.77% of the market share as of 2017 (The China Banking Regulatory Commission 2018, p. 184). It consists of the aforementioned four largest state-owned banks plus the Bank of Communication, a joint-stock bank. Whereas they currently belong to the same cluster, each has a different story of development. As briefly mentioned above, the four specialized banks were all associated with the government in one way or another before they finally emerged as separate financial institutions.

The Agricultural Bank of China (ABC) was the first to become independent among the group, before which it had several rounds of establishment and mergers in response to the economic situation at the time. In July 1951, the Agricultural Cooperation Bank was established by the PBC to provide financial services for rural regions' social and economic development. It was merged with the PBC one year later to support the latter's rural financial work. In 1955, the central authority decided to form an independent agricultural bank to facilitate the cooperative agriculture movement and crack down on the rural usury activities that were rampant in China at the time. However, due to functional overlap, the state decided to merge this bank with the PBC in 1957. In 1963, the government intended to unify fund management for agricultural projects and hence reestablished the ABC. Two years later, it was again merged with the PBC, also due to the overlap of their functions (Lardy 1998, p. 249; Zhao 2018). In February 1979, the ABC gained independence as a separate bank, having been designated by the government a specialized bank focusing on financing the rural economy.

Shortly afterwards, in April 1979, following the instructions of the State Council, the Bank of China (BOC) was separated from the PBC and placed under the direct leadership of the State Council (Liu 1986, part II-10). This movement enabled the BOC to focus on foreign-related businesses with the plan of serving China's opening-up economic strategy. Therefore, its main functions were handling foreign exchange, settling international payments, and selling bonds on the international market. In October 1979, the current China Construction Bank (CCB) surfaced as an actual bank. The CCB nominally existed except during two periods: from 1958 through 1962, it was subordinated to the Ministry of Finance, and from 1970 to 1972, it was part of the PBC (Liu 1986, part II-13). However, it could hardly be termed a bank, as its only role was to disburse funds for construction projects designated by the state to be funded by the public budget. It was only in 1980 that the CCB started to engage in real banking business, absorbing deposits and allocating loans for construction programmes.

The largest bank in China today, the Industrial and Commercial Bank of China (ICBC), was established in 1984 to take over the credit and savings businesses from the PBC. As reported, the savings deposits transferred from the PBC to the ICBC accounted for 87.8% of the total volume at that time, and working capital loans and fixed asset loans made up 64.6% and 86.7% of the total market value, respectively (ICBC n.d.). With such a volume of capital, the ICBC immediately became the most prominent financial institution in China.

Unlike the four state-owned banks, the Bank of Communication was the first joint-stock bank in China and had a unique history. It was initially formed in 1908 following a proposal by a high-ranking official of the Qing Dynasty named Liang Shiyi, who hoped to redeem the Beijing-Hankou railway from the Belgians. In the end, the bank financed more than half of the fund and successfully facilitated the redemption. In 1934, it opened its first branch in Hong Kong, and its mainland institution was subordinated to the Ministry of Finance in 1952. After 1958, except for its Hong Kong branch, its businesses were subsumed into the PBC and the CCB. Following the economic reform, it was reestablished in 1987 and headquartered in Shanghai.

Together, these banks form the 'big five' group, and the name implies their dominant status in China's financial system. While the banking structure appeared to have been modernized, their operations were not—they were still operating as governmental arms, intervening in the economy whenever the state deemed it necessary. In other words, the restructured financial system was still in the service of the planned economy and supported the then money-losing SOEs; therefore, it possessed no autonomy in responding to the market. This mechanism was in operation throughout the 1980s until a hyperinflation crisis interrupted it.

From 1993 to 1994, fuelled by Deng's 1992 Southern Tour, China ignited enthusiasm for investments, especially fixed assets. As a result, the prices of construction materials, particularly steel, started to surge in 1993, and soon after, inflation reached consumer products. As the data show, in 1994, the overall price index experienced a steady upwards trend starting in June and peaking in October, when the inflation rate of the overall consumer price hit 27.7%, with food items being hit particularly hard, reaching 44.5% (Chang and Hou 1997, pp. 73 and 75). While the trigger of this hyperinflation was debatable, this national inflation crisis forced the government to deepen the reform of its banking system. Therefore, from 1994 through 2010, another round of transformation took place. This time, the reform focused on the management structure of the 'big four'.

As mentioned above, for decades, China's SOEs were zombie companies at best, and most of them lost money year after year. Over this period, state-owned banks worked as financial sponsors of these public companies, which meant that the four specialized banks, by channelling unfettered financial resources to keep the SOEs afloat, had accumulated many nonperforming loans (NPL). The official ratio of NPLs, as one study showed, reached 30% in 1996 (Shih 2008, p. 27). To rescue its financial system, the government had to lift these enormous burdens from state banks. Consequently, the reform of the banking sector had to go hand in hand with the reform of SOEs. As it unfolded, following the conclusion of SOE reform, four bad banks, also called asset management companies (AMC), were set up in 1999,[12] with each receiving NPLs from one of the 'big four'. The idea of setting up the AMCs was to buy the NPLs from the state banks at face value (amounting to RMB 1.4 trillion) and thus clear their balance sheets and prepare them for IPOs (Sullivan and Curcio 2018, p. 55) with the expectation of improving the performance of these banks by exposing them to open competition. From 2005 through 2010, the 'big four' plus the Bank of Communication went public on both the Shanghai and Hong Kong Stock Exchanges. By 2010, after the Agricultural Bank of China had completed its listing, the five largest banks in China had finished their final major transformation and had been structurally stabilized.

Network of National Commercial Banks

In addition to the 'big five', China hosts another group of large-scale national joint-stock banks. In total, there are twelve of them, most of which emerged around 1990. There are three private banks in this block, and the rest are controlled through various mechanisms by either the central government or local governments. The CITIC Industrial Bank (1987) is the banking arm of the China International Trust and Investment Company, which is a state-owned investment company. The China Everbright Group set up the Everbright Bank (1992), an SOE focused on insurance, securities, investment management, etc. The Huaxia Bank (1992) was formed by the Capital Iron and Steel Group, China's largest steel and steel-related products producer. Finally, the Minsheng Bank, which was acclaimed as China's first private bank, opened for business in 1996. Its original shareholders were almost entirely non-state-owned enterprises, and it stands out as a specialist in supporting small and medium-sized businesses.

The remaining members of this group are the China Merchants Bank (1987), Hengfeng Bank (1987), Shanghai Pudong Development Bank (1988), China Guangfa Bank (1988), Industrial Bank (1988), Bohai Bank (2005), and two other private banks, Pingan Bank (1987)[13] and Zheshang Bank (2004). While most of them are under state ownership, the emergence of these large joint-stock commercial banks nonetheless diversified the banking sector. Together with the 'big five', they formed China's tier-one commercial banks, and their total assets accounted for 54.58% of market value as of 2017 (The China Banking Regulatory Commission 2018, p. 172).[14]

Regional Banks, Foreign Banks, and Nonbank Financial Institutions

China's regional banks have vast coverage of basically every corner of the country. By and large, they constitute two sublevels of commercial banks. Tier two is the group formed by banks set up in urban areas, or city banks; often, they are backed by local governments at either the provincial or municipal level, and most were established between 1990 and 2010. According to the CBIRC annual report, there were 134 of these banks as of 2017, with assets amounting to 12.56% of the market share (The China Banking Regulatory Commission 2018, pp. 172 and 184). The third tier is the largest in number, consisting of 2260 institutions located throughout the country. There are three forms, rural credit operative banks, rural commercial banks, and rural cooperative banks, which occupied 12.44% of China's total banking assets as of 2017 (The China Banking Regulatory Commission 2018, pp. 172 and 184).

In addition, postal banks and foreign banks are also participants in the Chinese market. However, the former, while significant in number (in total, there were 1625 of them as of 2017), assumed only 4.12% of the market share. Concerning foreign banks, while China promised that upon its accession to the WTO in 2001, it would open its financial market to foreign capital within five years, the market share of foreign banks in China is still minimal. By the end of 2017, there were a total of 39 foreign financial institutions operating in China, accounting for only 1.2% of the market share (The China Banking Regulatory Commission 2018, pp. 172 and 184).

Various types of nonbank financial institutions have been surfacing since the mid-1980s. As of 2017, there were 437 nonbank financial institutions in the Chinese financial market, accounting for 4.37% of the market share (The China Banking Regulatory Commission 2018, pp. 172 and 184). They engage in a wide variety of financing activities in domestic and foreign markets, and many are state-controlled via SOEs. Specifically, four financial asset management companies, as briefly noted above, were initially set up as bad banks for the 'big four', and they are still operating today. In addition, there are trust and investment companies that primarily take on long-term investments; the best known are the China International Trust and Investment Company and the China Foreign Economic and Trade Trust Company.[15] Also of importance are financial companies, which are the largest in number. These companies are the in-group financial institutions of enterprise groups. In China, large-scale conglomerates, for instance, groups with registered capital of no less than RMB 800 million,[16] are allowed to open their own financial companies to facilitate internal financial transactions and engage in external financial activities. Second, financial leasing companies appeared in 1981 as foreign joint ventures to assist Chinese firms in acquiring foreign capital goods, such as technical upgrading and modernization. Last, there are dozens of specialized financial companies, such as consumer finance companies, auto finance companies, and currency brokerage companies.

5.1.3.2 Governance of State Commercial Banks

The reform of the ownership structure shows merely one aspect of China's financial system. To gain a more comprehensive view, the internal mechanism of the corporate governance of these banks must also be scrutinized. As noted above, the key purpose of reforming the financial sector was to improve its performance and thus its ability to assist China's economic development. The central authority achieved this goal via learning managerial know-how by inviting experts, namely, foreign financial institutions, to sit on the boards as strategic consultants while controlling decisive voting power by holding a lopsided proportion of shares. In other words, neither the structure of shareholders nor the internal operative mechanism of these commercial banks has undergone substantive reform. As the previous section has laid bare the shareholder structures, the following section examines the governance mechanism, namely, the new board structure after the restructuring and some aspects of the operative mechanisms.

Technical Role of Foreign Institutional Investors

As stated above, before the structural reform of the banking system, China's state banks were barely banks in the modern sense. They were operating as the moneybags of state-owned industrial and commercial enterprises. The enormous accumulated amount of NPLs finally paralyzed the whole system. Hence, financial talent was desperately needed to transform these newly reshaped institutions into real modern commercial banks.

The reform guideline for state commercial banks, as stated in 2005 by Zhou Xiaochuan, the then PBC governor, was to follow the experience of industrial SOEs, meaning to reform the share system and list a small portion of the shares (Ling 2005). These measures were deemed highly successful by the authorities. Nevertheless, the importance of corporate governance, or a modern operating system, was widely acknowledged by leaders in China's financial sector (Hu et al. 2006; Ling and Zhao 2003), and board meetings, as the key forum for banking governance, would be changed from the former 'single voice carries all' to 'welcoming different voices' (Hu et al. 2006; Ling and Zhao 2003).

Additionally, the authority acknowledged the importance of learning from advanced financial institutions and opened some spots on the banks' boards or initiated particular cooperative programmes to import such skills. A string of representatives of seasoned foreign banks was invited to join the boards of these newly restructured state banks as strategic advisers. For instance, the HSBC was paired with the BoCom; the Bank of America and Singapore's Temasek were invited to provide board members to the CCB; the BOC placed representatives of the Royal Bank of Scotland and Temasek in the boardroom, and Goldman Sachs representatives sat as a partner of the ICBC. These consultants provided guidance for corporate governance, risk management, and other banking and financial skills (Howson 2009, p. 134). The internal management and regulatory framework of China's financial system were on the path to closing the gaps with their international counterparts (Bottelier 2006).

Nevertheless, while these foreign banks assumed chairs in the boardrooms, their role was rather confined due to their minimal shares. They were invited to be investors because of their financial know-how, which China was in need of at the time. However, no decision-making power whatsoever was shared (Howson 2009, p. 139). Put bluntly, while some structural reforms of corporate governance were made, outsiders were excluded from the substantive aspect, namely, the real power.

The Invisible Hand of the Party Committee

The diversified board structure of the state banks showed the central authority's determination to improve these banks' performance by enhancing their technical skills. This meant that the operations of the state banks were expected to follow market rules, and for such purposes, the authority ensured that both the Chinese Company Law and the Commercial Bank Law were in place for corporate behavioural guidance and regulatory purposes. Nevertheless, the law books do not tell the whole story of the management style of China's state banks.

At play in this scenario was China's unique political system, which featured an omnipresent Party committee. Sometimes also called a 'disciplinary committee', it is an organization that is present in literally every state institution, whether industrial SOEs, public institutions such as schools and hospitals, or state-controlled banks (Howson 2009, p. 161). The major role of the Party committee in these banks could be roughly categorized as corporate governance and personnel appointment (Huang and Orr 2007). In general, the Party committee governed state banks at the macrolevel, participating in activities such as selecting overall bank strategies and ensuring compliance with social and legal responsibilities (Hu et al. 2006, p. 72;

Zhang 2005). Additionally, at the top of the agenda was personnel appointments. The directors and top managers of state banks were usually selected by the Party from ranking party members (Howson 2009, pp. 144–145). For this reason, some have termed the Party committee the fourth committee to the banks (Zhang et al. 2006). However, the rights and obligations of the fourth committee are not stated in related laws, which has made the internal structure somewhat opaque to outsiders.

The Party's control over the banks' key operations and management guaranteed that the banks' highest-priority operation was to serve the nation's macroeconomic strategies rather than being responsible to their shareholders, although the most significant shareholder was the state itself. In other words, the Party committee stood above the shareholder meetings. This power structure implied that the interests of shareholders and the banks' strategies were subject not to market rules but to state and national economic concerns. Thus, it was argued that given that the overall control of China's banking system was in the hands of the ruling Party and that it would not prioritize shareholders' interests, the reform of the banking system was hardly substantial, and internal governance was not entirely within the purview of the related legal system (Howson 2009, pp. 152–153).

5.1.3.3 The Chinese Capital Market

Unlike the banking sector, China's capital market was formed at a relatively late stage of the reform, and like the banking sector, it was heavily dominated by the state, with private capital representing only a fraction.

Bond Markets

Before the economic reform, no bond market proper existed in China. The first bond issuance by the Ministry of Finance took place in 1981. In 1984, enterprises, for the first time, were granted the right to issue bonds. Despite this late start, China's bond market has grown in leaps and bounds, especially since the turn of the century. As of 2021, the Chinese bond market had reached 4200 billion *yuan* in bond issuance, with the bond trading volume reaching 17,110 billion *yuan* (CCDC Research 2022, p. 2). China's bond market is currently composed of two parts: the interbank bond market and the exchange market. The former, a quote-driven OTC market, was the avenue for institutional investors and played a dominant role in China's bond market (State Council 1996). In contrast, the exchange market was an order-driven market that complemented the market by taking on smaller institutional participants and individuals.

After decades of development, the Chinese bond market has reached a certain level of complexity, as numerous types of bonds are traded on the market. Although the market was somewhat diversified in terms of categories, it was still a government playground, which is utterly telling when the issuer structure of these bonds is examined (Walter and Howie 2012, pp. 98–102).[17] By and large, bond issuers in China can be classified in three major types, namely, governments, financial institutions, and corporations. The most significant share of the bond market was held by governments, which accounted for 62% of the market share in 2021 (treasury bonds 29%, local government bonds 33%) (CCDC Research 2022, p. 89).[18] Second place belonged to financial institutions, specifically, central bank bills issued by the PBC, policy financial bonds issued by China's three policy banks, and other general financial bonds issued by commercial banks and nonbanking financial institutes. Finally, the corporations represented the smallest portion, making up only 2% of the total amount in 2021 (CCDC Research 2022, p. 90; Wu 2005, pp. 240–242).[19] Regarding the ownership structure, China's commercial banks and corporations that were capable of issuing bonds were primarily state-owned, which demonstrated that on the whole, the Chinese bond market was state-dominated (Walter and Howie 2012, Chaps. 4–5).

Equity Markets

Like the bond market, China's equity market was a latecomer, emerging only a decade after the reform started; at present, there are three national markets for stock exchanges. The Shanghai Stock Exchange (SSE) and the Shenzhen Stock Exchange (SZSE) opened back-to-back at the end of 1990. As of 2018, there were 3584 companies listed on the different boards of the two markets, with market capitalization reaching 43.50 trillion RMB, which was equivalent to 48.32% of GDP (The China Securities Regulatory Commission 2018, pp. 27–31).[20] In 2013, the third market, called National Equities Exchange and Quotations (NEEQ), an OTC market, opened for business in Beijing. Within these three trading avenues, China has built a three-tier stock market structure serving different types of companies.

Tier one, or the Main Board Market, consists of three boards. Together, the two Main Boards offer a stock trading platform for the most influential public companies in the Chinese territory, as many of them are SOEs. In 2004, the SZSE opened the Small and Medium-Sized Enterprises Board. The requirements for being listed on the SME Board are identical to those for the Main Boards. However, the label 'small and medium-sized' does not indicate the size of the companies; rather, it refers to the number of floating stocks these companies issue (Walter and Howie 2012, pp. 164–167).

Tier two, also called the Second-Board Market, now has two boards in operation. The first one, the ChiNext, opened in 2009 on the SZSE. It is a NASDAQ-style market and was set up in the hope of serving innovative and high-tech firms that are not yet qualified for listing on the Main Board Market. In July 2019, the Sci-Tech Innovation Board (also called the STAR Market) opened on the SSE. Like ChiNext, it aims to attract high-tech companies that work in areas related to national development strategies or focus on core technology innovations. As of June 2020, 115 companies were listed on the STAR Market, and its market capitalization amounted to RMB19.68 trillion.[21]

Tier three is the national OTC market (the NEEQ), also called 'The New Third Board',[22] which opened for business in January 2013. Its primary concern is facilitating share transfer, equity and bond financing, and asset restructuring. By 2018, 10,691 companies had been admitted to the NEEQ, and it had a total market capitalization of RMB 3.45 trillion (The China Securities Regulatory Commission 2018,

p. 31). In 2021, China opened the Beijing Stock Exchange. However, its role in China's capital market is still unknown.

At present, three groups of shareholders are actively participating in China's stock market. Parent companies of listed firms and securities firms together hold the most significant shares, amounting to 61% of market value. Individual investors, in contrast, account for only one-quarter of the market. The remaining market shares (14%) are held by various institutional investors, such as mutual funds, insurance companies, qualified foreign investment institutions, trust and enterprise funds, and social security funds (The China Securities Regulatory Commission 2014, pp. 21–22). While most shares are held by institutional investors, which are regarded as mature and following a long-term vision, the Chinese stock market is volatile. It has long been argued that the Chinese market cannot be analysed by economic fundamentals, as it is essentially policy-driven. While market volatility is not unusual in a transitional economy, the degree seen in China is considered rather extreme. After its establishment, the market soared in 1993, 2000, 2007, and 2015 and collapsed each time (Wu 1997, 2001). The latest and most telling occasion happened in mid-2015. From December 2014 to June 2015, the Shanghai Composite Index rose over 150% percent, climbing from 3234 on 31 December 2014 to a peak of 5166 on 12 June 2015. However, it nose-dived to 3507 on 8 July and then plunged to 2927 on 26 August, falling by approximately 43% in just two months. As a result, over 1400 companies filed for trading halts, and new IPOs were temporarily suspended. This wave of turbulence lasted for half a year and did not end until February 2016 (Wang et al. 2019).[23]

5.1.3.4 The Informal Financial Market

An Overview of China's Informal Financial Market

After rounds of reforms, the Chinese financial system changed from the previous monobanking system to the current multicomponent structure, covering the central bank, commercial banks, policy banks, and numerous lower-level credit cooperatives. However, while this modernized structure provided the Chinese economy with various channels for financing, the most vibrant economic sector, small private enterprises, did not assume a fair share of loans. As introduced, China's financial system was an underdeveloped state playground. This reality had threefold implications. First, financial institutions were disproportionately dominated by the state, and private money had barely any weight. The most illustrative example was China's banking system, with the capital market being filled with state-owned banks and enterprises; privately owned banks emerged only in 1996 and remain small in number today. Second, the capital flow was unidirectional, from state-owned banks to state-owned enterprises. Outsiders, especially small and medium-sized private businesses, which were considered to be higher risk, could barely receive loans from these big banks (Tsai 2002, p. 2).[24] Third, because the financial market was immature, categories of financial products were limited in kind, which left constrained channels for financial activities for both investors and borrowers.

In short, there were two sets of structural conflicts in China's financial market: the increasing private money vis-à-vis limited choices of investment channels and the capital demand of small private businesses vis-à-vis constrained financing sources. These conflicts became severe as the opening-up policies became deeper and the demand from both sides of the financial market grew, especially in regions with booming private economies. This reality was illustrated by the sheer volume of capital demand in some underground markets, which is unfolded below.

Under such financial conflicts, the rise of China's informal financial market became inevitable, especially in provinces that became prosperous in the 1990s, such as Zhejiang, Guangdong, and Fujian Provinces. In these places, private businesses, which had long been disfavoured by the state-dominated capital market, turned to rich private investors who were tired of leaving their cash sleeping in deposit accounts and were in desperate need of better returns. The two found their match in the underground capital market.

Informal finance in China appeared to be both robust, in the sense of being long lasting and widespread in certain regions, and fragile, as it lacked formal regulation and thus involved high risks when things went wrong. In a sense, both features originated from China's insufficient financial system and gaps in the legal system. The forms of informal finance examined in this study had several features. They possessed institutional features that were tacitly acknowledged by their participants, such as well-structured and compliant procedures for doing business. They were of a certain size, so that a number of participants were involved, and their financial significance was visible in a certain period or region. They operated outside China's financial regulatory framework, which meant they were unsupervised by the Chinese government and thus functioned via informal social norms, self-discipline, and mutual trust.

For a period of time, the authorities turned a blind eye to informal financial activities (Tsai 2002, Chap. 4).[25] However, by the end of 1990, the scale and potential risks of the growing curb market struck a nerve with the central authority, which stressed the necessity of addressing the issue (Tsai 2002, p. 1). This section provides an overview of the forms and some features of informal financial activities in China in recent memory.

First, in recent decades, with the rising need of businesses for credit and financing, various types of informal finance emerged throughout the nation, and many coexisted simultaneously. Common forms were interpersonal loans, pawnshops,[26]rotating credit associations, trade credit among retailers and wholesalers, and private money houses. Each had its own particular group of clients, which suggests that various kinds of financing needs also coexisted in Chinese society.

Below, we take the rotating credit association as an example to show some characteristics of China's traditional folk finance. The Rotating Savings and Credit Association (ROSCA), also called *Hui* in Chinese, is, as Ardener (1964) put it, 'an association formed upon a core of participants who agree to make regular contributions to a fund which is given, in whole or in part, to each contributor in rotation' (p. 201). This type of association has a long history in China, and its recent thriving can be dated back to the late nineteenth century (Smith 1899, p. 152). In modern China, it reappeared in the southeast coastal regions, where the private economy was growing robustly. In general, there are currently three types of *hui* in China, namely, *chenghui*, *biaohui*, and *taihui*.

Chenghui normally appears among a small group of friends and relatives. The purpose of these associations is mutual aid rather than financial gains (Committee of Wenzhou Chorography 2020, p. 486). *Biaohui*, in contrast, is for earning profits. As the name '*biao*' (meaning 'bid' or 'auction') suggests, the allocation of the lump-sum fund of each period is decided by auction; therefore, the highest bidder obtains it. *Taihui* is a pyramid-structured association, similar to a Ponzi scheme; it has been explicitly outlawed (Meng 2018). Today, participants in *hui* extend to strangers, people outside kinship groups, and circles of friends, which has eliminated the initial purpose of mutual aid and turned these to purely profit-seeking associations. Therefore, the traditional norms that bring participants into compliance, such as mutual trust, have been weakened, and potential risks have arisen (Tsai 2002, p. 169).

Second, the location of active informal finance groups indicates strong regional particularities. Although it is reasonable to speculate that informal finance may be widespread in the nation, the levels of magnitude and pervasiveness show geographic features. As mentioned above, Zhejiang, Fujian, and Guangdong were the provinces where informal finance grew relentlessly, and coincidentally, these were also the places that hosted large numbers of private and often small-scale industries that relied heavily on informal finance for businesses. In contrast, the northeast region, where local economies were dominated by large-scale SOEs, experienced far fewer troubles with informal finance. This circumstance demonstrates that the appearance of informal finance may be linked to China's regional economic structures.

Case Study of Wenzhou's Underground Financial Market

While less globally famous than Shanghai, Wenzhou is a renowned city in China. A prefectural city in Zhejiang Province (south of Shanghai), it became a household name in China for local people's investment acumen and the wealth they accumulated in the opening-up years. Behind these people's economic success was the robustly growing private economy in the region (Lin 2017, Chap. 5). In 2011, these formerly successful Wenzhou businesspeople again hit a nerve in the nation, only this time for a large number of local entrepreneurs escaping from their debts. Two of them, deeply indebted, jumped from high-rises due to their incapability of repaying their loans, and many other private business owners fled (Barboza 2011). What they had in common was that they were all involved in underground lending as either borrowers or loan sharks (Jacob and Rabinovitch 2011).

These incidents brought the city's large underground financial network to the surface. It was a huge and complex underground web that consisted mostly of family members, friends, relatives, and colleagues, close and distant. As estimated by the local PBC branch office, nearly 90% of local households had joined this informal credit business, and more than half of local enterprises had participated in this informal market, which amounted to a capital volume of approximately 110 billion *yuan* as of 2011 (Mackenzie 2011). As one can imagine, within such a vast network, a single default in the capital chain could trigger a domino effect. It was reported that during the first nine months of 2011, eighty-four local business owners either fled or went into hiding because of their debts (Tao 2011).

The flurry of incidents ultimately drew attention from Beijing and forced the central authority to directly intervene and formulate a policy framework. In October 2011, the then premier Wen Jiabao paid a visit to the city for the purpose of calming the crisis and showing the central government's determination to institutionally address the tension between private capital and the real economy (Wenzhou Government 2012). A year later, the State Council issued the General Scheme of Wenzhou Pilot Program for Comprehensive Financial Reform, a region-specific policy designed to frame and guide local folk financial activities.

This document is a general framework of policy guidance for private capital. By and large, it has three main foci. The foremost emphasis is placed on innovating and diversifying financial institutions and their functions, such as supporting private investors becoming shareholders in local publicly owned financial institutions and encouraging private investors to form financial institutions tailor-made for the local economy.[27] Second, the scheme made explicit the importance of building up a social credit system as a form of market supervision. Third, it envisaged designing risk prevention mechanisms and a complete precautionary regulative structure. This was the first pilot programme for regulating folk finance, and it is still the only one in China. In a bid to systematically and institutionally steer private capital, the programme was intended to incorporate private capital from outside the established financial system into the state framework by creating a new form of institution. It was also regarded as a laboratory for China's attempts at future financial reforms.

5.1.3.5 Legal Institutions of the Financial System

The significance of a functioning financial system to economic development has been widely treated theoretically and empirically (Goldsmith 1969; Gurley and Shaw 1955; Schumpeter 1934). Nevertheless, the structure of the financial system that facilitates economic growth is still a subject of debate, especially concerning the role of the Central Bank or the state's intervention in the financial system (Norton 2000, Chap. 3). The above sections have shown that China's financial institutions have diversified over the years, although the governance of the banking system was liberated only on a limited scale. This section turns to the formal rule structure that entrenched the function of the financial system to help understand the role of finance in facilitating economic growth and the institutional factor behind the rise of informal finance, as described above.

Regulatory Structure of the Banking System

In China, the financial system is regulated by the PBC (ministry level) and the China Banking and Insurance Regulatory Commission (CBIRC),[28] which are subordinated to the State Council. Initially, the banking system was placed within the purview of the PBC. In 2003, the government established the China Banking Regulation Commission (CBRC) to take over regulatory responsibility for the banking sector from the PBC. Nevertheless, regardless of the changing of the regulatory institution, the Chinese financial system is not independent of the government, as the State Council is perpetually its ultimate authority. Therefore, it is reasonable to speculate that political considerations occasionally constrain the ability of China's banking sector to respond to market mechanisms, as is clear when the related rule arrangements are considered.

Similar to the creation of legal institutions for other sectors, China constructed a multilevel legal system for its financial sector. Of significance to the economy are the Law of the PRC on the People's Bank of China (1995, revised in 2003) and the Law of the PRC on Commercial Banks (1995).[29] The status of the PBC as a real central bank has been legally clarified since 1995 (Article 2).[30] Operating as an actual central bank, the PBC concentrates on monetary regulation, such as monitoring RMB (Chap. 3), using a toolkit of monetary policy instruments to monitor macroeconomics (Chap. 4), and supervising financial institutions (Chap. 5).[31]

Planned Financial Liberalization

Given the entrenchment of legal institutions for financial activities, the ability to channel financial capital into the real economy is crucial for the role of capital in facilitating economic development. While market-oriented reform deepened in the 1990s, China's financial sector showed its rather conservative side. To a certain extent, the Chinese government liberated the system via formal laws, although in a finely crafted way aimed at selected development goals.

Prior to the reform, the interest rate was fixed and remained low (Yi 1994, p. 77). The reform loosened the PBC's control over financial institutions. While the PBC still decides interest rates, it has adopted a floating rate system that grants financial institutions autonomy to decide within the range.[32] Furthermore, some lower-level financial institutions, such as rural and urban credit cooperatives and nonbank financial institutions, were granted discretionary power to break through the official rate ceiling if necessary (World Bank 1990, p. 25). Such discreet financial liberation helped state banks absorb and retain deposit savings (Laurenceson and Chai 2003, p. 10) that would later be used to fund SOEs. As the data show, SOEs received state bank loans at a minimum lending rate (Laurenceson and Chai 2003, p. 13). Hence, the moderately reformed financial control over interest rates in effect guaranteed SOEs cheap loans, which were essential in developing their economic performance (Laurenceson and Chai 2003, p. 9).

Another financial control that was critical to economic development was credit. Under the planned system, China was micromanaging credit plans, such as specifying the source and destination of each loan (Chai 1981). The reform transformed this substantive approach to supervision. Commercial banks were given discretion to make loan decisions (Law on Commercial Bank, Article 3 and 35), although their loan business should be in line with the needs of the national economic and social development plan and guided by the state's industrial policies (Law on Commercial Bank, Article 34). In other words, the state reformed its supervision mode by providing more leeway for banks' financial activities and retaining indicative control. However, while more latitude was given for loan approval, the scope of the impact was not exaggerated, as the loans distributed to SOEs dwarfed those granted to other economic participants (Laurenceson and Chai 2003, p. 9).

Capital Market Rules for the Rich

As noted above, China's capital market took off relatively late and was filled with SOEs, especially in the initial years. In theory, the capital market offered a forum, an alternative to the credit market, for fundraising and hence could help companies with limited access to the banking system; on the other hand, it could enhance economic efficiency by drawing otherwise idle cash into the market to pump up companies with development potential (Cho 1986). Norton (2000) highlighted four aspects of regulation that are essential for legal frameworks of the capital market in emerging economies (pp. 136–138): the scope of the law to cover specific regulatory issues and related administrative processes, clarification of the role of governmental supervision, sufficient level of information disclosure, and suitable accounting principles and auditing standards.

Suffice it to say, China's Securities Law (1998) has not met these formal qualifications.[33] It clarifies its application to specified categories of securities, including stocks, corporate bonds, and other securities confirmed by the State Council (Article 2). The issuing procedures are elucidated in chapter two, in response to concern about transparency, by providing formal rules for information disclosure over stocks and bonds (Article 58–66). Nevertheless, the high threshold of IPOs and strict state control over market access have effectively prevented small-scale enterprises and start-ups from raising funds from the equity market (Article 43–49) (Laurenceson and Chai 2003, Chap. 6).

Also standing out are the Regulations on the Administration of Corporate Bonds, which stipulate that Chinese enterprises with legal person status are eligible to issue corporate bonds (Article 2). In other words, all forms of firms or organizations other than companies are legally excluded from the Chinese bond market. Furthermore, this regulation made it clear that the scale and composition of corporate bonds are determined annually by the joint decision of the National Development and Reform Commission, the PBC, the Ministry of Finance, and the CSRC (Article 10). Second, this article embedded the private segment of the bond market into state plans, depriving these investors of certain rights to determine the volume and category of their corporate bonds. By legally constraining the eligibility of enterprises and the amount and categories of corporate bonds, this law effectively created a group of entities that are extruded from the bond market, which, to some extent, prepared a potential pool of clients for China's curb market.

With the help of many formalized legal institutions, China's capital market, on the whole, was a demarcated playground for governments, banks, and large companies. In essence, as most bank assets and large companies in China are state-owned, the Chinese capital markets, both bond and equity, were indeed a hotspot for state capital rather than private money.

Overall, the state has reformed its former instructional style of supervising financial activities and has adopted a more indirect and structural approach to macro-managing financial institutions. Via financial repression (Li 1994), the state pooled savings and channelled them into SOEs by calibrating deposit and loan interest rates; by maintaining a high threshold of the equity and bond markets, the state ensured that SOEs were the primary beneficiaries of the capital market. While the financial sector was still state-orchestrated, state intervention was indeed transformed into structural intervention. To the extent that the law has entrenched financial activities that helped channel savings into productive investments and SOEs, the reformed financial system did facilitate China's economic development except that it was achieved via well-calculated financial liberation for SOEs' benefit and at the expense of the private sector's access to funding.

5.1.4 Reform of the Foreign Trade Institution and Its Rules

In 2013, China, surpassing the U.S., became the largest trader in the world. This surge was not unpredictable, as China had deliberately designed its economic reform strategy to build an export-oriented economy. As a result, international trade has played a significant role in Chinese economic development in recent decades. At its peak, the share of merchandise trade in GDP climbed to 63.9% (2006). While the percentage has been declining since 2016, trade was still assumed to be approximately 35% of GDP as of 2020.[34]

Given the importance of trade to China's economy, it is hard to imagine that before the reform, China was largely an isolated country, imposing an import substitution regime with an array of policy instruments to restrict foreign trade, for example, the control of trading rights, the control of domestic pricing of trading goods, the rate of forex and the flow of foreign currency. Since the economic transformation started unfolding, the shackles that restricted foreign trade were broken one after another, and the volume of trade climbed continuously. When China acceded to the WTO, its total trade leaped from 38.52% of GDP in 2002 to 64.47% of GDP in 2006.[35] In the meantime, China comprehensively reconstructed its legal system for foreign trade with the intention of making it uniform and transparent.

The following sections first review the key points of China's trading regime before the reform. Then, it focuses on the institutional adjustments that were crucial to China's trading system. Finally, the last section probes the legal framework for international trade, including its general structure and China's changes upon its accession to the WTO.

5.1.4.1 Trading Regime in the Prereform Years

In October 1950, China intervened in the Korean War. In response, the United States and later the United Nations imposed a retaliatory trade embargo on China. Throughout the 1950s, China's international trade heavily relied on the Soviet Union and other communist countries, and this reliance peaked in 1959, when nearly half of China's international trade was associated with the Soviet Union (Naughton 2018, p. 398).

In the late 1950s, the relationship between China and the Soviet Union deteriorated, and the two parties finally cut ties in 1960. In the wake of the Sino-Soviet split, China altered its trading strategy from relying on a single partner to diversifying its trading network. From 1959 onwards, the Chinese government expanded its trading relations with western Europe,[36] Japan, Canada, Australia, and neighbouring communist countries, such as North Korea, Vietnam, and Outer Mongolia (Chen 2006). In expanding its trading network, China shifted its previous Soviet-reliant strategy towards self-reliance and adopted a conservative attitude towards international trade. This self-dependent policy, partly due to China's limited foreign exchange reserve at the time, required the government to balance its imports and exports. Because of the need to import advanced machinery, the export amount was determined by the import plans; in other words, exports served imports by earning foreign currency to finance the importation of advanced equipment. This strategy continued throughout the 1960s and ended in the early 1970s when China resumed its trading relationship with the U.S. Whereas most countries had reestablished their trading relations with China after the Korean War, the U.S. continued the trade embargo until 1972, when President Nixon visited China and agreed with then premier Zhou Enlai to normalize Sino-U.S. relations, including ending the decades-long trade embargo.

From 1950 through 1972, China maintained a relatively stable trade volume with hardly any discernible increase. As Fig. 5.2 shows, its trading performance started as low as 1135 million dollars in 1950. While there was slow growth in the ensuing years, the level fell immediately when China and the Soviet Union split in 1960. Although the volume rebounded as China expanded its trading partners in the wake of the split, the breakthrough of trade volume did not occur until Beijing normalized its trading relationship with the U.S. in 1972. As the data show, immediately after the reestablishment of Sino-U.S. trade relations, in 1973, for the first time since 1950, the total trading value jumped to two digits, reaching $11,000 million, almost double the number in 1972 ($6300 million). It maintained an upwards trend afterwards and reached $20,640 million on the eve of the commencement of the opening-up reform.

5.1.4.2 Institutional Evolution of International Trade

China's foreign trade system experienced a chain of liberalization movements over the years. It went from a centrally controlled regime to a market-driven system in roughly two decades (Lardy 1991). The most decisive conversions were the decentralization of trading rights and the loosening of control over foreign exchange. These

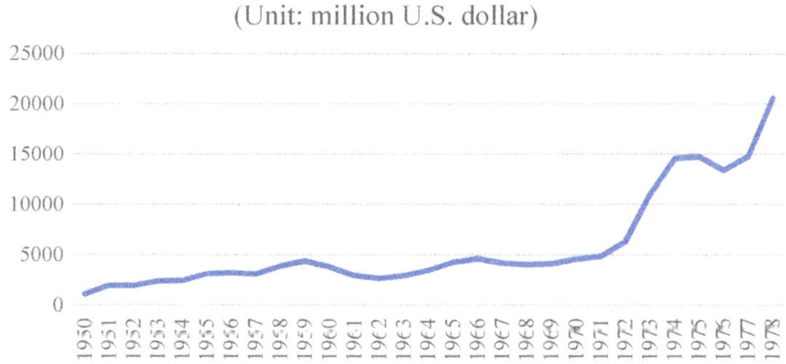

Fig. 5.2 Volume of China's foreign trade, 1952–1978 (Generated by data collected from the 1984 Almanac of China's Foreign Economic Relations and Trade)

two aspects marked the changes that laid the institutional foundation of international trade upon which further trading policies, such as tariffs, tax rebates, and import and export licences, were built.

Liberalizing Trading Rights

Before the reform, China's international trade was monopolized by the central government. In 1953, the Ministry of Foreign Trade classified trading products in fourteen categories and set up fourteen foreign trading companies (FTC) for each category.[37] In addition to two transportation companies,[38] these sixteen state-owned companies monopolized China's international trading activities, and each of them was associated with a related ministry. For instance, the China National Metals and Minerals Import and Export Corporation was affiliated with the Ministry of Metallurgical Industry. In 1958, the Central Committee of the CCP reiterated that no company except these mandated companies and their subsidiaries was allowed to engage in international trade (CCCCP 1958, pp. 409–411). The state kept a tight grip on its monopoly for decades, and trading rights were only incrementally delegated after the reform years.

In 1984, the State Council issued a policy document to reform China's foreign trading system (State Council 1984). In this document, the government ended the trading monopoly and allowed other companies and enterprises to participate in such business, but their rights to trade were subject to the approval of the Ministry of Foreign Trade and Economic Cooperation (MOFTEC). Additionally, China established a Foreign Trade Agent System that allowed enterprises without trading rights to join the international market by using FTCs as trading agencies. These changes marked China's first attempt to lift its control over the trade monopoly in the pursuit of its opening-up policy. As a result, by 1988, there were 5000 foreign trade companies, and over 10,000 manufacturing enterprises had been granted direct export and import rights (Naughton 2018, p. 406). These policies were later legalized in the first Foreign Trade Law of the PRC in 1994.

The next major step in trading rights control took place after China accessed the WTO. In pursuance of its WTO commitments, China promulgated a new Foreign Trade Law in 2004, expanding lawful 'foreign trade dealers' to 'legal persons, other organizations, or individuals' (Article 8).[39] Moreover, administrative control of foreign trade was reduced to registration, replacing the former approval procedure (Article 9). Hence, at the turn of the century, the Chinese government had liberalized trading rights for most common products and technologies and minimized administrative regulation (Article 16).[40]

Liberating the Foreign Exchange Regime

In addition to gradually loosening control over trading rights, foreign exchange (forex) regime changes, which would directly influence the pricing mechanism of trading goods, were of equal significance to China's international trade system. The reforms had two aspects: shifting the forex rate mechanism to a market-oriented mechanism and granting FTCs the right to retain foreign exchanges.

The exchange rate in China has a long history of government intervention, from being tightly controlled in the beginning to being relatively loosened as reform deepened. For example, from 1952 through 1980, China applied a single exchange rate system, with the government setting a fixed forex rate to serve its import and export plan. The fixed exchange rate with the dollar was usually pegged at 2.46 *yuan* (Lardy 1991, p. 148). Moreover, all trade firms were required to sell foreign exchanges that they earned from trading to the Bank of China, the only bank officially designated to deal with forex at the time. In other words, before the reform, the government controlled both the price and liquidity of foreign exchange in an absolute sense. However, as the trading right was gradually decentralized, this heavily regulated forex system was simultaneously freed in the hope of facilitating international trade.

There were practical reasons for the adoption of a single fixed forex rate system and the overvaluation of the *renminbi*. By then, China was desperate to improve its global buying power to import advanced machinery in order to build industrial plants to accelerate its modernization. However, this strategy worked only during a particular period when China's import value outpaced its export value; when the export value began to increase, this strategy began to have damaging effects. Eventually, after decades of overvaluing its domestic currency, China experienced a severe financial loss, with 3.18 billion yuan appropriated to the Ministry of Foreign Trade in 1980 to address the losses resulting from foreign trade transactions (Hu 1982, p. 496; Lardy 1991, p. 67). This triggered its first round of reform of the forex system.

From 1981 onwards, China adopted a dual-track exchange system to address the financial loss and granted FTCs the right to retain specific amounts of foreign exchange to stimulate foreign trade. This dual-track system was composed of an official rate for all economic activities and an internal settlement rate for trading transactions in the initial period (1981–1984) (State Council 1980). After 1985, while keeping the official rate intact, China replaced the internal settlement rate with the forex transaction system by establishing foreign currency swap markets. The first Foreign Exchange Transaction Centre was set up in 1985 in Shenzhen, and the Shanghai swap centre opened the next year. This dual system remained in action until 1993. Companies with extra forex were allowed to sell it for domestic currency within these swap markets in the hope of improving forex utility. The rates of forex sold in these centres ranged from six to seven, and the price was apparently set by the state (Lardy 1991, p. 58). In the meantime, the *renminbi* began a continuing process of devaluation, depreciating from 1.49 to the U.S. dollar in 1980 to 4.78 in 1990 (Lardy 1991, pp. 148–149).

In 1994, as China set out to deepen its reform and opening-up strategy, the dual-track system came to an end and was replaced by a 'system endorsing a market-based, unified, and regulated floating forex rate', as announced by the State Council (State Council 1994, pp. 557–563). At the same time, the currency-retention right of FTCs was replaced by a compulsory banking exchange system.[41] After this round of adjustment, the *renminbi* was immediately pegged to the U.S. dollar and devaluated to 8.61. After that, the price of the *renminbi* was kept at a relatively stable level, and the Chinese foreign exchange reserve began to accumulate rapidly.[42] In 2005, within the regulated floating system, the government substituted a currency basket peg for the U.S. dollar peg.

The above two institutional transforms were by no means the only adjustments to the Chinese trading system. Over the years, China also tried several strategies to boost its foreign trade, such as introducing import and export licensing, granting tariff and domestic tax rebates, and designing new forms of international trade, such as export processing and compensation trade. Nevertheless, the above two changes were of particular significance because they constituted the framework of China's international trade system upon which the effects of further trade incentive policies could be expanded.

5.1.4.3 Legal Environment of International Trade

China's legal institution of foreign trade was evolving along with its changing policies. Broadly speaking, the transformation revolved around China's accession to the WTO, as many of the changes reflected WTO requirements. This section employs a comparative perspective to examine the general legal system for foreign trade and then identify the specific legal adjustments that occurred upon accession to the WTO. Finally, it ends with a case study of China's WTO disputes to provide examples of the impact of WTO rules on China's related legal practices.

Legal Framework of International Trade

In 1994, China enacted its first national law on foreign trade, the Foreign Trade Law of the PRC. It covered general trading issues such as foreign trade business operators, the import and export of goods and technology, international service trade, foreign trade orders, foreign trade promotion, and legal liabilities. To a great extent, this law formalized a general order of foreign trade (Article 27–31) in a broad-brush manner, with some substantive rules concerning restrictions on trade in goods and technology (Article 16–21) and services (Article 24–25). It also categorized lawful trade dealers in licenced organizations (Article 8), and with this rule, individuals and other unauthorized organizations were excluded from direct participation—they were allowed to participate in foreign trade by forming agreements of agency with those who received such legal rights (Article 13) (Gao 2005).

In November 2001, after fifteen years of waiting and negotiating, China acceded to the WTO and became its 143rd member. Around 2001, in its final effort to join the WTO, China made great efforts to revise its legal system. To conform to WTO rules, China undertook two general categories of legal efforts, namely, formalizing its legal structure for international trade and revising concrete legal articles that were considered inconsistent with WTO rules. WTO rules required China to guarantee that its legal system was uniform and transparent and to provide a judicial review of foreign trade affairs; this part is discussed in the following subsection. Additionally, China's Accession Protocol involved much painstaking work to review its laws, regulations, and rules to ensure that they aligned with WTO rules (Clarke 2003).

As reported by the Ministry of Foreign Trade and Economic Cooperation (MOFTEC), China reviewed many thousands of legal documents at different levels, domestic laws, and international treaties, and identified nearly a thousand as needing either repeal or revision (Clarke 2003, p. 104).[43] In addition to revising large numbers of trade-related legal documents, China worked hard to issue new laws, regulations, and rules to supplement its legal system for foreign trade. As a result, from 2001 through 2006, China issued over three hundred trade-related legal documents at different levels, surpassing the total number of laws enacted in recent decades.[44]

Among these legal updates, the newly revised Foreign Trade Law (2004) is worthy of particular notice. By and large, it followed the general structure of the 1994 version, legalizing foreign trade activities with abstract rules for trade orders and specific terms for unlawful situations. Three chapters were added to this law concerning foreign trade-related intellectual property protection, foreign trade investigation, and foreign trade relief, which were not addressed in the 1994 version. As the names suggest, these rules complemented the law for more complex international trade activities, which China might engage in after joining the WTO. This law is worth specific attention because it granted individuals lawful status to directly participate in foreign trade (Article 8) and simplified trade administration by replacing the former licensing system with registration (Article 9). These two institutional changes effectively lowered the bar of market access (Chow 2003).

Legal Adjustments upon Accession to the WTO

In addition to revising specific articles, more importantly, China examined its formal legal structure for issues such as uniformity and transparency and expanded the scope of its judicial reviews due to its WTO obligations. The Protocol on the Accession of the PRC set out general rules for administration and laws that China had to comply with upon admission. According to section I.2.A of the Protocol, the Chinese government was to apply uniform administration within its entire trade regime and apply all levels of 'laws, regulations, and other measures' in a 'uniform, impartial, and reasonable manner'. In other words, the privileges shared by some regions, such as SEZs or minority autonomous regions,[45] were no longer applicable to international trade, as all levels of rules became subject to uniform application. Section I.2.B made particular reference to China's special economic areas, mainly regarding the transparency and impartial application of the rules. The most crucial provision was section I.2.C, which set forth transparency obligations requiring China to enforce only 'published and readily available' 'laws, regulations, and other measures' that were relevant to international trade. This article effectively ruled out Party directives or other nonlegal rules governing international trade, thus 'purifying' the regulatory system pertaining to foreign trade. The judicial review procedure set forth in section I.2.D conformed to China's Administrative Litigation Law and judicial system except that it substantially expanded the scope and included the WTO rules.

The transparency requirement pushed the Chinese government to take a series of measures to address the legal system beyond the trading sector. In response to the general rules regarding transparency, China confirmed a full list of official publications and the departments responsible for them where trade-related laws and regulations could be identified (WTO 2001a, para. 325–336). This confirmation of the designated publication list covered issues pertaining to foreign trade and trade-related corporations operating in China, the administration of imports and exports, customs laws, regulations and procedures, import and export duty rates, bilateral trade agreements, etc. In addition to disclosing legal documents, certain mechanisms for facilitating transparency obligations were set up. As a result, the Department of WTO Affairs was established, and its WTO Notification and Enquiry Centre was assigned to handle China's transparency commitments.

Another significant effort concerning transparency was the promulgation of the Legislation Law in 2000. This was China's first endeavour to officially specify its legal system's internal mechanism. Upon its implementation, China for the first time clarified the hierarchy of its legal system, the scope of laws at each level, the legislative powers and procedures of both the central and local legislatures, and the responsible departments and procedures for solving legislative conflicts. Thus, substantive articles of the Legislation Law provide foreign trade parties with a holistic picture of China's legal system. Moreover, by exposing the structure and specifics of the legal system to both domestic and international examination, the Legislation Law, to a certain extent, also met the uniformity obligation that China had promised to fulfil. While no official confirmation was performed, the specific timing of its promulgation suggests that it could have been an effort to meet China's transparency commitment to the WTO.

Additionally, to guarantee the enforcement of rules, China confirmed that it would 'designate independent tribunals, contact points, and procedures' for reviewing the 'implementation of laws, regulations, judicial decisions and administrative rulings of general application' relating to the WTO rules (WTO 2001a, para. 76–79; WTO 2001b, p. 4). This obligation effectively expanded the scope of China's Administrative Procedure Law and brought the Chinese court system to the forefront.

In China, not all levels of the courts have judicial power to review or invalidate legislation (Balme and Dowdle 2009, pp. 1–23).[46] The courts' only power over governmental actions is to review concrete administrative actions performed by an administrative agency while implementing laws, regulations, and rules under the Administrative Litigation Law of the PRC.[47] The most significant feature of this power is that the courts review only concrete and specific administrative actions. That is, all levels of administrative regulations, rules, and general orders and decisions are not subject to review, much less the law. However, the Chinese government's commitment to the WTO eliminated this limit. According to paragraphs 78 and 79 of the Report of the Working Party, in addition to confirming the impartiality and independence of tribunals, China made two substantial changes to its original system. One was to include judicial decisions on the review list, and the other was to significantly expand the range of judicial review of administrative actions. As confirmed in paragraph 79, administrative actions subjected to judicial review were extended to general applications of trade-related rules stated in the Protocol, which, in effect, included administrative actions that were laid down in the GATT 1994, the GATS, and the TRIPS, such as national treatment, conformity assessment, and regulation of services. Hence, China's commitment to judicial review, although excluding more aggressive revisions, such as judicial review of legislation, effectively extended the range of administrative cases concerning foreign trade.

Therefore, in terms of both structure and content, China's legal system was subjected to extensive and substantial adjustments around the turn of the century. After 2001, the Chinese laws in the book regarding international trade appeared to be uniform, transparent and backed by the expanded power of judicial review. However, to reconstruct is one thing, and to enforce is another. To examine how these legal obligations have been carried out in action, a review of the WTO cases that China has been involved in since 2001 is informative.

According to the WTO statistics as of 2019, since China joined the organization in 2001, China has been involved in a total of 244 cases, actively as the complainant (21 cases), as a third party (179 cases), or passively as a respondent (44 cases).[48] The 44 cases against China are fertile soil for examining the extent and conformity of China's legal compliance regarding international trade.

Of these cases, 16 involved China's general commitment to the uniform application of law and transparency issues,[49] with the most cited articles being the GATT X[50] or, more precisely, the GATT X: 3(a) (14 times), and several references to Part I para. 2(A) and (C) of the Protocol of Accession.[51] The remaining cases were brought up for various reasons associated with China's trading commitments in different agreements, such as the SCM, TRIMs, and GATS. During its first two decades as a WTO member, China faced 16 charges regarding its implementation of general legal commitment, accounting for roughly one-third of the total cases against it, and 28 charges, or two-thirds, regarding the enforcement of particular trading commitments.

Furthermore, among the 44 cases, half were concluded by the DSB, requiring China to bring measures or laws at issue into conformity with its obligations. Except for two cases that were brought to compliance proceedings,[52] China claimed that it had fully implemented the DSB's recommendations and rulings in the remaining 20 cases. These implementations resulted in China either terminating or revising the rules at issue, as in the cases of DS414, DS425, DS431, DS432, and DS433, or promulgating new regulations, as in the cases of DS394, DS395, and DS398. Regarding the results of the remaining cases, 12 are in consultation,[53] 6 were settled by agreement with the complainants,[54] and 4 recent ones are still in the panel-composition stage.[55]

WTO Rules Impact on China's Practice of Law—A Case Study

The incompatible structures between China's legal institutions and the WTO rule system were underlined by legal scholars before China became a member of the organization (Ostry 1998). As noted above, China put painstaking effort into bringing its substantive rules and legal procedures into line with the WTO rule system. Of particular interest to the present study is China's transparency obligation under Article X of the GATT and section I.2 of China's Accession Protocol. These obligations, such as publishing trade-related rules in a timely manner and administering rules uniformly throughout the nation, are crucial for guaranteeing the predictability of international trade. The following case closely examines China's compliance with these rules after its accession to the WTO.

In 2009, three complainants, the US, the EU, and Mexico, requested consultations with China with respect to export restraints that China had imposed on various raw materials.[56] Among other claims, the complainants alleged that China's export restraints were inconsistent with its commitment to export duties, export quotas, minimum export price requirements, and export licensing requirements under the Accession Protocol, Accession Working Party Report, and Articles X:1 and X:3(a) of the GATT 1994.[57] Upon investigation, the panel concluded that China had acted inconsistently with the above rules in regard to its administration and allocation of export quotas and minimum export price requirements. The panel (also the Appellate Body) therefore recommended that the DSB request that China bring 'the existing measures at issue into conformity with its obligations under the GATT 1994, China's Accession Protocol and China's Working Party Report' (WTO 2012, p. 95).[58]

On 28 January 2013, China reported to the DSB that it had promulgated the 2013 Tariff Implementation Program and the 2013 Catalogue of Goods Subject to Export Licensing Administration, had removed the export duties and export quotas for raw materials at issue, and had thus fulfilled its obligations under the WTO rule system.

The transparency issue raised in this case concerned China's failure to publish trade-related documents promptly. By nature, such inconsistent actions arose from the tension between the enforcement of general rules, such as Article X of the GATT, and substantive obligations under such rules. While general rules provide overarching coverage of situations to the greatest extent possible, their implementation entails a high level of care and dedication. Moreover, the space between general rules and substantive obligations often offers opportunities for political manoeuvre, if needed. For instance, nations may selectively implement their duties according to nation-specific concerns or interests (Biukovic 2008). That said, one must admit that China has improved a great deal with respect to its transparency commitment under the WTO rules (Gao 2017). These changes had not happened even when Beijing resolutely pursued market-oriented economic reform a decade ago—a scenario that indicates the power of external international pressure to drive the reform of China's legal institutions.

5.2 Internal Characteristics of the Law

5.2.1 Characteristics of the Economic Relationship

The dominant economic relationship of the Chinese market took a significant turn as the reform entered its second decade, departing from a largely planned economy to a promarket economy. With the planned feature waning, the state, while still omnipotent in many regards, began ceding its economic territory to private hands. As could be reasonably expected, the types of economic participants diversified as the grip of the state loosened. Specifically, the 1990s saw the enlargement of the pool of private participants in both number and kind, especially the forms of private enterprises; therefore, an economic complex with public and private actors sharing different sectors of the economy emerged throughout the period.

First, a diversified group of economic participants was formed. While the state still dominated the economy, the mode of domination was transformed after the sweeping reforms of SOEs. After that, the SOEs no longer regulated every corner of the economy—the authorities retreated from spheres that were less consequential to the national economy, such as light industry and tourism, and concentrated on the lifelines of the state economy, such as energy, national railways and airways, and finance. By carving out less critical economic areas, the state continued to participate in the economy as a dominant power in most crucial economic areas but left a large portion of the economy open to various types of private capital.

The private economy entered a booming decade by entering the economic spheres that the state had opened. As a result, the categories of private participants varied along with granted legal status. In the previous decade, private enterprises had been deemed a capitalist economic form and had therefore been illegal; the private economic sector was open only to individual businesses with a cap on the number of employees. These restrictions were no longer workable following the reforms of SOEs, as legitimacy was granted to private companies. Thus, during this decade, both individual and private legal persons became legitimate economic actors and formed a significant economic force for participation in the economy. Therefore, the parties entitled to economic participation were significantly diversified due to the structural reform of SOEs, and a new economic structure began to develop—one that featured state companies, which, though less in number, still held robust control over the national lifelines of the economy, and private investors, who were abundant in number but dominated less important economic spheres.

Second, along with the expanded pool of economic participants, the autonomy of these actors in economic activities was also expanded. The freedom they gained had two dimensions: autonomy over the legal entities that private capital was allowed to form and the expanded economic spheres opening to private money. The former type of freedom was similar to internal autonomy in legal status, as private capital could choose the types of enterprises that best suited its businesses, a move that marked a breakthrough in the economic system. Therefore, private capital, extended from the previous economic type of individual businesses, welcomed entities such as companies and partnerships during the next decade and thus formed a club filled with multiple types of private participants.

Furthermore, along with the diversified participants, more economic spheres opened their doors to private money as the state retreated from its role in those less important areas—a win in terms of external autonomy in economic activities. Among these areas of significance was the foreign trade right, which was formerly monopolized by the state and now was opened to private companies and individuals. In addition to the expanded economic spheres, the internal regulation of economic production also took an autonomous turn. Following the structural reform of SOEs and the promulgation of the Company Law and related legal documents, firms in this decade were no longer the production arm of the state economy to fulfil economic commands. They gained full autonomy from economic production and internal management and therefore shifted to companies in the modern sense.

Third, following the changing economic structure, the dominant economic relationships also took a significant turn from a mainly public–private relationship to private economic relationships representing an ever-growing proportion of the economy. To put the overall economic reforms into perspective, the nature of the majority of the economic sectors, including industrial, commercial, and foreign trade, had taken a private turn due to the growing number and expanded spheres of economic areas. Without the state placing production orders, economic transactions took place mainly between private parties, whose economic decisions, again without the state's intervention, started to react to market principles. Along with the swelling market for the private economy, the need for wage labour became evident, leading to the rise of the free labour market.

The only exception, at that time as now, was the financial sector. While it had been fundamentally restructured in the 1990s, its public ownership was not subject to the reform and therefore had been left intact, as was the dominant role of the state in financial access to the economy.

5.2.2 *Formation of the Rules—A Case Study of Company Law*

As noted in the above section, the significant effort, and thus the main outcome of economic reforms in this decade, was the transformation of SOEs. As a result, the activities performed by companies, especially private ones, played a growing role in the economy. As a result, the law responded accordingly (Fang 1995). The first endeavour was the adoption of the Company Law in 1993 (Huo 1995). As private firms started to take up shares in the economy, the rules concerning their activities became crucial to the overall economic performance during this period. Hence, before launching the large-scale SOE reform, the central authority had to address related legal structures (Art and Gu 1995). After over a decade of development, with growing knowledge of private enterprises and in a bid to further boost the private sector, the

1993 Company Law was heavily revised in 2004 to respond to changing social and economic needs (Dickinson 2007). The following section examines the two company laws promulgated in different contexts for their roles in responding to their particular economic purposes. The study unfolds in two aspects: the internal structure of the laws and their external functions that the state intended, focusing on the rules regarding capitalization.

The first formal Company Law of the PRC was promulgated in 1993. However, before that, because China allowed no private firms to exist, the government issued a law only for its SOEs, the Law of the PRC on Industrial Enterprises Owned by the Whole People (1988). Therefore, before the reform of SOEs commenced in 1996, the government released the Company Law to prepare the legal framework for the upcoming structural change in domestic firms (Fang 1995, pp. 151–198).

The purpose of the Company Law (1993), as Article 1 stated, was, among other things, 'to maintain social and economic order and promote the development of a socialist market economy'. It covered two types of corporations, namely, limited liability companies and shareholding companies. The law consisted of eleven chapters, and apart from the general rules that formed chapter one, the main body laid down regulations for the establishment and organization of the two types of companies (Chaps. 2 and 3), the issuance and transfer of shares (Chap. 4), corporate bonds and financial affairs (Chaps. 5 and 6), and corporate mergers, separation, and bankruptcy issues (Chaps. 7 and 8).[59]

As China's first formal company law, sanctioned when the country was on the verge of entering a market economy, rigid and substantial regulations addressed various aspects of corporate behaviour, especially registering capital and financing issues.

For limited liability companies, Article 23 divided corporations according to the types of their main business and stipulated a different registered capital requirement for each type. Explicitly, it stated that for companies whose primary businesses were production (Article 23 (1)) or wholesale (Article 23 (2)), the registered capital should be no less than 50,000 *yuan*; companies with retail as their primary business should register no less than 30,000 *yuan* (Article 23 (3)); and companies focusing on technology, consulting, or services, needed 10,000 *yuan* of registered capital (Article 23 (4)). For shareholding companies, the minimum amount of registered capital was 10,000,000 *yuan* (Article78). These required amounts of capital had to be paid at the time that the company was registered (Howson 1997).

Additionally, there was difficulty accessing means of financing. In the early 1990s, China's capital market was in its embryo stage, as discussed in the previous section. The limited financing channel was made worse by strict control of eligibility to access the capital market, where the law set a relatively high benchmark. For IPOs, companies had to possess no less than 50 million *yuan*, and to issue corporate bonds, shareholding companies had to have a net worth of no less than 30 million, or 60 million for limited liability companies (Article 161).

These strict amounts of registered capital for establishing companies and financing stipulated in the law revealed that the authority was extremely cautious about setting up companies. In the early 1990s, when China was still in a very early stage of economic development, the required registration capital was quite a high threshold for private investors. The capital market, as mentioned above, was virtually the playground of state companies, given the high threshold for access. This rigid requirement for private capital, while appearing to be in stark contrast to China's desire to accelerate its economic development, reflects the cautious attitude of the government towards China's then immature social and economic background—the need to protect the new field from high-risk investors and thus curb potential risks (Gu 2006, pp. 247–286). In other words, the rules laid down in China's first company law were tailor-made for the social and economic environment of the time. The law was subject to amendment when the time came, which occurred at the turn of the century.

In 2004, a group of legal experts was organized by the Standing Committee of the NPC and the State Council to discuss the revision of the Company Law, which was regarded as insufficient in the new era (Jiang 2006). In explaining the reasons for revision, the legal office of the State Council listed a string of reasons and stated that the old Company Law could not fulfil its role of promoting economic development, as the economy had been deeply reformed in the previous decade. Among other concerns, problems associated with capital issues were industriously elaborated. In general, it reported that the capital threshold was too high to establish companies and thus restrained private investment and that the rules for corporate financing, namely, equity, bond issuance, and company listing, were too strict to meet companies' financial needs (Shi 2014). Based on these and other concerns, the 1993 Company Law was heavily revised, with 13 articles deleted, 91 revised, and 44 added (Wang and Huang 2006, pp. 231–232).

Before going into the details of the new Company Law, let us first provide an overview of it. The 2005 Company Law incorporates thirteen chapters, two new ones concerning the equity transfer of limited liability companies (Chap. 3) and the eligibility and obligations of executives, supervisors, and senior managers (Chap. 6). Furthermore, the new law legalizes the form of a one-person limited liability company (Chap. 2 (3)), which was not previously allowed, in a bid to diversify business modes. Thus, to a great extent, the new Company Law vigorously reacted to the profoundly changed Chinese economic environment, as is illustrated by examining the details of the rules (Gu 2006, pp. 367–375).

To facilitate private investment, the 2005 Company Law eliminated the rules that differentiated types of businesses for registered capital and lowered the capital threshold to thirty thousand *yuan* for all types of limited liability companies (Article 26) and five million *yuan* for shareholding companies (Article 81). Additionally, instead of requiring capital to be paid when registering, the new law allowed capital to be paid in instalments over a period ranging from two to five years, depending on the type of business (Wei 2014).

As shown in the context of the two company laws, the changing internal structures exhibited the response of the law to the evolving external economic environment. As mentioned above, the first Company Law was issued to prepare for the then upcoming reform of SOEs, as many of them would be converted into private companies. At the time of early marketization, the 1993 Company Law was strict in setting up companies based on the high requirement of registered capital. Thus, the rules were substantive in terms of regulating corporate behaviours. However, after more than ten years of economic reform, the Chinese economy was at a full-fledged stage in which corporate governance had had years of development; thus, certain restrictions might no longer have been necessary and needed to be lifted to advance the economy (Xi 2009). In response, the heavily revised 2005 Company Law was born to adapt the law to the changing social and economic environment. Related articles that were either revised or deleted during the revision showed the unmistakable effort of the law to better utilize private capital and promote the economy or, in other words, to address economic needs.

5.2.3 Application of the Rules

On 12 April 2004, the Wanhua Industrial and Commercial Development Company applied to the local Administration for Industry and Commerce to change the name of the company, the registered list of shareholders, the legal representative of the company, and part of the content of the company's bylaws. To support the application, the company submitted a set of documents, including two equity transfer agreements, a resolution of the shareholders' meeting confirming that all shareholders had agreed on the transfer of the equities, and a revised version of the company's bylaws. However, in 2006, one of the company's original shareholders sued in the local court, claiming that she had neither been aware of the so-called shareholder meeting nor transferred her equities as one of the company's shareholders. She further claimed that she had not known of the existence of the resolution. Therefore, she asked the court, among other claims, to invalidate the resolution of the shareholder meeting and the transfer of her equities (Supreme People's Court 2007).

As the court investigation revealed, the company in dispute, founded in 1995, had been formed by four individuals with registered capital of 1,060,000 *yuan*. Mr. Wan had contributed 1,000,000 *yuan*, and the other three shareholders had divided the remaining shares equally. That is, Wan held the absolute majority of the shares, which granted him the right to summon interim shareholder meetings and transfer company shares individually.[60] He used his rights well. According to the court investigation, the so-called shareholder meeting had not occurred, and the resolutions and related agreements of share transfer were manufactured by Wan and then used to apply to change the company information, as mentioned above.

The focal point of the case signals the tension between the formal application of the law and the consideration of case particularities. In formally following the law, the court had to admit the legal effectiveness of the resolution of the shareholder meeting and the transfer of the shares, as Wan's absolute voting power backed both. On the other hand, such a strict application of the law would confirm de facto one-person rule, thus harming the other shareholders' interests. Between formal and substantive consideration, the court chose the latter and sided with the minority shareholders.

The ruling in the case had two different rationales of reasoning concerning the application of the law. First, the court endorsed a rather strict dogmatic interpretation of the law regarding the meeting procedure. Article 43 of the Company Law (1993) reads, 'Where a temporary meeting is proposed by the shareholders representing 1/4 of voting rights or more... a temporary meeting shall be held'. Article 39 (1) stipulated that 'the discussion methods and voting procedures of the shareholders' meeting shall be prescribed in the articles of the association unless it is otherwise provided by this law'. The articles of the company's bylaws on the above issues, as quoted by the court investigation, did not stipulate otherwise. Therefore, the action gained legal validity once it conformed to the requirements of the law. While the law expressly stipulated the legal procedure of summoning temporary shareholder meetings, it did not stipulate the required number of shareholders in attendance to make the meeting legal. Additionally, the law and the bylaws did not specify a particular procedure and method of voting. Therefore, in this particular case, the focal issue was whether the fact that the smaller shareholders did not attend the meeting would reduce the legal effectiveness of the meeting and, therefore, its resolution. Here, the court stressed the formal requirement of the meeting. In its reasoning, the court asserted, 'The essence of changing the contents of the bylaws, the transfer of the shares, etc. via shareholder meetings is to allow shareholders to implement their rights and decide their legal relationship with the company. Hence, in fact, the attendance of shareholders and the presentation of their true meaning are the prerequisites of the legal effectiveness of the shareholder meeting and its resolution'. At this point, the court applied a formalistic interpretation of the rules for shareholder meetings, as the formal aspects, namely, the attendance and presentation of shareholders, were regarded as preconditions for the meeting and its resolution to be legally valid. Hence, in this case, the fact that the minority shareholders were absent from the meeting was regarded as inconsistent with the formal requirements for shareholder meetings.

However, while the court insisted on the formal aspect of the rules about meeting procedures, it took a substantive turn regarding the rules for voting powers.

Article 39 (2) of the Company Law explicitly expressed that 'a resolution made at a shareholders' meeting on increasing or reducing the registered capital, merger, split-up, dissolution or change of the company form shall be adopted by the shareholders representing two-thirds or more of the voting rights'. Additionally, Article 40 stipulated that 'the resolution on revising the bylaws shall be adopted by the shareholders representing two-thirds or more of the voting rights'. Additionally, Article 41 read, 'the shareholders shall exercise their voting rights at the shareholders' meetings on the basis of their respective percentage of the capital contributions'.

In this particular case, the defendant, Wan, held an absolute majority share of the company and thus the absolute deciding voting power over company affairs. The facts that Wan alone could legally hold a shareholder meeting and vote on the issues mentioned in Article 43 and 44, the court reasoned, 'did not imply that the process of his personal decision-making could equal the actual convening of a shareholders' meeting, nor did his individual will equal the effect of the resolution of the meeting'. Hence, the court denied the existence of the shareholders' meeting and thus repudiated the legality of its resolution. Here, the formal requirement of the law for the two-thirds voting power to make a meeting resolution effective was not formally applied, but the fact that the absence of minority shareholders was referred to as the reason for invalidating the meeting resolution showed that the court applied a substantive interpretation of the rule for voting power (Cheng 2010).

Hence, by stressing the necessity of shareholders expressing their ideas and, in fact, voting on discussed issues, the court endorsed the rather strict formal application of the law to the format requirement for shareholders' meetings. Then, the very fact that invalidated the meeting resolution—the absence of minority shareholders—was used as the case particularity to reject the formal application of the articles on voting power (Howson 1997, pp. 140–141 and 148–150). In summary, the court formally applied the law on meeting procedure and substantively applied the law regarding the voting power of shareholders to the same case fact.

As the court reasoned, the purpose of shareholder meetings was to allow shareholders to implement their rights and decide their legal relationship with the company. It revealed that the guiding principle behind the court's alternate use of formal and substantive interpretations of different rules was to protect minority shareholders and to refute Wan's claim even though he held over 90% of the voting power—a particular substantive result achieved via flexible interpretation of related rules.

5.3 The Expansion Stage of the Formation of the Legal Profession

Coupled with China's visibly improving economic performance and fledgling legal institutions was China's equally expansion of legal education in this period. China's higher education in general was expanding in the 1990s, although at a moderate speed. The increase in undergraduate enrolment remained between 5 and 10% from 1992 to 1998. However, the number of postgraduates grew much more quickly, usually increasing by more than ten percent each year and reaching 20.9% in 1998 (Ying 2008, p. 99). Legal education expanded from a few dozen top universities in the early 1980s to approximately 240 institutions by 2000 (Ji 2005, p. 20). Correspondingly, the percentage of enrolled law students increased from 2% in 1990 to 5.4% in 2001 (Ying 2008, pp. 117 and 120). In 2000, 19,806 law graduates accounted for 4% of national college graduates (Ji 2005, p. 20). Moreover, as a survey suggested, law was increasingly becoming one of the most popular majors among China's top high school graduates (Zhao 2009). In the meantime, China's law education was being formalized and standardized in terms of both hardware and software.

5.3.1 Institutional Environment of Legal Education

Based on the previously established multilevel legal education system, the Chinese authority made efforts to unify legal education in the 1990s. In this part, the discussion of legal institutions has two general focuses. First is an introduction to the expanding scale of legal education in general, related to issues such as the numbers of law departments and law graduates, to provide an overview of the size of the legal profession in the coming years. Second is a focus on the characteristics of the Chinese academic environment, which, as a soft environment, socialized the coming generation of law professionals in a subtle but no less influential way (Zhu 2009, pp. 83–86).

A decade into the restoration of the higher education system, the central government found it difficult for the education system to keep up with the growing need for legal talent as the economy expanded. Against the rapidly advancing economic background, China's legal education responded. In 1993, the legal community held a national conference to discuss issues related to legal education, while the idea of a 'legal service market' emerged and was accepted (Ji 2005, p. 3). The marketization of legal education was first and most visibly seen in numbers. In contrast to previous decade, when legal education had been conducted at various levels, after the 1990s, law education was concentrated and offered only by universities. The growing formalization of legal education led to a flourishing period for law departments. It was estimated that in 2000, there were approximately 240 university law departments nationwide, nearly double the 127 in 1993. In less than ten years, the number of law graduates had jumped from 10,695 in 1993 to nearly 20,000 in 2000, accounting for four percent of regular college graduates that year (Ji 2005, p. 20). Even more dramatic growth was seen in the expanding body of law teachers. According to national statistics, there were merely 2174 law teachers in 1987, combining lecturers, associate professors, and professors; this number jumped to over 10,397 in 2000 (Ji 2005, p. 20).

In the Chinese education system, high school graduates gain access to university education by passing the national university entrance exam, also known as *gaokao*. The examination is composed of six separate subjects: Chinese, English, and mathematics as uniform examination subjects for all high school graduates, plus history, politics, and geography for students of humanities or physics, chemistry, and biology for those who want to pursue a career in science and engineering. However, the structure of China's *gaokao* shows a gap between high school education and law studies in universities. In other words, China's new law students, who normally enrol at age eighteen or so, possessed no prerequisite legal knowledge or university learning experiences compared to American juris doctors.

China adopted a three-tier degree system similar to those of most other countries—bachelor's, master's, and doctoral degrees. A formal LL.B. normally requires four years of university studies plus an externship before graduation. The doctoral stage is a research-focused period of study, and Ph.D. candidates must attend one year of classes and write a doctoral thesis to receive the degree, which usually takes a minimum of three years.

A more complicated stage of legal education is the master's stage. Traditionally, the master's stage of study was pursued by students interested in an academic career, as these programs were primarily research-oriented. Nevertheless, in response to the expanding market demand, the central government installed a practice-oriented master's-level legal programme in 1996 named juris master. It mimicked the American JD model and was open only to students who had completed undergraduate studies in majors other than law (or the equivalent). Unlike candidates for the LLB, applicants for the JM degree needed to possess some elementary legal knowledge and demonstrate it in the entrance examination, which included two legal sections testing basic knowledge of civil law, criminal law, constitutional law, jurisprudence, and Chinese legal history. The course structure of the JM was similar to that of the LLB but more concentrated, allowing students to finish within three years.

The JM degree was well received in the country, as the number of universities offering the degree gradually expanded from only a handful of universities in 1996 to 28 universities in 2001 (Sun 2001, p. 235). The Chinese legal market thus welcomed a further influx of potential legal professionals by opening the door of legal study to people with nonlegal backgrounds. As Professor Ji (2005) pointed out, the Chinese legal profession was experiencing a wave of a great leap forwards, albeit just in a numerical sense.

Whereas the numbers of law departments and enrolled regular law students experienced visible changes during this period, the software of legal institutions, the academic tradition of legal study, in contrast remained relatively static. The academic tradition in the Chinese context featured a one-way relationship between students and teachers and students and their textbooks (Kraus 1989, pp. 121–125; Ji 2016, p. 239).[61] It was centred on the traditional authoritarian status of the teacher in relation to his or her students—a thousand-year academic tradition that unsurprisingly survives to the present day, was inherited by modern learning relationships and therefore remains a vital tone of the institutional environment. The teacher's authority was also transmitted to textbooks and other teaching materials, as domestically prestigious scholars edited the majority of these materials. In other words, communication between students, teachers, and learning materials consisted of the students receiving and uncritically accepting and teachers transmitting authoritatively. These basic academic traditions would prove detrimental, especially to legal study, as it requires constant reflection and critical thinking for advancement.

Formalized university-level legal education with a diversified degree structure served as an institutional framework in which law students found themselves. However, in addition to this relatively visible feature, Chinese university campuses also have an unspoken atmosphere of authoritarianism (Abramson 2006, p. 342)[62] in which students' role is to be passive knowledge receivers. The impact of the soft environment would be furthered by the curriculum structure and teaching method, as discussed in the following sections.

5.3.2 Curriculum Structure and Teaching Materials

The first systematic exposure to law for Chinese legal-career seekers is the undergraduate study of law in the LLB or JM programme. While the two are different degree levels, the structures of their curricula are similar, as they are both designed for people without prior legal knowledge. Therefore, as the first stage of legal study, the social space and social forces that law students confront are essential in forming their related dispositions (Bourdieu 2018). That is, the elements that constantly appear in this stage, such as study materials, course structures, teaching methods, and evaluation systems, especially the bar exam, by constituting the initial environment of legal study, are of significance in socializing and therefore shaping these future legal professionals.

By and large, the critical elements within the first educational environment can be classified in two groups: the substance group, including course structures and learning materials, and the relational group, including the style of teaching interactions and evaluation systems, which is the focus of the following two sections. Regarding the former, the legal courses constitute the contents and the structure of the legal knowledge of these students. The contents are the building blocks of the knowledge body, and the structure determines the scope and breadth of this knowledge. In other words, by examining the specific law classes taken by students in their initial years of legal study, we can unveil the substantial elements and the corresponding features of the first social space they encounter. At the same time, this will help us discern some missing elements in this stage, which might be of equal importance in 'misshaping' legal professionals.

Course Structures

In general, the legal courses that undergraduates are obligated to take in order to graduate include mandatory courses and optional courses. During the three to four years of law classes, students in Chinese law schools must complete sixteen so-called core courses of China's legal education: jurisprudence, constitutional law, Chinese legal history, civil law, criminal law, commercial law, intellectual property law, economic law, administrative law and administrative litigation law, civil litigation law, criminal litigation law, public international law, private international law, and international economic law. In addition, some law schools also include labour law, social security law, and environmental and natural resources protection law as mandatory courses.[63] Legal courses other than these are optional, and the offerings differ among universities.

As listed above, the course structure shows a balance among different legal sectors. Major legal areas, either public or private laws, domestic or international laws, or substantial and procedural laws, are all well represented in this list. As well covered as it appears, this list of courses focuses on positive law. The most overlooked area of legal study in the Chinese context is interdisciplinary study of the law and the economy. These courses are particularly essential to a transforming society such as China, as this is the way to study 'which particular legislative program of reform ought to be instituted' (Kennedy 1983, p. 5). Given that the government strongly emphasized using the law to serve the economy, it seems rather odd that studies on the relation between the law and the economy or the interaction of the law and other social spheres have made no appearance in the course structures of law schools.[64]

Another feature that stands out from the list of core courses is the strong practice-oriented focus. Many of these courses are about China's positive laws, manifesting a strong pragmatic inclination of legal education that corresponds well with the common political slogan that legal education is in the service of China's socialist economic construction. Consequently, courses such as the history of legal thoughts and Western legal theories are not obligatory. Although there are classes about jurisprudence and Chinese legal history, they do not centre around theoretical debates. For instance, the common contents of *jurisprudence* courses appear to be instructional textbooks informing students about what 'is'. Furthermore, the usual contents of such textbooks introduce the idea of 'jurisprudence' on the basis of China's positive laws and the so-called socialist legal system.[65] Chinese legal history deals with legal phenomena throughout China's thousands of years of history, introducing, for instance, types of punishments, significant historical codes (i.e., *tanglüshuyi*),[66] and ancient marriage customs. In other words, the course design is limited to introducing historical events from China's legal history. In addition to domestic laws, there are three courses on international law. However, unlike Western international law courses, Chinese legal education singles out economic-related international laws and clusters them into a separate course. These three related international law courses mainly introduce international institutions, treaties, and their origins. They are also positive legal courses tasked mainly with introducing practices and rules concerning international affairs.

Given that all Chinese law students take mandatory courses as a prerequisite for graduation, the structure and contents of these courses can, to a certain extent, reveal the legal knowledge framework of Chinese legal professionals. Therefore, in addition to the above general discussion of the features of the courses, a closer look at the textbooks used by students might be helpful to form a more comprehensive view of China's legal education.

Course Contents—An Example

To facilitate legal education, since the early 1990s, the Ministry of Education has initiated a series of projects to standardize national legal education by editing legal textbooks. It organized a committee of Chinese legal experts to accomplish this project. As a result, there are many versions of legal textbooks on the market, covering all departmental laws and other legal issues, such as jurisprudence, legal history, and Western and Chinese legal thought. While not mandatory for use, these textbooks, as they are usually edited by nationally renowned legal experts in related areas and are widely supported by the authorities, are perceived as the first choice for law classes.

For an overview, the cluster of law textbooks published by the Higher Education Press (the HEP) is taken as an example for analysis. The HEP is the publishing branch of the Ministry of Education, a publisher that excels in editing college and higher-level textbooks.[67] In general, these textbooks are composed of two major parts: an introduction to the law in general, which usually covers issues such as the origin and basic principles of the law, and a breakdown and specific elaboration of each component of the law. For example, in the Economic Law textbook (Qi 2014),[68] the contents are as follows:

Part I General Introduction

Chapter 1 The birth and development of economic law.
Chapter 2 The concept and objects of economic law.
Chapter 3 The value, function, and basic principles of economic law.
Chapter 4 The legislative system of economic law.
Chapter 5 The obligatory and implementation system of economic law.

Part II Law of Market Regulation

Chapter 6 General introduction of market regulation law.
Chapter 7 Antitrust law.
Chapter 8 Law against unfair competition.
Chapter 9 Consumer protection law.
Chapter 10 Law of product quality.

Part III Law of State Investment and Management

Chapter 11 General introduction of the law of state investment and management.
Chapter 12 Law of state assets.
Chapter 13 Law of state investment.
Chapter 14 Law of state enterprises.

Part IV Law of Macroeconomic Regulation

Chapter 15 General introduction of macroeconomic regulation.
Chapter 16 Law of the plan and industrial policy.
Chapter 17 Fiscal law.
Chapter 18 Tax law.
Chapter 19 Financial law.
Chapter 20 Price law.

In general, classes in economic law are taken in the second or third semester of undergraduate study. Typically, the course would be completed in one semester, which is approximately 32 hours of classes. It is the usual time allocated for law classes other than major courses, such as civil law and criminal law, which generally run for several semesters due to their significance. Consequently, there is not enough time to cover all the topics listed in the textbooks. A common method of time allocation is to concentrate on part I and selectively assign the remaining topics.

The list of contents shows broad coverage of legal areas of economic laws, and the internal structures of these laws are introduced similarly: the teaching of these particular laws is limited to general introductions. For example, in chapter 8, Law against unfair competition, the chapter contains three sections: the general introduction of anti-unfair competition law, a description of typical anti-unfair competition behaviour, and the implementation of anti-unfair competition law. It is telling that classes based on this textbook structure are usually devoted to elaborating doctrine and concepts, intending to fill students with conventional understandings of related concepts and doctrines. Alternatively, the idea of law teaching is to instruct students only in what has been written in black-and-white. To a certain extent, the structure and contents of the legal courses then largely define or constrain the teaching method.

5.3.3 Pedagogic Features

From the 1980s to the 1990s, while the institutional aspects of legal education and teaching materials evolved as legal education matured, the pedagogic style remained intact. Several sides of the teaching method applied in Chinese law schools could be perceived. Today, although not widely acknowledged, it is no secret that Chinese universities, especially in humanities and social sciences, adopt the spoon-feeding method in instructing younger generations (Kraus 1989, pp. 121–125). It is a negative approach to education in the sense that such a method does not invite students to actively participate in the class, which stifles the development of critical thinking abilities that are crucial to further advancing in related fields. That said, teaching methods are not an independent element in pedagogy. How law teachers cultivate students is primarily bound by factors such as the overall academic tradition of the field, the goal of legal education, and the teaching materials they use. Moreover, students' early learning habits also play out in this context.

In the Chinese context, especially in the years when legal education geared up to produce legal professionals for economic development or sometimes claimed to be building a socialist society, as mentioned in political agendas (Li 1995; Qiao 1993), the goal of legal education is unmistakably pragmatic. In other words, it aims to produce an army of practical lawyers who can help the state navigate through economic transitions and address potential social and economic needs as the economy becomes more complicated and market reform deepens.

Nevertheless, while the goal of legal education is relatively straightforward, the process of legal education does not appear to support this goal. As mentioned above, the academic atmosphere and tradition of Chinese universities are hierarchical and authoritative. Course structures and contents are based mainly on positive Chinese laws. Moreover, the widely used textbooks are doctrinally based. Altogether, it is not surprising that the majority of Chinese universities have taught and still teach law in a theoretical manner for practical purposes.

In an atmosphere where teachers hold absolute authority, the most common pedagogic approach is one-way transmission. This style of teaching does not invite or encourage discussion. With textbooks compiled by nationally famous legal scholars, teachers lecture on legal propositions, legal concepts, principles, etc. Legal cases may be referred to for the further elaboration of legal propositions. From a relational perspective, in law classes, the teacher and textbooks are the primary sources of knowledge, and the students are mostly passive receivers. Given that China's legal system is mainly akin to the civil law system, the continental style of lecturing is naturally the first choice of Chinese law schools. Some have argued that, in addition to the statute law tradition, the academic tradition of the civil law system, which stresses legal texts rather than case analysis, is more easily adapted to Chinese traditions (Zhu 2009, p. 85).

Moreover, the two active parties in the class, the teacher and the students, are also major contributors to the mundane and inactive teaching method. For faculty members, the Chinese education system adopts a rigid promotion system that stresses the number of publications and governmental grants for research projects, leaving educators little incentive to develop their teaching abilities or diversify their teaching methods. In other words, teaching is a peripheral activity for many law teachers, as it has little to do with their career promotions and remuneration.

On the students' side, as mentioned earlier, Chinese legal education usually started at the undergraduate level before the JM was established in 1996. This suggests that Chinese law students start legal courses when they are still constrained by the high school spoon-feeding learning style and are not experienced in the interactive learning mode. Therefore, to a great extent, students find that the highly criticized Chinese teaching style suits them well. These accumulated and ingrained learning habits further deepen the mode of rigid thinking, a process of forming the habitus of mechanically applying legal doctrines, i.e., concepts, legal propositions, and theories, to real-world cases.

Taking the two factors together—students' previous learning habits and teachers' low interest in teaching—it is unsurprising that China's law schools have formed such a deep-rooted teaching style, as all parties find it rather comfortable until the students enter the real world. It is challenging for Chinese law graduates to adjust to the uncertainties of practising law, as their university education has not been trained in such legal skills (Zhu 2009, p. 85).

5.3.4 Evolving Evaluation System

The Chinese evaluation system for legal education, or the legal profession entrance examination, evolved along with the formalization of university studies. Evaluating the education results is a measure to test the extent to which 'a valid realization of knowledge' has been achieved (Bernstein 1974, p. 363). The focus of this section is not to examine the substantial contents of the measurement of legal knowledge, although some will be mentioned. Rather, the major interest of the investigation is the changing format of the judicial examination system, or the threshold of the legal profession. It therefore also touches on the growing standards for entering the legal profession as a reflection of improving the criteria for legal education.

As mentioned in the previous chapter, the first national bar exam was introduced in 1986; before that, the lawyer credential was within the purview of provincial governments.[69] When lawyers' credentials were formalized, the selection process for judges and prosecutors had yet to be formalized. It was not until 1995, along with the promulgation of the Law of Judges and the Law of Prosecutors, that a standard examination system was applied to judges and prosecutors. In 1999, the Supreme Court issued a provisional version of the testing system for junior judges.[70] It stipulated that all junior judges and assistant judges should pass the national examination (Article 2), composed of written and oral exams, and only those who passed the written examination were eligible to take the oral examination (Article 9). The judges' entrance examination was open to people working in the court system, lawyers, law school teachers, and other legal professionals (Article 6).

From the first appearance of the national bar exam in 1986 to the addition of the two separate exams for judges and prosecutors in 1995, China held these three parallel examinations for the three types of legal professionals until 2000,[71] when the government unified the three exams into a uniform judicial exam for legal professionals—lawyers, judges, prosecutors, and notaries. Over those fifteen years, China held twelve bar exams and four exams for judges and prosecutors (1995, 1997–1999), and by 2000, 117,260 people had been certified as lawyers (Sun 2001, p. 1271).

For an overview of the evaluation system for China's first generation of domestically trained legal professionals, one could take a close look at the structure of the bar exams in that period. In the following, the papers of the 1993 bar exam are taken as an example to assess the tests designed for people entering the group. According to the Centre of China Bar Exam, the office in charge of the exam, in 1993, over 88,000 people registered for the bar exam and approximately 74,000 sat for it; the majority of the candidates possessed a formal legal education background at the undergraduate level and were under 35 years old (Centre of China Bar Exam 1994a). Approximately 20,000 participants were expected to acquire a lawyer certificate (Centre of China Bar Exam 1994a).

In general, the design of the exam was intended to test the practical ability of prospective lawyers. Therefore, the centre accentuated candidates' ability to understand and apply the law and placed less emphasis on memorizing. To complete the exam, the participants had to sit for four written exams, each of which had to be completed within three hours. The exam was designed to test four main aspects: basic knowledge of the law, substantial laws and regulations, procedural laws and regulations, and legal system and practice (Centre of China Bar Exam 1994b). Overall, the exams were patterned as multiple choice, true-or-false questions, completions, case analysis, and short-answer questions. Although there were four written tests, they were not designed to test particular laws but rather presented were in a diffuse manner, with each paper testing all possible legal issues, incorporating both civil and criminal issues, substantive and procedural[72]—a unique style of testing from today's perspective.

The layout and focus of the original papers of the 1993 bar exam were as follows: papers one and four stressed the ability to memorize and the application of the law in real life. To test the memorization of legal concepts and legal propositions, questions were presented in the form of gloss explanations and short-answer questions in paper one and completions in paper four, where candidates had to lay out the characteristics of the three types of foreign enterprises and describe the features of the three types of domestic companies. In addition, the ability to apply law was tested in revising economic contracts and writing legal consulting opinions based on given case details.

The ability of case analysis was tested via various types of cases. For instance, paper two had ten multiple-choice questions designed on the basis of concise case scenarios; seven more detailed and complicated cases, each followed by several questions patterned as short-answer or multiple-choice questions, and one true-or-false question testing the knowledge of legitimate criminal procedures. Paper three allocated 20% of the credit to each of the five short cases, which were to be answered subjectively with the aim of testing the candidates' ability to demonstrate legal judgement and reasoning skills. The remaining cases were presented as objective items, with multiple-choice or true-or-false questions. As a whole, the four examination papers, while diverse in the forms of questions, all appear to be less substantial in volume, as there were fewer questions than those in the present-day bar exam.

Nevertheless, the structure and contents of the early version of the bar exam were more informational than critical. This is the lens through which we can gain an overall idea of China's early criteria for becoming a legal professional. They are also crucial in the sense that the quality of legal professionals would impact China's legal development in general and the application of the law in particular.

5.4 The Facilitative Role of Law and the Market Economy

The 1990s were a booming period for China's formal laws and thus the completion of the legal system. First and foremost, the Constitution made a fundamental change in the private sector as constitutional barriers were lifted. Economic areas that had been neglected in the preceding decade all received attention from the legal field, including laws for different types of economic entities, such as companies and partnerships; laws for foreign trade and financial affairs; laws for economic activities such as anti-unfair competition laws; and the first Chinese labour law. In addition to the high coverage of economic spheres, the laws promulgated in this period showed improvements in formal qualities, a legislative phenomenon that echoed the rapid expansion of legal education.

The advancement of economic laws in this decade suggests that the room for policy papers to manoeuvre had become much narrower, and formal laws started to play a central role in navigating the economy. The tendency for formal laws to guide economic affairs demonstrated that the state in the 1990s was retreating from direct and substantive interventions; the laws that appeared in this period no longer aimed for microlevel management of the economy. Instead, most of them made general issues their subject matter, such as broad categories of economic entities, behaviours, and relationships. Although the degree of generalization varied in the internal structures of these laws, the overall general characteristics guaranteed the universal application of the law, which indicated that other laws had shifted from an instrumental to a facilitative role.

On the whole, unlike the laws stipulated in the preceding decade, the laws put into force during this stage tended to build a comprehensive legal framework for economic issues in general, demonstrating that the authority was forgoing its role of babysitting economic affairs, indicating an intention to develop general and formal laws to guide the economy. The change of tone on the legal front corresponded to the change in the political attitude towards the economy, as in the 1990s, top leaders decided to accelerate the marketization process of China's economy, and the law was there to help.

Indeed, on the legal front, visible efforts were made to facilitate the structural change of the economy. For example, the first Chinese Company Law was enacted in 1993 against an economic background where the authority was trying to reform the structure of the public sector, and the timely arrival of the formal Company Law could help smooth the process of privatization and corporatization in the late 1990s. As a socialist country, China long had ideological barriers to legalizing and changing the private economy, and the Constitution made several amendments to gradually legalize private economic activities, which was a critical move towards the marketization of the economy. Moreover, to facilitate China's accession to the WTO and integration into the global market, the legislature adjusted thousands of laws and regulations, either repealing or revising them; in addition, it promulgated China's first Legislation Law to formalize legislative work and clarify the internal structure of the Chinese legal system.

Against this economic and legal background, China's legal education system soon found it difficult to keep up with the growing need for talent as the economy expanded. China's legal education system responded with a focus on both its hardware and software. As a result, significant changes were made to its institutions and teaching materials.

Starting from a multilevel institutional structure, China formalized its legal education in the early 1990s, and from then on, law study was offered merely by universities. In this period, law departments and enrolled regular law students experienced a visible increase. Along with institutional formalization, the course structure and teaching materials were also revised. The authority designed a core course structure for legal education and mandatory courses for LLB and JM degree programmes. In the meantime, governmental projects for editing standardized legal textbooks were underway. Overall, Chinese legal education underwent a quite comprehensive evolution in this period, formalizing institutions, course structures, and learning materials.

Correspondingly, the evaluation system for legal education, or the entrance exams for the legal profession, also evolved. The bar exam for lawyers and the exams for judges and prosecutors started to be held at the national level and regularly. The standard of these exams improved, as was seen in the design of the exams, which stressed the practical ability of prospective legal professionals and placed less emphasis on memorization. Also worth mentioning is the growing number of legal experts, as many more were certified and joined the group. Such changes are not surprising given the improving standards of legal education in this period.

These aspects of legal education are crucial because the formal qualities of legal education may influence the formalization of the law. Moreover, given the direct role of legal professionals in law application, the formalization of legal education would impact the law in action in general.

In conclusion, as the market reform of the economy accelerated, the law responded. In this period, the formalization of the law helped qualify law for a facilitative role in the economic transformation: the general coverage by the law of economic areas, the timely emergence of particular laws for specific economic reforms, etc. A similar role of the law was also seen on the international stage, where Chinese laws made concessions to international rules to facilitate China's international trade. These characteristics of the law indicate the reduced intervention of the state in the economy and a change in the role of the law from the micromanager of the planned economy to a macrofacilitator of the market economy. However, as we have seen in the financial sector, China's legal formalization benefited mostly the state sectors and other established market actors, and at this point, legal formalism may have also been a contributor to the rise of social inequalities, which is addressed in chapter six.

Notes

1. This refers to Jiang's political slogan 'Three Represents'—the CCP shall always represent the developing requirements of China's advanced productive force, the direction of China's advanced culture, and the fundamental interests of the majority of the Chinese people. This was Jiang's main political idea, first announced in 2000.
2. One interpretation of Deng's endorsement of law as the dominant instrument of governance was to end the arbitrariness and thus the chaos China had experienced during the Cultural Revolution; see Lubman (1999, p. 124).
3. The first attempt at reforming the SOEs in the 1980s turned out to be unsuccessful; see chapter four of this work.
4. Concerning the size of collectively owned TVEs, as Huang showed, in 1996, there were 23.4 million TVEs, of which only 1.5 million were collectively owned. The 23.4 million TVEs employed 135.1 million workers, of whom 59.5 million were hired by collective TVEs.
5. Data available at http://www.sasac.gov.cn/n2588035/n2641579/n2641645/index.html. Accessed 25 October 2019.
6. On page 360 of the Communique of the State Council (1988), the proposal for the constitutional amendment said the revision suggestions were made according to 'the practice of recent years' reform of the economic system and the development following the opening-up'.
7. It is interesting to note that the CCCCP made the amendment proposal. In China, the NPC has the right to revise the Constitution, but no legal document mentions the right to propose constitutional amendments.
8. To name but a few, there are the Company Law (1993), Anti-Unfair Competition Law (1993), Law on the Protection of Consumer Rights and Interests (1993), Labour Law (1994), Law on Township Enterprises (1997), and Partnership Enterprise Law (1997).
9. The 1999 amendment also revised Article 6. The original version reads, 'The basis of the socialist economic system of the People's Republic of China is socialist public ownership of the means of production, namely, ownership by the whole people and collective ownership by the working people'. It was revised to 'In the primary stage of socialism, the State upholds the basic economic system in which the public ownership is dominant and diverse forms of ownership develop side by side and keeps to the distribution system in which distribution according to work is dominant and diverse modes of distribution coexist'.
10. Details about the socialist transformation are discussed in chapter three of this study.
11. Lardy (1998), who extensively studied China's financial sector, noted that China's newly formed PBC controlled huge financial capital but lacked experience and expertise in managing the financial system efficiently, such as lacking the ability to supervise emerging commercial banks, poor disclosure practices, and a weak financial accounting system. Hence, improving the economic efficiency of state banks was considered a crucial factor of China's effort to restructure the state-owned banking system.

12. The arrangements were as follows: the China Cinda Asset Management for the CCB, the China Oriental Asset Management for the BOC, the China Huarong Asset Management for the ICBC, and the China Great Wall Asset Management for the ABC.
13. Its predecessor was the Shenzhen Development Bank, which was founded in 1987. Its largest shareholders at the time were the Shenzhen Investment Management Company and the Shenzhen International Trust and Investment Company, both owned by the Shenzhen government. The Pingan Insurance (Group) Company of China bought it in 2012 and renamed it Pingan Bank.
14. The percentage is manually calculated according to data from the annual report.
15. The Ministry of Finance wholly owns the CITIC, and the state wholly owns the FOTIC via the Sinochem Group.
16. For detailed requirements for establishing an in-house finance company, see Article 7 of Measures for the Administration of Finance Companies of Enterprise Groups.
17. The development of China's bond market was believed to finance the national budget needs, which could explain why participants in the bond market included many actors that, in one way or another, were linked to the state.
18. Since 2016, the research centre of China Central Depository and Clearing Co., Ltd. has compiles the Zhongguo zhaiquan shichang gailan/Overview of China Bond Market annually.
19. Wu assessed China's corporate bond market as 'extremely underdeveloped', which he argued was due to China's inappropriate positioning of corporate bonds to serve state investment and insufficient institutional support, i.e., the OTC market and capable institutional investors.
20. These data do not include the STAR Market's market value, as it opened in 2019.
21. Data acquired from the official website of the STAR Market, available at http://star.sse.com.cn/market/stocklist/. Accessed 25 June 2020.
22. In 2001, China established its first OTC market, which is now called 'The Old Third Board'. It was established to receive shares of delisted companies. However, due to very few companies being listed on the board and most of them being of poor quality, this market is not active, although it is still operating.
23. In contrast to scholars criticizing overspeculation as the cause of China's stock market volatility, there is also research indicating that the driving force behind China's equity market was government policies rather than economic factors.
24. According to a calculation made by Tsai (2002), the state banking system in aggregate allocated less than one percent of its loans to China's private sector by 2000.
25. Tsai's field investigation revealed that many local governments were aware of and some even actively participated in informal financial activities.
26. Among all types of informal finances, pawnshops are the only one that has been institutionalized by formal rules, a ministry-level administrative regulation called the Pawn Management Approach (2005).
27. Such as microloan companies, investment companies, capital mutual-aid agencies, and credit-loan branches for small enterprises.
28. In January 2020, the China Insurance Regulation Commission and the China Banking Regulation Commission merged and formed the current CBIRC.
29. Also worth noting is the Trust Law of the PRC (2001), the Banking Supervision Law of the PRC (2003), and the Anti-Money Laundering Law of the PRC (2006).
30. Article 2 reads, 'The People's Bank of China is the central bank of the People's Republic of China. The People's Bank of China shall, under the leadership of the State Council, formulate and implement monetary policies and exercise supervision and control over the banking industry'.
31. The supervision right for the banking system was transferred to the CBRC in 2003.
32. Law on People's Bank of China Article 23 (1) (2) and the Law on Commercial Banks Article 31 and 47.
33. The legal framework of the capital market also includes the Law of the PRC on Securities Investment Funds (2003) and the Regulations on the Administration of Corporate Bonds (1987), which stipulated specifics for investment funds and corporate bonds. In addition, the

legal issues of government bonds are separately regulated by the Regulations on Treasury Bills of the PRC (1981). Additionally, Regulations on the Risk Disposal of Securities Companies (2008) structure precaution mechanisms for possible malpractice or risks.

34. Data mentioned in this section are available at https://wits.worldbank.org/CountryProfile/en/Country/CHN/StartYear/2005/EndYear/2020/Indicator/NE-TRD-GNFS-ZS. Accessed 18 Mar 2023.
35. Here, 'trade' refers to the sum of exports and imports of goods and services measured as a share of gross domestic product.
36. Western Europe refers to Britain, West Germany, France, and Italy.
37. These 14 trading companies are all state-owned, covering all categories of possible commodities, such as machinery, mineral products, technology, chemistry products, food, tea, cigarettes, and grains.
38. These are the China Land Transportation Corporation and China Shipping Corporation.
39. For the purposes of this law, 'foreign trade dealers' refers to legal persons, other organizations or individuals who have fulfilled the industrial and commercial registration requirement or other practice procedures in accordance with the law and engage in foreign trade dealings in compliance with this law and other relevant laws and administrative regulations.
40. Some strictly regulated goods, including precious metals such as gold and silver and other natural resources, are subject to approval.
41. This policy was applied only to domestic companies.
42. China's foreign exchange reserve was $21.1 billion at the end of 1993, and since 1994, it has sustained accumulative growth, reaching $28.47 trillion by 2010. Data gathered from the State Administration of Foreign Exchange database, available at http://www.safe.gov.cn/safe/tjsjkbcx/index.html. Accessed 15 June 2020.
43. To quote the author, the MOFTEC reported that it had reviewed 'over 1400 laws, regulations, and similar documents, including six statutes (of which five were revised), 164 State Council regulations (of which 114 were to be repealed and 25 amended), 887 of its ministry regulations (of which 459 were to be repealed and 95 amended), 191 bilateral trade agreements, 72 bilateral investment treaties, and 93 tax treaties. In the first two months of 2001, the various ministries and commissions of the State Council reportedly reviewed some 2300 laws and regulations, of which 830 were identified as in need of repeal and 325 as in need of revision'.
44. The English versions of texts of legal documents and statistical numbers of laws in each sphere are available at https://www.lawinfochina.com.
45. China has five ethnic minority regions. All of the local governments possess a certain leeway in promulgating issues that are particular to their regions.
46. It was argued that China's less-developed court and constitutional systems might be among the reasons for the absence of a judicial review system, which is more common in nations that possess mature constitutional systems.
47. Articles 2, 12, and 13 of the Administrative Litigation Law.
48. Data gathered from the WTO website. Available at https://www.wto.org/english/thewto_e/countries_e/china_e.htm. Accessed 15 Jun 2020. From a comparative perspective, China's caseload as a respondent appears to be moderate, as the U.S. and the E.U. have been charged 155 and 87 times since 1995, respectively.
49. The sixteen cases are DS342, 394, 395, 398, 407, 431, 432, 433, 450, 501, 508, 509, 517, 549, 568, and 589. Common issues regarding transparency include not publishing trade-related rules in a timely manner and inconsistency of rule administration at local levels. See also the case study in the next section.
50. GATT Article X concerns publication and administration of trade regulations, and Article X:3 (a) refers to uniform, impartial and reasonable enforcement of members' laws, regulations, decisions, etc.
51. Part I para.2(A) refers to uniform issues; related cases are DS508, 509, and 549, and part I para. 2(C) concerns transparency issues; cases include DS450, 501, and 568.
52. The two cases are DS427 and DS483. China was ruled to be noncompliant in the former, and the latter is still proceeding.

53. The 12 cases are DS387, 388, 390, 407, 419, 450, 451, 501, 519, 549, 568, and 589.
54. The 6 cases are DS358, 359, 372, 373, 378, and 489.
55. The 4 cases are DS508, 509, 542, and 558, except that DS508 has an established panel but has not yet been composed.
56. DS394, 395, and 398.
57. Case summary is available at https://www.wto.org/english/tratop_e/dispu_e/cases_e/ds395_e.htm. Accessed 10 Feb 2022.
58. WTO, China—Measures related to the Exportation of Various Raw Materials, WT/DS394/R, WT/DS395/R, WT/DS398/R, 271–281. For the conclusions of the Appellate Body over the issue, see WT/DS394/AB/R WT/DS395/AB/R WT/DS398/AB/R. Available at https://docs.wto.org/dol2fe/Pages/SS/directdoc.aspx?filename=Q:/WT/DS/398ABR.pdf&Open=True. Accessed 10 Feb 2022.
59. The remaining chapters of the law were rules on branches of foreign companies (Chap. 9), legal responsibilities (Chap. 10), and supplementary rules (Chap. 11).
60. Such rights were granted by Article 40, 43, 44, and 72 of the Company Law (2005).
61. As elaborated by Professor Ji, the old-fashioned Chinese teaching style was like 'full-class-time teaching', which encouraged 'students providing standardized answers' and stressed 'memorization of legal provisions' with an exam orientation.
62. One illustration is the default working relationship between students and teachers. Students were obligated to do secretarial and some research assistant work for supervisors without a formal contract. Such relationships were described by Abramson (2006, p. 342) as 'fiefdoms ... to polarize the law school along political lines, breeding students with loyalty to the specific legal perspective of their advisor ... [and] some of the work seemed, from the context of American academic standards, to exceed the bounds of acceptable practice'.
63. For instance, Shanghai Jiaotong University.
64. Such courses are currently available in some top law schools in China.
65. For instance, Zhang WX (ed) (2018) Falixue/Jurisprudence. Law Press China, Beijing, and Sheng ZL (ed) (2001) Falixue/Jurisprudence. Peking University Press, Beijing.
66. This is the Criminal Code and associated commentary used in the Tang Dynasty, also named the Tang Code.
67. A brief introduction of the press and its significant status in publishing higher education textbooks is available at https://www.hep.com.cn/aboutus. Accessed 20 September 2021.
68. This series of textbooks was commissioned under two key state projects: the eleventh five-year plan of textbooks project and the textbooks for the twenty-first century. Both were funding projects for editing high-standard textbooks for university education.
69. Article 9 of the Provisions Regulations of Lawyers (1980).
70. Interim Procedures of the Examination of Junior Judges and Associate Judges (1999).
71. The lawyers' qualification exam was held from 1986 to 2000, and the first unified judicial exam was held in 2002. However, in 2001, preparations were being made for the unified judicial exam, and the exam was thus suspended.
72. The introductions to the 1993 bar exam were summarized upon the four original exam papers published by China Lawyer, volumes four through seven, 1994.

References

Abramson K (2006) Paradigms in the cultivation of China's future legal elite: a case study of legal education in western China. Asian-Pacific Law &Policy Journal 7(2):302-384

Ardener S (1964) The comparative study of rotating credit association. The Journal of the Royal Anthropological Institute of Great Britain and Ireland 94(2):201-229

Art RC and Gu MK (1995) China incorporated: the first corporation law of the PRC. Yale Journal of International Law 20(2):273-308

Balme S and Dowdle MW (2009) Introduction: exploring for constitutionalism in 21st century China. In: Balme S and Dowdle MW (eds) Building constitutionalism in China. Palgrve Macmillan, London

Barboza D (2011) In cooling China, loan sharks come knocking. The New York Times 13 October. Available at http://www.nytime.com. Accessed 21 Sept 2021

Bernstein B (1974) On the classification and framing of educational knowledge. In: Richard Brown (ed) Knowledge, education, and cultural change: papers in the sociology of education. Tavistock Publications, London

Biukovic L (2008) Selective adaption of WTO transparency norms and local practices in China and Japan. Journal of International Economic Law 11(4):803-825

Bottelier P (2006) Accelerating reforms in China's financial system. China Brief 6(24). Available at https://jamestown.org/program/accelerating-reforms-in-chinas-financial-system. Accessed 19 Feb 2022

Bourdieu P (2018) Social space and the genesis of appropriated physical space. Journal of Urban and Regional Research 42(1):106-114

Byrd WA (1983) China's financial system: the changing role of banks. Westview Press, Nashville

CCCCP (1958) Guanyu duiwai maoyi bixu tongyi duiwai de jueding/Decisions on common approaches to foreign trade. In: CPC Party Literature Research Office (ed) (1992) Jianguoyilai zhongyao wenxian xuanbian, 11 juan/Selected key documents since the establishment of the PRC, vol 11. Central Party Literature Press, Beijing

CCCCP (1988) Guanyu xiugai zhonghua renmin gongheguo xianfa gebie tiaokuan de jianyi/ Suggestions on the revision of several articles of the Constitution of the PRC. The Communique of the State Council 11:360. Available at https://www.gov.cn/gongbao/shuju/1988/gwyb198811.pdf. Accessed 14 Feb 2023

CCCCP (1993) Guanyu jianli shehui zhuyi shichang jingji tizhi ruogan wenti de jueding/Decisions on several issues of constructing a socialist market economic system. In: CPC Party Literature Research Office (ed) (1995) Shisida yilai zhongyao wenxian xuanbian, shang/Selected key documents since the 14th National Congress of the CCP, vol 1. Central Party Literature Press, Beijing

CCCCP (1999) Guanyu guoyou qiye gaige he fazhan ruogan zhogndа wenti de jueding/Decisions on several issues of reform and development of the SOEs. In: CPC Party Literature Research Office (ed) (2001) Shiwuda yilai zhongyao wenxian xuanbian, zhong/Selected key documents since the 15th National Congress of the CCP, vol 2. Central Party Literature Press, Beijing

CCCCP and State Council (2002) Guanyu jinyibu zuohao xiagang shiye renyuan zai jiuye gongzuo de tongzhi/Circular on further improving the work of reemployment of laid-off workers. In: CPC Party Literature Research Office (ed) (2003) Shiwuda yilai zhongyao wenxian xuanbian, xia / Selected key documents since the 15th National Congress of the CCP, vol 3. Central Party Literature Press, Beijing

CCCCP and the Political Bureau (1992) Guanyu jiaqiang zhengfa gongzuo, genghao de wei gaige kaifang he jingji jianshe fuwu de yijian/Opinions on strengthening political and legal work for better serving the reform and opening-up strategies and economic construction. In: CPC Party Literature Research Office (ed) (1993) Shisanda yilai zhongyao wenxian xuanbian, xia/Selected key documents since the 13th National Congress of the CCP, vol 3. Central Party Literature Press, Beijing

CCDC Research (2022) Zhongguo zhaiquan shichang gailan/Overview of China's Bond Market. Available at http://www.ccdc.com.cn/ccdc/cn/business/c150471295/c150471502/c150481996/20220420/160071278.shtml. Accessed 28 Mar 2023

Centre of China Bar Exam (1994a) 1993 Quanguo lüshi zige kaoshi zongshu/Summary of the 1993 national lawyers' qualification exam. China Lawyer 1:3

Centre of China Bar Exam (1994b) 1994 Nian quanguo lüshi zige kaoshi de youguan guiding/ Relevant provisions of 1994 national lawyers' qualification exam. China Lawyer 6:3

Chai JHC (1981) Domestic money and banking reform in China. Hongkong Economic Papers 14:37–52

Chang GH and Hou J (1997) Structural inflation and the 1994 'monetary' crisis in China. Contemporary Economic Policy 15(3):73–81

Chen X-z J (2006) China and the U.S. trade embargo, 1950–1972. American Journal of Chinese Studies 13(2):169–186

Cheng W-q (2010) Protection of minority shareholders after the new company law: 26 Case Studies. International Journal of Law and Management 52(4):283–308

Cho YJ (1986) Inefficiencies from financial liberalization in the absence of a well-functioning equity market. Journal of Money, Credit and Banking 18(2):191-199

Chow GC (2003) Impact of joining the WTO on China's economic, legal, and political institutions. Pacific Economic Review 8(2):105–115

Clarke C (2003) China's legal system and the WTO: prospects for compliance. Washington University Global Studies Law Review 2(1):97–118

Committee of Wenzhou Chorography (2020) Wenzhoushi zhi, vol 11 minsu/Wenzhou chronicles, vol 11 folk custom. The Commerical Press, Shanghai

Deng XP (1978) Jiefang sixiang, shishiqiushi, tuanjieyizhi xiangqiankan/Emancipating the mind, seeking truth from facts, forwarding with solidarity. In: Deng Xiaoping (1993) Deng Xiaoping wenxuan dierjuan/The selected works of Deng Xiaoping, vol 2. People's Publishing House, Beijing

Dickinson SM (2007) Introduction to the new company law of China. Pacific Rim Law & Policy Journal 16(1):1–12

Fang LF (1995) China's corporatization experiment. Duke Journal of Comparative and International Law 5(2): 149–270

Gao YF (2005) Foreign trade law in China and its revision. China: An International Journal 3(1): 50–73

Gao H (2017) The WTO's transparency obligations and China. Journal of Comparative Law 12(2):329–355

Goldsmith RW (1969) Financial structure and development. Yale University Press, New Haven

Gu MK (2006) Understanding Chinese company law: a comparative introduction. Hong Kong University Press, Hong Kong

Gurley JG and Shaw ES (1955) Financial aspects of economic development. The American Economic Review 45(4):515–538

Howson NC (1997) China's company law: one step forward, two steps back—a modest complaint. Columbia Journal of Asian Law 11(1):127–174

Howson NC (2009) China's restructured commercial banks: nomenklatura accountability serving corporate governance reform? In: Zhu M, Cai JQ, and Avery M (eds) China's emerging financial markets: challenges and global impact. Wiley, Hoboken

Hu CN (1982) Jiagexue/Price studies. Chinese People's University Publishing House, Beijing

Hu RF, Cheng Z, and Fu T (2006) Zhonghang shenqiu zhihang zai bao piaoju an/Another bill fraud case of Shenqiu branch of Bank of China explodes. Caijing Magazine, vol 13. Available at https://magazine.caixin.com/2006-06-12/100077662.html?sourceEntityId=100991494. Accessed 26 Feb 2023

Huang YS (2008) Capitalism with Chinese characteristics. Cambridge University Press, Cambridge

Huang RH and Orr G (2007) China's state-owned enterprises: board governance and the communist party. McKinsey Quarterly 1:108–111

Huo S (1995) The company law of the people's republic of China. UCLA Pacific Basin Law Journal 13(2):373–389

ICBC (n.d.) ICBC History (1984–2014). Available at http://www.icbc-ltd.com/ICBCLtd/About%20Us/ICBC%20History/. Accessed 20 June 2020

Jacob R and Rabinovitch S (2011) China SMEs rely on shadow financing for growth. Financial Times 19 October. Available at http://www.ft.com. Accessed 21 Feb 2023

Ji WD (2005) Legal education in China: a great leap forward of professionalism. Kobe University Law 39:1–22

Ji WD (2016) Legal education in China: reforms and requirements. Asian Journal of Law and Society 3(2): 237–246

Jiang ZM (1995) Jianding xinxin, mingque renwu, jiji tuijin guoyou qiye gaige/Enhancing confidence, clarifying tasks, actively pushing forward SOEs reform. In: CPC Party Literature Research Office (ed) (1997) Shisida yilai zhongyao wenxian xuanbian, zhong/Selected key documents since the 14th National Congress of the CCP, vol 2. Central Party Literature Press, Beijing

Jiang ZM (1997) Gaojü dengxiao lilun weida qizhi, ba jianshe you zhongguo tese shehui zhuyi shiye quanmian tuixiang ershiyi shiji/Holding high the great banner of Deng Xiaoping's theory, advancing the task of building-up a socialist country with Chinese characteristics towards the twenty-first century. In: CPC Party Literature Research Office (ed) (2000) Shiwuda yilai zhongyao wenxian xuanbian, shang/Selected key documents since the 15th National Congress of the CCP, vol 1. Central Party Literature Press, Beijing

Jiang TB (2006) Gongsifa xiugai ruogan lilun yu Shijian wenti yi: dui lici gongsifa xiugai de huigui/Theoretical and practical issues concerning the revision of Company Law, vol 1: a review of revisions of Company Law. Market Regulation 1:48–49

Kennedy D (1983) The political significance of the structure of the law school curriculum. Seton Hall Law Review 14(1):1–16

Kraus J (1989) Legal education in the People's Republic of China. Suffolk Transnational Law Journal 13(1):75–134

Kroeber AR (2008) China's economy: what everyone needs to know. Oxford University Press, Oxford

Kuhn RL (2004) The man who changed China: the life and legacy of Jiang Zemin. Crown Publisher, New York

Lardy NR (1991) Foreign trade and economic reform in China: 1978-1990. Cambridge University Press, Cambridge

Lardy NR (1998) China's unfinished economic revolution. Brookings Inst Press, Washington DC

Lardy NR (2014) Market over Mao: the rise of private business in China. PIIE Press, Washington DC

Laurenceson J and Chai JCH (2003) Financial reform and economic development in China. Edward Elgar, Cheltenham

Li KW (1994) Financial repression and economic reform in China. Praeger, Westport

Li P (1995) Yaowei shenhua gaige he fazhan jingji tigong youli de baozhi baozhang/Guarantee powerful legal protection for the reform and the economic development. In: CPC Party Literature Research Office (ed) (1997) Shisida yilai zhongyao wenxian xuanbian, zhong/Selected key documents since the 14th National Congress of the CCP, vol 2. Central Party Literature Press, Beijing

Li P (1998) Wei jiaqiang shehuizhuyi minzhu fazhi tuijin yifa zhiguo er nuli gongzuo/Working hard to reinforce socialist democracy and legal system, advancing the rule of law. In: CPC Party Literature Research Office (ed) (2000) Shiwuda yilai zhongyao wenxian xuanbian, shang/Selected key documents since the 15th National Congress of the CCP, vol 1. Central Party Literature Press, Beijing

Li P (2000) Jiaqiang lifa gongzuo, jianli you zhongguo tese shehui zhuyi falü tixi/Carry on legislative work, build up a socialist legal system with Chinese characteristics. In: CPC Party Literature Research Office (ed) (2001) Shiwuda yilai zhongyao wenxian xuanbian, zhong/Selected key documents since the 15th National Congress of the CCP, vol 2. Central Party Literature Press, Beijing

Lin Y-M (2017) Dancing with the devil: the political economy of privatization in China. Oxford University Press, Oxford

Ling HW (2005) Zhou Xiaochuan tan jianhang gaige/Zhou Xiaochuan addresses China Construction Bank's reform. In: Caijing Magazine, vol 24. Available athttp://finance.sina.com.cn/review/20051128/17002153616.shtml. Accessed 26 Feb 2023

Ling HW and Zhao XJ (2003) Jiang Jianqing xijie gonghang/Jiang Jianqing explains ICBC in detail. In: Caijing Magazine, vol 26. Available at https://magazine.caixin.com/2003-01-05/100079289.html. Accessed 26 Feb 2023
Liu HR (ed) (1986) 1986 zhongguo jinrong nianjian/1986 Almanac of China's Finance and Banking. China Financial Publishing House, Beijing
Lubman SB (1999) Bird in a cage: legal reform in China after Mao. Stanford University Press, Redwood
Mackenzie K (2011) China's shadow banking sector needs a bail-out, says SocGen. Financial Time 6 October. Available at https://www.ft.com. Accessed 21 Feb 2023
Meng HL (2018) 1986 Yueqing 'huian' fengbo: zuiming yicheng huiyi/1986 Disturbance of yueqing 'hui' case: the name of crime became history. Available at https://www.chinacourt.org/article/detail/2018/12/id/3603485.shtml. Accessed 19 Feb 2022
Naughton B (2007) The Chinese economy: transition and growth. MIT Press, Cambridge
Naughton B (2018) The Chinese economy: adaption and growth, 2nd edn. The MIT Press, Cambridge
Norton JJ (2000) Financial sector law reform in emerging economies. The British Institute of International and Comparative Law, London
Ostry S (1998) China and the WTO: the transparency issue. UCLA Journal of International Law and Foreign Affairs 3(1):1–22
Pei MX (2016) China's crony capitalism: the dynamics of regime decay. Harvard University Press, Cambridge
Qi DJ (ed) (2014) Jingji fa/Economic law, 3rd edn. Higher Education Publication, Beijing
Qiao S (1993) Nuli jianshe shehui zhuyi shichang jingji falü tixi/Work hard to build the legal system of the socialist market economy. In: CPC Party Literature Research Office (ed) (1995) Shisida yilai zhongyao wenxian xuanbian, shang/Selected key documents since the 14th National Congress of the CCP, vol 1. Central Party Literature Press, Beijing
Qiao S (1996) Jiakuai lifa, jiaqiang jiandu/Accelerating legislations, strengthening supervision. In: CPC Party Literature Research Office (ed) (1997) Shisida yilai zhongyao wenxian xuanbian, zhong / Selected key documents since the 14th National Congress of the CCP, vol 2. Central Party Literature Press, Beijing
Schumpeter J (1934) The theory of economic development (trans: Opie R). Harvard University Press, Cambridge
Shi TT (2014) Gongsi ziben zhidu gaige: jiedu yu bianxi/The reform of corporation's capital system: a commendation. Tsinghua University Law Journal 5:128–141
Shih VC (2008) Factions and finance in China: elite conflict and inflation. Cambridge University Press, Cambridge
Smith AH (1899) Village life in China: a study in sociology. F. H. Revell, Ada
Song LG (2015) State and non-state enterprises in China's reform. In: Chow GC and Perkins DH (eds) Routledge handbook of the Chinese economy. Routledge, London
State Council (1980) Guanyu maoyi waihui neibu jiesuan jiage shixing bafa de tongzhi/Report on the methods of implementing the internal settlement price of foreign exchange in foreign trade
State Council (1984) Guowuyuan zhuanpi duiwaijingmaobu guanyu waimaotizhi gaige yijian de baogao de tongzhi/Notice on the reply of the State Council to the MOFTEC concerning the reform of foreign trade system
State Council (1993) Guanyu jinrong tizhi gaige de jueding/Decisions on the reform of the financial system. In: CPC Party Literature Research Office (ed) (1995) Shisida yilai zhongyao wenxian xuanbian, shang/Selected key documents since the 14th National Congress of the CCP, vol 1. Central Party Literature Press, Beijing
State Council (1994) Guanyu jinyibu shenhua duiwai maoyi tizhi gaige de jueding/Decisions on further deepening the reform of foreign trading system. In: CPC Party Literature Research Office (ed) (1995) Shisida yilai zhongyao wenxian xuanbian, shang/Selected key documents since the 14th National Congress of the CCP, vol 1. Central Party Literature Press, Beijing

State Council (1996) Guangyu ge shangyeyinhang tingzhi zai zhengquan jiaoyisuo huigou ji xianquan jiaoyi de tongzhi/The notice on cessation of repo and bond trading by commercial banks in the stock exchanges

Sullivan LR and Curcio P (2018) Historical dictionary of the Chinese economy. Rowman & Littlefield, Lanham

Sun WZ (ed) (2001) Zhongguo falü nianjian 2001/The juridical yearbook of China 2001. Press of Juridical Yearbook of China, Beijing

Supreme People's Court (2007) Zhang zanjuan su jiangsu wanhua gongmao fazhan youxian gongsi, Wanhua, Wuliangliang, Mao jianwei gudongquan jiufen an/Yanjuan Zhang sue Wanhua Industrial and Commerce Development Co., Hua Wan, Liangliang Wu, and Jianwei Mao over shareholders' rights. Communique of the Supreme People's Court, vol 9. Available at http://gongbao.court.gov.cn/Details/9cde0357de27bb53c852a1bc313cb5.html. Accessed 28 Sept 2021

Tao XN (2011) Laoban paolu chao yinbao wenzhou weiji/The Wenzhou crisis ignited by runaways of local entrepreneurs. Available at http://finance.sina.com.cn/roll/20111013/063410612794.shtml. Accessed 19 Feb 2022

The China Banking Regulatory Commission (ed) (2018) Zhongguo yinhangye jiandu guanli weiyuanhui 2017 nianbao/The 2017 Annual Report of the China Banking Regulatory Commission. China Financial Publishing House, Beijing

The China Securities Regulatory Commission (ed) (2014) Zhongguo zhengquan jiandu guanli weiyuanhui nianbao 2014/The annual report of the China Securities Regulatory Commission 2014. China Financial & Economic Publishing House, Beijing

The China Securities Regulatory Commission (ed) (2018) Zhongguo zhengquan jiandu guanli weiyuanhui nianbao 2018/The annual report of the China Securities Regulatory Commission 2018. China Financial and Economic Publishing House, Beijing

The Export-Import Bank of China (2018) 2018 Annual Report. Available athttp://www.eximbank.gov.cn/aboutExim/annals/2018_2/201907/P020190718590373639140.pdf. Accessed 22 Feb 2023

Tsai K (2002) Back-alley banking: private entrepreneurs in China. Cornell University Press, New York

Walter CE and Howie FTJ (2012) Red capitalism: the fragile financial foundation of China's extraordinary rise. Wiley, Hoboken

Wang BS and Huang H (2006) China's new company law and securities law: an overview and assessment. Australian Journal of Corporate Law 19(2):229–242

Wang YC, Tsai J-J, and Li XW (2019) What drives China's 2015 stock market surges and turmoil? Asia-Pacific Journal of Financial Studies 48(3):410–436

Wei S (2014) Fading registered capital rules under the amended Chinese company law: sweeping changes in uncertain contexts. International Company and Commercial Law Review 25(8):270–282

Wenzhou Government (2012) Beijing: minjian ziben shou xianzhi yinfa jinrong fengbo/Background: financial storm triggered by constrained folk capital. Available at http://www.wenzhou.gov.cn/art/2012/5/7/art_1217151_1392208.html. Accessed 14 Mar 2023

World Bank (1990) China: financial sector policies and institutional development. World Bank, Washington DC

World Trade Organization (2001a) Report of the working party on the accession of China. Available at https://docs.wto.org/dol2fe/Pages/FE_Search/FE_S_S006.aspx%3FFullTextHash%3D1%2526MetaCollection%3DWTO%2526SymbolList=%22WT/ACC/CHN/49%22+OR+%22WT/ACC/CHN/49%2A%2522%2526languageUIChanged%3Dtrue%23. Accessed 14 Feb 2023

World Trade Organization (2001b) The accession of the PRC. Available at https://docs.wto.org/dol2fe/Pages/FE_Search/FE_S_S006.aspx?Query=@Symbol=WT/L/432&Language=ENGLISH&Context=FomerScriptedSearch&languageUIChanged=true. Accessed 14 Feb 2023

World Trade Organization (2012) Reports of the appellate body: China—measures related to the exportation of various raw materials, WT/DS394/R, WT/DS395/R, WT/DS398/R, 271–281. For the conclusions of the Appellate Body over the issue, see WT/DS394/AB/R WT/DS395/AB/R WT/DS398/AB/R, available at https://docs.wto.org/dol2fe/Pages/SS/directdoc.aspx?filename=Q:/WT/DS/398ABR.pdf&Open=True. Accessed 14 Feb 2023

Wu BG (1995) Zongjie jingyan, jinyibu jiada guoyou qiye gaige lidu/Summing up experience, furthering SOEs reform. In: CPC Party Literature Research Office (ed) (1997) Shisida yilai zhongyao wenxian xuanbian, zhong/Selected key documents since the 14th National Congress of the CCP, vol 2. Central Party Literature Press, Beijing

Wu JL (1997) Tantan 'touji': Hechu xunqiu da zhihui/On 'speculation': where to find macro wisdom. Joint Publishing, Hong Kong

Wu JL (2001) Shinian fenyun hua gushi/Opinions on stock market during its ten confused years. Shanghai Far East Publisher, Shanghai

Wu JL (2005) Understanding and interpreting Chinese economic reform. Thomson/South-Western, Singapore

Xi C (2009) Corporate governance and legal reform in China. Wildy, Simmonds and Hill, London

Yi G (1994) Money, banking and financial market in China. Westview Press, Nashville

Ying WJ (ed) (2008) Zhongguo gaodeng jiaoyu gaige yu fazhan 30 nian 1978-2008/30 years of reform and development of China's higher education. Shanghai University of Finance and Economics, Shanghai

Zhang XC (2005) Li Lihui xishu zhonghang chongzu/Li Lihui recounts in detail the restructuring of the bank of China. Caijing Magazine, vol 11. Available at http://finance.sina.com.cn/g/20050531/10381640069.shtml. Accessed 26 Feb 2023

Zhang WK and Yuan DM (2008) Zhongguo jingji gaige 30 nian, mining jingjijuan/China's thirty years of economic reform: the private economy. Chongqing Univerity Press, Chongqing

Zhang JW, Yu N, and Guo J (2006) Yang Kaisheng: Gonghang ziyou lu/Yang Kaisheng: ICBC has its path to forward. Caijing Magazine, vol 10. Available at http://finance.sina.com.cn/bank/plyj/20060517/14092574903.shtml. Accessed 26 Feb 2023

Zhao DG (2009) Gaokao zhuangyuan zhuangye xuanze diaocha/A survey on the choices of discipline by top gaokao scorers. Education and Vocation 34:42-43

Zhao FC (2018) Zhongguo nongye yinhang sanci feili de lishi yanjiu (1951–1965)/A historical study on the three times of establishment and abolishment of the agricultural bank of China (1951–1965). Dissertation, Hebeing University

Zhu RJ (1994) Xiandai qiye zhidu gaige shidian de jige wenti/Several issues on the pilot programs of modern enterprises system. In: CPC Party Literature Research Office (ed) (1997) Shisida yilai zhongyao wenxian xuanbian, zhong/Selected key documents since the 14th National Congress of the CCP, vol 2. Central Party Literature Press, Beijing

Zhu RJ (1997) Dali tuijin qiye gaige, jiji shishi zai jiuye gongcheng/Push forward the enterprises reform, actively implement reemployment project. In: CPC Party Literature Research Office (ed) (1999) Shisida yilai zhongyao wenxian xuanbian, xia/Selected Key Documents since the 14th National Congress of the CCP, vol 3. Central Party Literature Press, Beijing

Zhu RJ (2000a) Jiakuai wanshan shehui baozhang tixi, qieshi baozheng guojia changzhijiuan/Improve the social security system, guarantee the long-term political stability. In: CPC Party Literature Research Office (ed) (2001) Shiwuda yilai zhongyao wenxian xuanbian, zhong/Selected key documents since the 15th National Congress of the CCP, vol 2. Central Party Literature Press, Beijing

Zhu RJ (2000b) Tongyi sixiang, mingque renwu, bushishiji shishi xibu diqu dakaifa zhanlue/Unifying thoughts, clarifying tasks, grasping the opportunities to deploy the development strategies of the western region. In: CPC Party Literature Research Office (ed) (2001) Shiwuda yilai zhongyao wenxian xuanbian, zhong/Selected key documents since the 15th National Congress of the CCP, vol 2. Central Party Literature Press, Beijing

Zhu SL (2009) An institutional inquiry into legal skills education in China. Global Business and Development Law Journal 22(1):75–92

Chapter 6
The Integrative Role of Law, 2002–2011

Abstract This chapter explores the Chinese government's reaction to social inequalities following twenty years of tilted economic development (2002–2011). In effect, the central authority put its primary reform focus on loosening social mobility control by gradually dismantling the *hukou* institution, freeing the labour market, and building up the social insurance network. (6.1) Laws on the book have been formalized to a great extent; nevertheless, the judicial trial was evidently a pursuit of substantive results, as seen in the case study presented in this chapter. These features indicate that the Chinese legal system at the time was trying to correct social injustice via its judicial system. (6.2) Parallel to such social correction was the reformulation of China's legal education and the bar exam, both of which showed quality improvement. (6.3) Overall, in responding to the changed political agenda, the law in this period demonstrated its integrative function in bridging social and economic divergence. (6.4).

6.1 External Functions of the Law

6.1.1 Political Economy from 2002 to 2011

In the preceding two decades, the Chinese authority reformed the agricultural sector, industrial and commercial sector, foreign investment and trade, and financial sector, each to varying degrees of scope and depth. Following these reforms, the landscape of the Chinese economy and society was transformed tremendously. With rural areas implementing the HRS, the commune system built in the Mao era was dissolved and took with it the rural social welfare system. The immediate aftermath of the structural reform in the SOE sector led to millions of workers being laid off, and their living conditions became a pressing concern for the government. The inflow of FDI after 1978 converted China into a world factory, where the high demand for manual labour in coastal regions drew millions of rural surplus workers into the Pearl River Delta and Yangtze River Delta for jobs.

J. Hu, *The Role of Law in China's Economic Development, 1978–2011*,
https://doi.org/10.1007/978-981-99-9911-8_6

Twenty years of coastal area-biased development strategies helped the southeast area visibly outperform the rest of the nation. Urban preference policies, facilitated by the urban–rural binary household registration system, disfavoured rural regions economically and socially. As a once wholly publicly owned economy, the social welfare system at the time did not substantially extend to people outside the public sector, which left workers in the private sector, those laid off from former SOEs, and individual business owners at a disadvantage to the point that building full coverage of the social welfare system was a desperate need (Naughton 2018, pp. 237–256). On the whole, at the turn of the twenty-first century, Chinese society had become a society with glaring social differentiations, and social integration had become an urgent priority.

It was against this social and economic background that the Hu-Wen administration adopted a political agenda endorsing a 'scientific view of development' and building China into a harmonious society (Hu 2003, pp. 483–484; Wen 2008a, pp. 699–718). On the economic front, the government did not initiate new structural changes to the economy but adopted a moderate approach to consolidating and deepening the market economy (State Council 2001, pp. 39–48; Zhu 2001, pp. 487–512). As a series of related economic policies developed, the main priority for the market economy was to continue establishing and fledging the system (CCCCP 2003, pp. 464–482) by pushing the development of the capital market, reforming the investment system (State Council 2004a, pp. 747–754; State Council 2004b), furthering SOE reform (State Council 2003a), and continuing to encourage and support the development of the private economy (State Council 2005a, pp. 684–694).

However, a new front of social and economic concern was initiated at the turn of the century—addressing regional inequalities such as rural–urban divergence and uneven east–west development and building a comprehensive social security network. These aspects either had been largely neglected in the previous two decades of development or were consequences of previous uneven development strategies. To a great extent, the government could no longer afford to ignore them, as the deterioration of these spheres would result in social instability (Han 2008, pp. 13–33). In response, the central authority advocated building a harmonious society by concentrating on creating a social welfare network with full coverage of its citizens and relieving rural poverty by underlining the so-called three agricultural issues (Hong 2016, pp. 171–183).[1] The Party and the central government made a macroplan for these issues by continuingly incorporating them into the tenth and eleventh Five-Year national development plans. These documents, therefore, offer an overview of the issues that preoccupied the authority in those ten years.

In the suggestions for the Plan of the 10th National Economic and Social Development (2001–2005), the CCCCP, among other economic development concerns, stressed the fundamental role of agricultural issues (Sect. 1), the development of western areas (Sect. 6), and the completion of the social security system, employment promotion, and improvement of living standards (Sect. 13 and 14) (Zhu 2001, pp. 506–508). These suggestions were then keenly adopted by the central government (Mahoney 2008, pp. 99–128; Tang 2010).[2]

In his report on the tenth national economic and social development program, Premier Zhu included the concerns mentioned in the CCCCP's suggestions as the key focus of the State Council. He stressed the central position of the 'three agricultural' issues by advocating a comprehensive plan covering issues such as economic structural adjustments, rural financial support, public infrastructure construction, and poverty relief (Sect. 3). The plan for the development of the western region stressed the construction of infrastructure and urged the eastern region to offer support (Sect. 5). The completion of the social security system paid vital attention to the conditions of labourers laid off due to SOE reform, the public pension system, unemployment insurance, and public health insurance (Sect. 8) (Zhu 2001, pp. 754–778 and 772–774).

The CCCCP suggested that the eleventh Five-Year Plan should continue to focus on constructing the new socialist rural regions (Sect. 3), coordinating regional development (Sect. 5), improving employment, and accelerating the completion of the social security system; these were deemed indispensable components in establishing a harmonious socialist society (Sect. 9) (Wen 2005, pp. 1061–1085). These concerns were endorsed by the government in the following years (Roberts 2012). In the report on governmental work, then premier Wen explained the key points of the program outline of the eleventh national economic and social development plan: the central position of the 'three agricultural' issues, a coordinated regional development plan, and the construction of a harmonious society (with social security construction incorporated into it) (Wen 2005, pp. 1044–1060).

In 2008, Premier Wen reviewed the advancement of social security over the preceding five years and stated, in his government work report, that by 2007, millions of people in urban areas were covered by the public pension system (200 million) and public health insurance system (180 million) and over 730 million rural people had joined the new rural cooperative health insurance system (*xinnonghe*)—the direct benefit of these policies was that they incorporated people who had formerly been outside the public welfare and health system and had to rely on family support after retirement or illness into a national welfare system (Wen 2008b, pp. 299–300).

Given the changing focus of the central authority and enlightened by Goldmann (2020), this chapter, by tracing the development of the labour market and the welfare system, centres the Chinese government's efforts at social integration to examine the role of law in building an inclusive economy and facilitating social integration.

6.1.2 Reform of the Labour Market

To understand the Chinese labour market, we would lose perspective if we missed the hidden unequal institutional arrangement of household status because the structure of the Chinese labour market was closely intertwined with this unique household registration system (also called *hukou*).[3] This peculiar *hukou* system effectively divided the Chinese population into two categories—urban and rural. Moreover, due to policy bias, *hukou* identities were also linked to job opportunities, with rural residents facing strict limitations on seeking job opportunities in cities and being disfavoured in the labour market. Additionally, in China, the welfare benefits people are entitled to, even currently, are related to the category and location of the working units to which they belong.

In summary, to understand China's efforts to build a socially integrative community, especially the development of the welfare system, the transformation of its household registration system and the transition of its labour market must be considered. Thus, prior to the discussion of the welfare system, this section introduces the transformation of China's labour market and the *hukou* system.

6.1.2.1 The *Hukou* System and Labour Mobility

The changing flow of the labour force, or the transformation of the labour market, in the Chinese context served as an intersection where the social welfare system and economic strategies clashed. Specifically, the demand for economic growth required a certain level of labour flow that responded freely to market mechanisms. However, the old Chinese welfare system, combined with the unique household registration system, severely curbed and, for a period, even prevented labour force movement between rural and urban areas. Hence, the transformation of the Chinese labour market in the reform years also demonstrates China's tendency towards a fledgling welfare system—a response to unbalanced economic development over the years.

Among the many issues of the labour market, two aspects are of special significance to economic prosperity and social stability: freedom of labour movement and the improvement of welfare benefits for workers of rural origin. The former opened the doors of more advanced urban areas to rural workers, and the latter helped rural labourers integrate into their host cities. The following section traces the changes in these two points in the reform years.

The Chinese household registration system was designed in 1958 as a tool of social control. It was intended mainly to prevent migration from rural to urban areas (Leung and Xu 2015, pp. 23–24). Unlike the household system of other countries, the Chinese *hukou* was heavily attached to widely differentiated social benefits. Holding urban *hukou* status meant one had access to staple foods and meats, commodity grain, and better health and education services (Chan and Zhang 1999, p. 821). Hence, the system was much more than a statistical administration tool, as it also served the then political-economic goals.

However, after the rise of the industrial sector in urban areas and uneven national development due to regionally biased development strategies, labour demand became highly concentrated in eastern coastal regions. These developed regions, with more job opportunities and higher income, led to the flow of labour from less developed areas flooding into rich regions (Lin et al. 2004). However, under the rural–urban binary household system, urban employment was linked to household status. As mentioned before, rural residents, in principle, were not allowed to seek job opportunities in cities (Young 2013, pp. 53–60). Therefore, to enable the surplus labour force from rural areas to work in urban regions, institutional obstacles that curbed labour mobility and integration in Chinese society had to be lifted.

The old *hukou* registration system had a few channels for conversion. For instance, an individual could convert his or her rural *hukou* to urban *hukou* if he or she was employed by an SOE, received a university degree, or received admissions issued by urban *hukou* registrars (Regulations on Household Registration, Article 10). These thresholds of *hukou* conversion proved to be too high for the majority of the rural population and were therefore an unrealistic option for mobilizing China's abundant rural labour force for economic construction. In response to the tension between economic demand and institutional barriers created by keeping intact the system's fundamental features, i.e., its linkage with welfare benefits, some new types of *hukou* were created (Young 2013, pp. 66–77).

From the mid-1980s to 1992, the Chinese government developed several new types of *hukou* categories, of which the important ones were the temporary residence permit and the blue-stamp *hukou*, in a bid to mobilize the labour flow. In principle, rural residents above 16 years old who lived in cities for more than three months were eligible to apply for the temporary residence permit (Fu 2012, pp. 327–332). In other words, in effect, it opened urban employment and business opportunities to rural populations without additional conditions. However, while freedom of movement was granted, holders of such residential permits were excluded from the urban social welfare systems (Zhang and Li 2018), and rural workers holding temporary residence permits were denied access to the pension system, public health, and education system that urban residents enjoy.

In 1992, a new category called the blue-stamp *hukou* was designed (Ministry of Public Security 1992; Shanghai Government 1993). While it was not a regular *hukou* status and was subject to annual inspection, after some years, normally three to five years, it could be converted to regular urban *hukou* upon fulfilling certain conditions.[4] It was aimed at investors and urban real estate buyers. Unlike the temporary residence permit, it included some social benefits and rights. For instance, blue-stamp *hukou* holders were entitled to access to the public education system in cities, open businesses, and participate in other social benefits enjoyed by urban *hukou* holders.[5]

Owing to these institutional renewals, urban–rural migration increased dramatically following the lifting of movement control via the *hukou* system. The number of interprovincial migrants doubled in a decade, jumping from 11.83 million in the late 1980s to 27.53 million before the end of the twentieth century (Lin et al. 2004). In 1995, approximately 80 million working people in urban areas were from rural households, and 44 million held temporary resident permits (Renmin Daily 9 July 1995, p. 1). In 1997, a pilot scheme of *hukou* reform took place in small cities and towns. It allowed 450 selected towns and small cities to grant urban *hukou* to qualified rural residents (Ministry of Public Security 1997). It was estimated that in 2001, the number of migrant workers seeking job opportunities in cities reached over 90 million (Fan and Qie 2002).

However, while these newly created types of *hukou* and policy concerns helped the system channel the labour force from rural areas to cities, these institutional designs, except for the high-threshold blue-stamp *hukou*, did not help rural workers truly integrate into their host cities, as they were excluded from urban welfare systems and their children were denied entry into the local public education system (Guo and Zhao 2019).[6] This situation would be addressed by the Hu-Wen administration, which focused on delinking the social welfare benefit from *hukou* identities and thus converting rural workers into urban residents—the most fundamental effort that helped rural workers connect with their host cities.

6.1.2.2 Legal Framework for Labour Rights

The political concerns over these social issues soon translated into laws as the government deemed that the timing had matured. As a result, the Chinese legal system received a block of welfare legal documents as laws concerning social issues were overwhelmingly promulgated in this period. Broadly speaking, two main clusters of laws that emerged during the first decade of the twenty-first century manifested the legal front in addressing social issues—the rights of rural labourers and social insurance for people who were formerly outside the welfare system. This section introduces the legal system that created a legal defence web for people whose concerns had been neglected at the time when the economy was taking off. Below is an overview of the legal system for labour rights; social welfare laws are discussed soon after.

The cluster of labour-related laws, except for the first Chinese Labour Law enacted in 1994, appeared in this decade. It included the Labour Contract Law (2007), the Employment Promotion Law (2007), and the Labour Dispute Mediation and Arbitration Law (2008). Together with the Labour Law, these laws constituted the legal framework for labour rights. It was the legal response to the increased labour flow that had resulted from loosened control of the *hukou* system—as large numbers of rural labourers moved into more industrialized urban areas, the deficiencies of the Chinese labour law system in protecting workers of rural origin, such as unfavourable working situations and wage default, were constantly experienced by rural workers.

As stated above, the purposes of these laws were, among other things, 'to promote economic development…and social stability' (Employment Promotion Law 2007, Article 1), 'to construct and develop harmonious and stable labour relationships' (Labour Contract Law 2007, Article 1), and 'to facilitate the stability of labour relationships' (Labour Dispute Mediation and Arbitration Law 2008, Article 1). To achieve these goals, the Labour Law first offered general protection for workers and employers who formed labour relationships within Chinese territory (Article 2). The law granted workers within this legal framework a work shift of no more than 8 work hours per day and no more than 44 h per week (Article 36). In addition to public holidays (Article 40), employers must guarantee at least one day off per week (Article 38). Additionally, extra payments must be made for overtime work (Article 44). For those who have continuously worked for over a year, paid annual leave must be granted (Article 45).

Wages shall be distributed on the principle of 'equal pay for equal work' (Article 46 (1)), and the state adopted a minimum wage system, although the specific wage level was to be determined by each province (Article 48). Wages must be paid in cash (Article 50) and be raised as economic development advances (Article 46 (2)). In addition to providing a safe and sound working environment in general (Chap. 6) and special protections for female and minor workers (Chap. 7), employers, in cooperation with the state, must establish vocational training mechanisms to help workers develop and improve their working skills (Article 66–68). Furthermore, workers are entitled to social insurance at the time when they 'retire, suffer diseases or injuries, become disabled during work or suffer occupational diseases, become jobless, or give birth' (Article 73).

In addition to the substantial rights listed above, the law laid down formal rights for parties involved in particular labour relationships. Of significance were the legal force of the written form of labour contracts with specified contents (Article 19), conditions and procedures of dissolving a labour contract (Article 26), and procedures of labour dispute settlement and its legal force (Chap. 10). In addition, the legal framework for labour relationships was later supplemented by two specific laws on labour contracts (2007) and labour dispute mediation and arbitration (2008).

The Labour Contract Law has detailed legal regulations for each stage of labour contracts, from formation to enforcement, change, dissolution, and termination, together with particular regulations for special types of labour relationships such as collective contracts, worker dispatch service, and part-time employment. The most controversial rule for both sides of labour relations is Article 14, which stipulates legal conditions for labour contracts without a fixed term (Dong 2007, 2008a; Wang and Huang 2008). According to the rule, in addition to the situation in which both sides voluntarily form a contract, the law mandates that employers conclude a non-fixed-term labour contract with an employee under any of the following circumstances: the employee has worked for the employer for ten full years consecutively (Article 14 (2–1/2)); the labour contract is to be renewed after two fixed-term labour contracts have been concluded consecutively (Article 14 (2–3)), and the employer fails to sign a written labour contract with an employee after the lapse of one full year from the date when the employee began to work (Article 14 (3)).

The Labour Dispute Mediation and Arbitration Law expands legal regulations on the issues of dispute mediation and arbitration from a mere seven articles in the Labour Law into an independent statute. Building upon a three-dimensional dispute resolution mechanism laid down by the Labour Law—mediation (optional), arbitration (the precondition of bringing a case to court), and lawsuit—the arbitration law further institutionalizes the procedures of mediation and arbitration, making them standard and formal procedures of labour disputes. Therefore, once disputes arise, the parties can, in either oral or written form (Article 12), file a case with a local mediation committee (Article 10) and have the case mediated by citizens with legal knowledge (Article 11). Once an agreement is achieved, a written formal agreement is produced, although there are only soft constraints on both sides (Article 14). In the case of underperformance of the agreement, either party can bring the case to arbitration (Article 15).

The arbitration of labour disputes is administered at municipal and provincial levels (Article 17) and is free of charge (Article 53). Eligible arbitrators are selected from a pool of experienced legal professionals, such as former judges, law teachers, and lawyers with more than three years of practice experience. (Article 20). Before reaching a legal decision, arbitrators are obliged to mediate (Article 42), and once the adjudication is made, it is final (Article 47) and can be appealed only to the court (Article 48). Hence, after thirty years of economic reform and social transformation, the legal network for labour rights was created, with protections for substantive rights and procedures.

6.1.3 Reform of the Social Insurance System and Its Rules

The term 'social insurance' in the Chinese context refers to a social welfare system that incorporates five categories of social insurance, namely, the old-age pension, public health insurance, unemployment insurance, occupational injury insurance, and maternity insurance. Currently, it is compulsory social insurance and is reaching its target of full coverage. The concern of this section is the development of the four categories of social insurance (excluding maternity insurance) that the government has pledged to build for the entire Chinese population.

As discussed in the previous chapters, China had undergone over twenty years of economic reform by the turn of the century, sweeping almost all economic sectors, especially the industrial and commercial sectors. However, these economic changes did not leave society intact, and Chinese society evolved in an equally fundamental way (Saich 2004, pp. 268–274). A consequence of unequal labour rights between rural and urban residents was their respective welfare rights; in the Chinese context, the category of social insurance one enjoys. As mentioned, rural workers were denied access to urban welfare benefits and lived peripherally in their host cities. As the government perceived, these issues would cause social instability and jeopardize the fruits of the economic success achieved in recent decades (Hu 2003, pp. 483–484; Wen 2008a, pp. 699–718). Hence, the political focus shifted in part to addressing social issues before further economic reforms. The term 'harmonious society', as introduced in the above section, refers to, among other concerns, building a comprehensive social insurance system.

The pension and public health insurance systems, similar to the urban and rural systems, were substantially different; each is discussed in a separate section. The other two types, unemployment and occupational injury insurance, which had less regional disparity, are introduced without regional differentiation. By and large, all four categories of social insurance have experienced substantial changes over the years, be it the coverage of insurance, financial issues, or levels of protection. From a regional perspective, both urban and rural residents currently have many comprehensive social protections compared to the days before the reform, whether livelihood issues after retirement or public health concerns.

While all types of social insurance deserve equal attention, this study pays particular attention to the pension and public health systems, as both matter significantly to sustainable economic development and overall social stability. The other two are introduced before the end of the chapter.

6.1.3.1 Public Pension System

Before the reform, the then central authority issued the Regulations of Labour Insurance of the PRC in 1951. This was the first legal document for national-level social security concerns, and the issues covered included pension, health, occupational injury, and maternity (Article 12–16). However, it was not intended for all workers but applied only to particular state-owned enterprises and other economic entities with more than 100 employees (Article 2). This system was completely supported by enterprises, which were obliged to submit an amount equivalent to 3% of the total salary of their employees to the All-China Federation of Trade Union each month, and any disguised deduction of the amount from workers' salaries was explicitly prohibited (Article 7–9). The designated retirement age was 60 for male workers and 50 for females. Depending on the length of service, the pension rate ranged from 50 to 70% of the salary and would be dispensed until the worker's death (Article 15). This system lasted until 1969, when the national social insurance system was abolished and the burden of social security was shifted to individual enterprises (Ministry of Finance 1969).

Before unfolding the reforms, it is helpful to briefly examine the basic structure of the current Chinese pension system and the particular difficulties the country faced. Broadly speaking, the pension system has two accounts: the pooling account and the personal account. For example, in Zhejiang Province, the contribution to both accounts combined is a maximum of 28% of wages and is paid monthly by individual workers (8%) and their employers (maximum 20%)[7] by direct deduction from their monthly salaries (Social Insurance Law 2010, Article 12). The 8% paid by individuals goes to personal accounts, and the amount paid by employers goes to the pooling account. To be eligible to receive a pension after retirement, a worker must contribute to both accounts for at least 15 years (Social Insurance Law 2010, Article 16). This system may be functional in an ideal situation. However, if one considers the older generations who joined the workforce before the system existed and thus did not contribute as much as younger generations, the pension system was, in fact, severely short of funds to support the whole retiring group (Dong 2008b, pp. 33–38). The fund shortage was acute, and redesigning the system was a pressing issue, as China was foreseeably stepping into a greying society due to its decades of birth control. As briefly mentioned above, the pension system differed significantly in urban and rural areas due to the *hukou* system, as the following review shows.

Urban Households

The Chinese urban social welfare system has two parallel subsystems. One is for those employed in the public sector, such as governmental officials, teachers in public schools, and doctors (workers in SOEs were not counted as public employees). It was a privileged system established following the end of the Cultural Revolution and reformed in 2015 (State Council 2015).[8] This group was relatively small and was regulated by a separate set of policies and laws. What concerns this study is the pension systems for the majority of Chinese people outside the public system—those working in the private sector. This group includes workers employed by SOEs, collective enterprises, joint ventures, and other private enterprises. While they were covered by a less favourable national social welfare system at the time in comparison to those working in the public sector (Dong 2008b, pp. 33–38), people who had access to the system and were thus entitled to pensions were already the lucky ones, as the coverage of this system was relatively low in those years. The primary concern of the reform was to expand the coverage and incorporate those who had been outside the system.

By and large, policies at the national level evolved over the years to incrementally complete China's social insurance system. As explicitly stated in different policy papers, the general goals were to gradually build a social welfare system that corresponds to the developmental levels of the economy, fulfils the basic livelihood needs of people after retirement, and covers different types of employment (State Council 1991, 1995, 1997). Since the early 1990s, regional experimental reforms of the system have been searching for a workable structure.[9]

In 1991, upon reflecting on the old pension system, the State Council considered it necessary to reform the old pension system to ensure that it was in line with national economic and social development and thus launched the first reform of China's welfare system since 1978 (State Council 1991). By then, the system covered approximately 57 million workers and supported 12 million retired workers (Dong 2008b, p. 26). The most significant change made was to create a three-level contributor structure for the pension system. As mentioned above, the prereform pension system was supported by the state and enterprises; individual workers were exempted from contributing to the fund. The new policy fundamentally changed the funding structure, and a three-party contribution system, namely, the state, enterprises, and individuals, was designed. The initial contribution burden for individuals was a maximum of 3% of monthly wages and was expected to increase as economic development continued.

In 1995 and 1997, the State Council issued two policy documents to further complete the social insurance system. Both reiterated the general goals of building a pension system that is economically affordable, fits China's socialist market economy, and covers different types of workers (State Council 1995, 1997). As China is a large country with wide regional disparity, it proved too challenging to build a uniform national system for all Chinese people at the time; therefore, many different practices coexisted in the pension system during that period. According to a survey conducted in 1996, at least three different pension structures were operating in different provinces (He 1997, p. 57). This regional disparity was identified as an issue to be solved in a policy paper in 1997 (Dong 2008b, p. 49).[10]

Nevertheless, without a nationwide coordinating network, the pension coverage issues, while reiterated by the government throughout the years, had not been addressed substantially. A large number of Chinese people still had no social insurance of any sort by 2000, and this became a focal point of the Hu-Wen administration in the coming years because the goal of building up a harmonious society required that the government comprehensively include all people living in China. Furthermore, as a system restored only after 1978, the pension fund had minimal room to manoeuvre to support older people who had joined the workforce before the system was built

(Guo 2003).[11] The funding shortage was especially severe in regions with a large ageing population or that were economically disadvantaged. To eliminate lurking dangers that might result from insufficient funds, the central government implemented some experimental policies in the three northeast provinces, Liaoning, Jilin, and Heilongjiang, because of a lack of potential solutions (Dong 2008b, pp. 39–40).

In 2005, the State Council published a resolution to address, among other things, these lingering and unstable aspects of the system. It stated that ‘from now on and in the following period, the coverage enlargement of the pension system shall concentrate on workers in non-public sectors, urban individual businesses holders, and freelancers’ and ‘to gradually fill those empty personal accounts, … to continue the experiment in the three northeast provinces and other regions should work out their own solutions for the issue of “empty personal accounts”’ (State Council 2005b).[12]

Whereas the ‘empty personal accounts’ proved to be a rather hot potato for the central government, following the specific policy concern mentioned above, the coverage issue was relatively well addressed nationwide over the years. In 2011, the State Council further developed an ambitious political goal of achieving full coverage of the social pension system for urban citizens by 2012 (State Council 2005c). This document was of great significance in that it broke the work status constraints and incorporated all urban residents regardless of their employment situation—the final step in reaching the goal of a full-coverage pension scheme. As the national data show, the coverage ratio in urban areas reached over 90%, and more than one billion people joined the pension system.[13] However, while the urban pension system was a constant item on the governmental agenda, the rural population was less lucky (Giles 2021).

Rural Households

Rural society is crucial for China, not only because of its economic contributions but also, most importantly, because the large size of the rural population means that the well-being of rural people is the actual indicator of the overall living conditions of the Chinese people. Rural *hukou* status was the deciding factor in the welfare benefits to which the population was entitled. In the Mao era, the social welfare of rural areas, under the Standard Charter of the Advanced Agriculture Cooperatives (1956), was covered by the commune system plus some special policies designed for disadvantaged groups, such as the so-called five guarantees, referring to food, clothes, housing, medical attention, and funeral services, for disadvantaged people who had difficulty making a living. This community-based security network, with financial support drawn from the revenue of local agriculture cooperatives (Dong 2008b, p. 152), was disrupted by the Cultural Revolution.

From the dissolution of the People’s Commune until 1992, in rural areas, there was no systematically institutionalized social insurance system in rural regions; only some wealthy counties experimented with community-based trail-out of pension systems (Dong 2008b, p. 158). These modes were affordable only in a few affluent towns because they were funded mainly by local collectives, whereas the state, at that stage, was not investing money in the pension pool. In other words, rural pensions were operating in a self-sufficient way in a few economically advanced places. By

1989, approximately 190 towns had built such a collective-based pension system, covering roughly 900 thousand rural people (Zhao 2002).

In the 1990s, the first national-level trail-out of rural pensions was implemented based on a policy paper issued by the Ministry of Civil Affairs in 1992 (Ministry of Civil Affairs 1992). It clarified that rural pension funds relied mainly on individual payment, subsidized by collective revenue; the state would offer only policy preferences. In other words, the funding sources were similar to trail-outs in the 1980s, and no state money was pooled—peasants had to rely on themselves. Also worth noting was that the policy accentuated the importance of family support for old-age care (Ministry of Civil Affairs 1992, part 1). According to the document, individuals were to receive a pension from age 60 until death, and regulatory committees were set up in each county to monitor the system's operation. By 1992, nationwide, 170 counties had established pension systems based on the guidance of the paper, covering approximately 35 million peasants (Deng and Liu 2007, p. 103); this number reached 74.5 million in 1997 (Ministry of Civil Affairs 1997). Unlike the urban pension system, the rural system relied mainly on individual accounts, and there was no pooling account, as in the urban system. Hence, the so-called rural pension system was not social insurance but was more similar to a commercial pension system. It was mismanaged, and corruption was extensively observed in a commercial insurance survey conducted by the State Council in 1997. This led the State Council to conclude that 'currently, China's rural region was not prepared for universal social insurance', and related projects that had unfolded since 1992 were halted in 1999 (State Council 1999). Nevertheless, the situation was slightly better for those who worked in TVEs, as employees in collectives were covered by a separate legal framework called Measures of Pension Insurance System for the Employees of Township and Village Enterprises (1992).

From 2003 onwards, as an institutional design, a gradual resumption of rural social insurance took place in the Hu-Wen administration. It was announced in the sixteenth Party report in 2002 and was expected to unfold in a patchwork approach. The first places in which it was implemented were regions deemed economically capable and places where local peasants were in desperate need of such a system due to land expropriation in their areas (Ministry of Labour and Social Security 2003). As a result, rural areas in the southeast began implementing local rural social pension policies because of their better economic situations (Dong 2008b, p. 162). By 2005, 54.4 million peasants had joined the social insurance system, accounting for only 4.1% of the rural population (Ministry of Labour and Social Security 2005). Suffice it to say, the minimal rural pension system covered only those who were economically better off, and those living in interior regions and who were more in need of such a system still had to wait a few years.

In 2009, the government built a modern-style rural social pension system named Neo Rural Insurance (*xinnongbao*). As the policy paper stated, the principle of this system was to construct a social welfare network that 'guarantees subsistence needs, wide-coverage, flexible, and sustainable' in a rural insurance pension system to 'gradually ensure rural old-age support' (State Council 2009). The system was open to all rural residents above 16 years old (except students) who did not have an urban pension account, and participation in it was voluntary. General coverage targets were approximately 10% of counties nationwide in the first year of the program and full coverage by the end of 2020.

The newly designed pension system was composed of basic accounts and individual accounts, and the funding was to be pooled by individuals,[14] collectives, and the state together. In contrast to the urban system, the individual account in the rural system was pooled by both individuals and their collectives, and the state entirely funded the basic account. As a policy adjustment for regional inequality, the State Council provided clear policy support for less developed regions—the state would provide a 100% subsidy for the basic account for rural residents living in the central and western regions[15] and a 50% subsidy for people living in comparatively well-off provinces. This preferential policy substantially addressed inequalities that had been increasing due to China's uneven economic development since 1978.

As in the urban system, the minimum duration of contribution years was set at 15 years. From age 60 on, rural residents were entitled to receive a monthly pension until death, and those already age 60 in 2009 could still receive a basic pension without paying extra contribution. By the end of 2011, this new rural pension system covered 300 million rural residents, reaching an average coverage of 70%.[16]

6.1.3.2 Public Health Insurance

Urban Residents

Before the economic reform, China's urban region had two parallel health care systems for workers from different working units. In those years, both systems were fully funded by the state. However, they were not of national coverage, as only selected cities, normally economically better-off ones, were chosen for pilot programmes of the health insurance system.

One of the dual health care systems was for people working in the public sector. It was called 'free public medical service', meaning that all kinds of medical bills would be paid by public money. People eligible for this system were those working in all levels and branches of governmental offices and public institutions such as schools, research institutes, and hospitals and initially their family members as well (Dong 2008b, p. 52). The other system was called '*laobao*' and was open to labourers working in entities such as SOEs, joint ventures, and private enterprises. Medical bills, as the central government stipulated, would be paid by these enterprises.[17] While different types of workers were served, their coverage was similar (Dong 2008b, p. 53). Additionally, in both systems, individuals were not asked to pay for their medical expenses, nor did they have to pay an insurance fee of any sort. Hence, technically speaking, these systems were not health insurance in the common sense. They were more a type of welfare benefit directly offered by the state due to the beneficiaries' working status. Such a dual health care system existed for approximately 30 years, and by the end of the 1970s, the two systems covered over 75% of urban workers, both working and retired, amounting to 137 million people (114 million under the *laobao* system and 23 million under the free public health service system) (Dong 2008b, p. 53).

As they were fully funded by the state and enterprises, the two systems turned out to be too economically burdensome. The financial difficulties soon became acute, and throughout the 1960s, the State Council issued several policy papers to delimit the coverage of free medical services and to designate a proportion of bills for individuals to pay (Ministry of Public Health and Ministry of Finance 1965; State Council 1957a). Nevertheless, as these minor changes did not affect the funding structure, these systems were still too expensive, especially for enterprises. The situation became particularly worse when SOEs were delinked from the public fund and put on the track of self-sufficiency as part of the SOE reforms. Therefore, new structures to support a sustainable health care system were needed.

From the 1980s until 1998, the state tried different health care insurance mechanisms in selected cities or provinces. For instance, in 1989, Shenzhen and Hainan tried to incorporate health care into the social insurance system and thus initiated a comprehensive reform of the welfare system.[18] In 1994, the State Council issued a document aiming to reform workers' health insurance system and selected two cities for the experiment (State Commission for Restructuring et al. 1994). The experiment intended to construct a health care system similar to the pension system—combining personal accounts and social accounts and trying out a prototype for national health insurance.

At the end of 1998, the State Council issued a decision stating a political goal of building a national basic health insurance system. The insurance mechanism was designed to be paid both by employers (6% of salary) and employees (2% of salary), thus reducing the financial burden of enterprises (State Council 1998). It was designed to cover all types of working units in urban areas, public and private. After that, the population possessing health insurance jumped from 20 million in 1999, the first year of implementation, to 137 million by the end of 2005, a nearly sevenfold increase (National Bureau of Statistics and Ministry of Labour and Social Security 2005, pp. 580–581; National Bureau of Statistics and Ministry of Labour and Social Security 2006, Sect. 11–25; State Council 2009).

Nevertheless, while its coverage expanded as reform deepened, this health insurance system was not open to citizens who were not employed by the public sector or enterprises, such as individual business owners, freelancers, and housewives. A relief package was created in 2007 when the State Council issued another policy paper for carrying out experiments in selected cities (State Council 2007); following this, the number of urban residents covered by public health insurance doubled, jumping from 13,783 in 2005 to 25,226 in 2011 (Ministry of Health 2012, p. 318).

Rural Residents

Before the reform, in rural areas, approximately 2234 county-level hospitals and 51,600 outpatient clinics were operating nationwide (Zhang et al. 1994). An early attempt at health insurance took place in 1955 when a local health centre in Shanxi Province tried a cooperative approach to its collective health system by pooling funds from individual peasants and their collectives for medical purposes. A similar practice was duplicated in other provinces (Dong 2008b, p. 68) and was applied nationwide after Mao's endorsement (CCCCP 1965). Public health care was then incorporated into the People's Commune as one of its critical functions for commune life. Until 1976, 90% of production teams had a medical system, and 85% of the rural population was covered (Li 2002, p. 74). After the Cultural Revolution, such a cooperative health system was institutionalized by the Rule of Rural Cooperative Medical Service (provisional) in 1979. However, it was poorly managed and declined rapidly in the 1980s. According to a survey conducted in 1989, only 4.8% of villages still had cooperative medical services (Gu et al. 1998).

Throughout the 1990s, while the central government was claiming to develop a rural health care system and while many research and policy agendas covered related issues, no concrete measure was deployed to materialize the construction of such a system. In 1996, only 9.6% of villages in China had some sort of cooperative system covering medical expenses, and, worse still, the majority of them were in affluent coastal areas (Qian 2002). The needs of those who resided in the vast poorer regions were not addressed throughout the 1990s, and by 2002, nearly 80% of the rural population had no health insurance at all (Statistical Information Centre of the Ministry of Public Health 2005). Regardless of low coverage and poor management, as reported, the mechanism tried out in these places—pooling money from both individuals and collectives—proved to be a workable framework for rural areas.

In 2002, drawing on previous experiences, the State Council issued a decision that set a political goal of building a basic rural cooperative health insurance system nationwide by 2010 (CCCCP and State Council 2002, pp. 756–766). Shortly afterwards, in 2003, a more concrete system arrangement for the cooperative was laid out (State Council 2003b). For instance, the funding was to be pooled at the county level, and the funding was to be contributed by individuals, collectives, and governments, both central and local. This program, also called *xinnonghe*, was officially initiated in 2003, expanded gradually, and had achieved almost full coverage by 2011, as over 832 million people, accounting for 96% of the total rural population, had joined the program (Ministry of Health 2012, p. 317). The financial input of the government was also expanding rapidly. In 2003, the fiscal contribution to the fund was only 10 *yuan* per person per year; it was raised to 80 *yuan* in 2008 and 240 *yuan* in 2012 (Ministry of Public Health and Ministry of Finance 2008; Ministry of Public Health, Ministry of Finance, and Ministry of Civil Affairs 2012).

6.1.3.3 Unemployment and Occupational Injury Insurance

Unemployment Insurance

Unemployment was not a genuine concern during the years when the economy was centrally planned, as the allocation of the labour force was an integral part of the planned economy. Thus, for a few decades, the state was in charge of arranging workers into different working units to serve the purposes of the economy and rearranging them when unemployment occurred. However, some policy papers published in the 1950s dealt with related issues, such as provisional measures of relief and reallocation for unemployed workers (Ministry of Labour 1950; State Council 1957b). In this system, neither labour nor enterprises had autonomy in employment issues; on the other hand, unemployment insurance was technically unnecessary.

The planned economy retreated as market reform took place, as did the uniformly orchestrated appointment system. Unemployment became institutionally possible, and the necessity of related insurance came to light (Hurst 2009). In 1986, the State Council created an institutional design for unemployment insurance for SOE workers (State Council 1986). As the name suggests, this provision applied only to SOE workers, and three years after it was announced, by 1989, approximately 136 thousand unemployed people had received relief payments, an amount equivalent to approximately 25% of the average SOE salary (Dong 2008b, p. 95). This system operated throughout the 1990s, with only moderate updates in 1993 (State Council 1993). In 1998, when the SOE reform resulted in a considerable number of layoffs, this system offered timely help for over fifteen million workers (Dong 2008b, p. 96).

In 1999, the State Council issued the Regulations of Unemployment Insurance, which made significant revisions to the previous framework. For instance, the new regulation enlarged the eligible group for the payment from previously merely SOE workers to employees of all types of enterprises; job holders in private enterprises and joint ventures were from then on entitled to payment when they became unemployed. Moreover, the regulation set a flexible and more considerate range for the payment amount, putting the payment amount between the minimum wage and minimum subsistence level, according to local developmental levels. However, protection under the regulation was aimed at workers who had formerly had regular employment, and people working in areas other than the above types of entities, for instance, freelancers, graduates who had not yet found jobs, and workers with rural residency, were excluded.

Occupational Injury Insurance

The earliest legal protection for occupational injury appeared in 1951; the Regulation of Labour Insurance, issued by the then State Council, made preliminary arrangements for work-related injury and death (Article 12). It was supplemented by a ministry-level regulation for occupational diseases issued by the Ministry of Health in 1957 (Ministry of Public Health 1957).

However, the 1951 regulation covered only certain types of economic entities (Article 2), i.e., enterprises with over one hundred employees, workers in public transportation systems, and state-owned construction companies; people who worked for smaller enterprises or joint ventures were not protected. Undoubtedly, it was inadequate as the economy developed, and the coverage was expanded along with the transformation of the economy. In the 1980s, several experimental insurance programmes were tested in approximately ten cities. The guideline of the new injury insurance was to build a system combining occupational injury insurance, prevention, and recovery, improving the insurance coverage and payment level (Dong 2008b, p. 109).

In 1992, an evaluation standard was issued for occupational injury and diseases. In 1996, a provisional measure to institutionalize occupational injuries was promulgated as a conclusion of the early trials (Ministry of Labour 1996), and city-level public funds were pooled to guarantee payment. These measures applied to all kinds of workers within the Chinese territory, and the definition of occupational injury was expanded to increase its range of protection, including transportation accidents while commuting as work-related injuries. Furthermore, the standard institutionalized an evaluation system for work-related disability levels, making compensation more workable. By 1998, over 35 million workers were protected by insurance (Dong 2008b, p. 111). This provisional measure was translated into the Regulation of Occupational Injury Insurance in 2013, and shortly afterwards, it was also applied to the work injuries of rural workers (Ministry of Labour and Social Security 2004). In 2007, over 121 million workers had potential work-related injuries or disease covered by insurance (Dong 2008b, p. 114).

6.1.3.4 The Legal Structure of Social Welfare Benefits

The legal construction of the social welfare network was underway simultaneously with laws for labourers' rights. Today, the legal systems for social welfare benefits can be divided into two main stages, with the uniform Social Insurance Law promulgated in 2010 as the watershed. Before this, both China's pension system and public health insurance were heavily regulated by policies, with numerous policies targeting different issues, as described in the previous section. On the legal front, the majority of the rules addressing welfare concerns were issued by the State Council as administrative-level regulations addressing particular welfare concerns. Examples are the Regulations on Unemployment Insurance (1999) and the Regulations on Occupational Injuries (2003). Pension and health insurance issues were regulated chiefly at local levels with the general guidance of policy papers issued by the State Council. The 1951 Labour Insurance Law (Article 15–16) and the 1994 Labour Law (Chap. 9) briefly mentioned welfare issues, but both applied only to labourers affiliated with certain types of working units, and people without a formal labour contract were excluded from both systems.

Such institutional inequalities were rectified via a series of rules on welfare rights, culminating with the promulgation of the Social Insurance Law (2010), which formalized the legal institution of social welfare networks. Broadly speaking, the law entitled individuals living within the territory to welfare rights of pension, health care, occupational injury, unemployment, and maternity insurance (Article 2). The law also materialized these welfare benefits by structuring financial and administrative institutions for implementation.

Specifically, beneficiaries, regardless of their occupational status, were entitled to a pension at retirement age if they had contributed to the fund for at least fifteen years (Article 10 and 16), and the pension payment lasts until the death of the beneficiary (Article 17). Furthermore, the law established a triple-party system to guarantee the payment, which obliged individuals, employers, and the state to contribute to the fund (Article 11). The payment was subject to adjustment in the situation of wage increase or inflation (Article 18). For interprovincial labourers, the system ensured that the pension would transfer with the beneficiary (Article 19), which to a great extent guaranteed labour mobility. Health care insurance was institutionalized with formal rules similar to those of the pension system, legalizing beneficiary coverage, the financing mechanism, and the administrative structure. In addition, substantive rules were formulated for excluding certain medical bills, such as third-party liability and overseas medical treatment. (Article 30).

In the case of injury occurring during work, under certain conditions, the victim was entitled to occupational injury insurance benefits under the law. Unlike pension and health care insurance, the injury insurance fund was raised solely from contributions made by employers for this particular purpose (Article 33), and all employers opening businesses within China were obliged to pay occupational injury insurance for their employees (Article 2). To be entitled to the payments, the victim had to follow the appropriate administrative procedures (Article 36). The rules for these administrative procedures were detailed in the Regulations on Occupational Injuries (2003). For a worker to be eligible for the benefit, the injury must be certified as a work-related injury by the Labour Security Administration Department, with supporting documents (Article 18–19). In case of disability, the victim must apply for verification of the degree of physical disability (Chap. 4). These were the preconditions for receiving payment. The regulation was formulated with primarily substantive rules, specifying situations that were or were not applicable to the regulation. Hence, before receiving insurance, the victim must undergo many administrative procedures.

Unemployment insurance benefits were accessible only to employees of urban enterprises who had paid the premium for more than a year and were involuntarily unemployed (Article 45).[19] The benefits were dispensed after unemployment information was registered with the related social insurance department (Article 50). The maximum payment period was limited to twenty-four months, depending on the years of contributions made by the unemployed person and his or her employer (Article 46). While unemployed, the individual would still be covered by health care insurance but exempted from paying the fee (Article 48).

Moreover, institutional behaviour crucial for these welfare benefits, such as collecting premiums, regulating insurance funds, and other administrative tasks, was formalized by general rules and supervised by local governmental branches (Chaps. 7–9). While China had yet to build a judicial review system, legal remedies for wrongful administrative acts could be accessed via administrative procedure laws. For instance, in cases where a related administrative organ failed to fulfil a duty, such as issuing a pension or paying insurance money, the parties were entitled to file an application for administrative reconsideration or to file a lawsuit against the specific administrative entity (Administrative Reconsideration Law, Article 6; Administrative Procedure Law, Article 11).

6.2 Internal Characteristics of the Law

6.2.1 Characteristics of the Economic Relationship

Entering the third decade of economic reform, China's economy took a structural turn from a mainly planned economy featuring state orders to a complex economy featuring diversified economic relations. Whereas the economic structure had taken a market-oriented turn over the years, the labour structure and the labour market lagged behind. Institutional constraints curbed the free movement of the labour force, and the segmented urban–rural welfare system added further barriers that prevented rural residents from seeking employment and settling in economically advanced areas. The focus of economic reform, therefore, in this period shifted to the labour market and the welfare system that mainly impacted rural labour benefits. Hence, this section discusses the characteristics of economic relations in terms of the diversifying structure of the Chinese labour market and changing labour relations due to the complicated labour market.

With the arrival of large numbers of rural-origin workers, the economy was no longer constrained by the local labour force, and the Chinese labour market had become much more diversified by the turn of the century. It was estimated that in 2001, approximately 90 million rural labourers were working in cities (Fan and Qie 2002). To a great extent, this mobility helped the flourishing of the urban economic sector, where employment numbers, especially in the tertiary sector located in coastal regions, rose by almost 50% from 1990 to 2001, while rural employment remained static (National Bureau of Statistics of China 2003, pp. 126–127). Nevertheless, the influx was significant due to the ensuing complication of labour relationships. Unlike the labour relationship formed between the public sector and urban workers, the one between private enterprises and rural workers was usually less formal and sometimes illegal (Congressional Research Service 2016).

One reason was that the diversifying background of the labour force was shaking up the job allocation system, the formality of which was controlled by the state power. Before the reform of SOEs, China had no so-called labour market, as the government assigned jobs to individuals in what could be termed a planned labour allocation system, corresponding to the planned economy (Bian 1994). However, the economic structural reform broke up this allocation system as the state ceded its domination to private enterprises and individuals; this gave birth to the free labour market in the modern sense, and rural workers vigorously entered this market (Naughton 2018, pp. 139–145). Consequently, the Chinese labour market was filled with labourers of multiple origins and thus different labour relations, which brought the related legal system into question (Naughton 2018, pp. 216–219).

In addition to regular labour relations, such as employment by state sectors or regular labour contracts formed between two urban parties, the labour relations formed between rural *hukou* holders and urban employers were constantly found to be outside then legal institutions. These informal labour relations soon became a factor that tested social stability, as labour rights were constantly infringed upon and had no adequate legal protection, such as wage default and inadequate labour protection (Halegua 2008). Moreover, the separation of *hukou* and the welfare system made these newly formed labour relations unstable, with workers with rural backgrounds being excluded from urban public service systems and their children being excluded from local public schools, as mentioned above (Fan and Chen 2014, pp. 17–35).

In retrospect, twenty years of economic reforms had gradually liberated the commodity market and the labour market. However, unlike the former, the emerging labour market faced problems beyond economic terms, such as the social integration and welfare conditions of migrant workers (Xu et al. 2021). These issues were brought to the surface by the gap between existing legal institutions and transforming social practices as a result of the surge in rural workers moving to urban areas. Facing new social issues, the central government, in the first decade of the twenty-first century, actively engaged in building legal institutions to address these problems.

6.2.2 *Formation of the Rules—A Case Study of the Labour Contract Law*

The legal framework for labour-related issues would emerge only in 1994. It was a time when the central government initiated a structural reform of the economy and subsequently reformed the old job-assignment system and the lifelong employment secured by the state sector. In other words, a labour market emerged following the deepening reform of the economic structure. Against this backdrop, the first Chinese Labour Law was enacted. It was the sole national-level law on labour-related issues in the following decade until the Labour Contract Law and the Labour Dispute Mediation and Arbitration Law were passed in 2007–2008. To date, the legal network in China covering labour issues is composed of these three laws plus administrative-level rules and local regulations.

The timeline of these laws suggests that by and large, the legal system concerning labour-related issues has developed substantively over the years. It developed from a singular Labour Law, which lightly touched on issues related to a raft of rules and measures concerning certain labour rights, to a legal system structured by multiple levels of laws for different types of concerns. This section takes the Labour Contract Law as an example to examine the internal characteristics of the law.

Overview of the Labour Contract Law

The Labour Contract Law was created with several goals. First, while not expressed explicitly in the law, it was promulgated against the social background of mounting wage defaults, especially in cases concerning rural labourers who formed a factual labour relationship with employers without signing formal labour contracts.[20] Hence, the central purpose of the law, as stated in Article 1, was to 'clarify the rights and duties of both parties of labour contracts, protect the legal rights of the labourers, and build and develop harmonious and stable labour relationships'.

Before discussing the law, let us first consider an overview of the structure of the law. Like the uniform contract law for economic transactions, the 2007 Labour Contract Law outlined its contents along the timeline of contracts, from the rules of formation, enforcement and changes in labour contracts to rules concerning dissolution and termination actions (Chaps. 2–4). Additionally, a chapter provided special rules for three particular types of labour relations: collective contracts, worker dispatches, and part-time employment (Chap. 5). By and large, the law created mixed rules, with some adopting a formal style and others substantiated by listing concrete situations for application.

Formal Characteristics of the Labour Contract Law

The formal characteristics of the law were most visible in rules concerning the validity of critical stages of contractual behaviour, for instance, the rule of a legally valid form of formulating, changing, and dissolving labour contracts.

Specifically, labourers, regardless of the types of industry they belonged to or the types of organizations they worked for, would find that their contractual labour rights were protected by the law as long as they had formed a formal written labour contract with their employers (Article 10). In other words, the rules for a legally valid labour contract were universally applicable to different types of economic or social organizations, whether corporations or partnerships, privately owned or state-owned. Similarly, the specific types of industry, whether commercial companies, specialized service agencies, or manufacturing firms, were irrelevant to the validity of labour contracts. The emphasis on format guaranteed the general applicability of the rules to various types of labour contracts in various types of industries.

In a similar vein, contract changes would be valid as long as they were made in written form, and the only condition the law stipulated for changes was that they be made in a 'negotiated agreement between the employer and the labour' (Article 35). That is, the law was hands-off regarding substantive factors related to such changes, for instance, specific reasons for change or the particular contents of changes. The law was concerned with the format of change—the written form. Hence, the rule achieved universality of application by leaving substantive elements involved in changing a labour contract outside its realm.

A contract can typically end in many possible ways. For example, it may end because of the expiration of the contract, the dissolution of the employer, or an employee's situation, such as retirement or death. Additionally, the contract may be dissolved by the will of one of the parties, regardless of whether the agreed-upon working years have been completed. However, the Chinese Labour Contract Law adopted a divergent attitude towards the two parties on the latter issue. The law granted labourers a formal right to exit from a labour contract as long as they offered their employer thirty days' written notice before leaving (Article 37). Therefore, labourers found themselves in a relatively free situation regarding their employers because the law placed no conditions on reasons for dissolving a labour contract; instead, the law subjected the right to leave a working position to formal rules—a technical guarantee of the rules' universal application to various reasons of dissolution. For employers, on the other hand, the law substantively transformed the form of the rules, as is shown below.

When the three parts are taken together, it is clear that the rules on the legal validity of formulating, changing, and dissolving a labour contract (when triggered by labour) had formal characteristics and were therefore capable of universal applicability. However, the law took a substantive turn regarding other issues that may occur in labour relationships.

Substantive Characteristics of the Labour Contract Law

One substantive feature was the illustrative style of the rules. A common structure of such rules is conditioning certain legal effects on listed particular situations. In other words, when the concrete situation that had occurred was not among the illustrated situations, these substantive rules would lose their applicability, resulting in a much narrower range of application. In the Labour Contract Law, there were indeed many such rules. A rather influential group of rules was those for different situations of ending labour contracts.

As briefly mentioned above, the rules regarding employers' rights to dissolve labour contracts were formulated, in contrast to labourers' rights, in a substantive manner. Employers would find their hands bound when they wanted to dissolve labour relationships with their employees, as the law confined their position by enumerating legitimate reasons for dissolving labour contracts. Articles 40 through 42 substantiated the applicable situations in which the employer could legally dissolve labour contracts, from individual cases to conditions of mass layoffs. This structure of rules, as a result, limited the application of the law to particular listed situations.

Likewise, legal consequences of nullity or termination of labour contracts (Article 26 and 44) were constrained by listing particular conditions. These rules therefore limited the possibilities of rescinding labour contracts. Additionally, the rules entitling employees' economic compensation upon the dissolution of a contract were provided in a similar manner (Article 46). Thus, employees would find that only for particular reasons listed by the law would they be entitled to the legal right to claim economic compensation from their employer.

In summary, the above analysis of the rules shows that the law was composed of different types of rules, and it is therefore difficult to provide a general evaluation of the characteristics of the Labour Contract Law. However, a brief discussion of the concrete rules indicates that those concerning forming and maintaining labour contracts were put in a formal and general manner, which could ensure their universal application. On the other hand, the rules took a substantive turn in regard to issues that normally would bring the contract to an end, whether it was actively dissolved by the two parties or ended for other reasons, and thus would apply only to particular situations that the law explicitly listed.

6.2.3 Application of the Rules

On 21 March 2012, Mr. Hou suffered an injury to his left index finger while working on a machine. The damage was later diagnosed as a comminuted fracture and was subsequently identified as a tenth-degree disability, an official recognition that entitles the victim to claim a subsidy. Hou had a formal written labour contract with his employer, which confirmed their labour relationship between 1 March 2011 and 28 February 2012. The two did not renew their labour contract; nevertheless, they continued the labour relationship until 24 August 2012, when Hou was informed that he was fired due to constant violation of internal regulations. In the following years, Hou brought several cases against his employer. Among the many legal issues arising in the disputes, some put the court and the law to the formalistic test and therefore are of interest to the current study (Supreme People's Court 2015).

The first issue concerns the 'formulation of the labour relationship'—the legal status of the forms of the labour contract, which put to the test the formal application of the legal requirement of the written form of a labour contract.

On 8 October 2012, Hou filed a case with the local labour arbitration committee to, among other appeals, restore his labour relationship with his employer. The case went through arbitration and the first-instance court and was finally appealed to the Shanghai No.1 Intermediate People's Court. The court confirmed the legal status of the actual labour relationship during the period (1 March 2012–24 August 2012) after the formal written contract had expired. The court argued that the grounds for such confirmation were that the two continued their labour relationship and the employer was still paying for Hou's social insurance and wages. Moreover, on 17 April, the defendant had applied, as the employer, for occupational injury identification on behalf of the plaintiff. The court thus concluded that the two parties were in effect in a lawful labour relationship since March 2012, a phenomenon usually termed a 'factual labour relationship' in China.

It is worth mentioning that the so-called factual labour relationship is a widespread practice. Although both the Labour Law (Article 19) and the Labour Contract Law (Article 10) explicitly stated that labour contracts should be in written form, in practice, the forms of contracts have been much more flexible. In response to the gap between the law and practice, in 2001, the Supreme People's Court issued a legal interpretation of equivalent legal effect to the law to reconcile the legal situation with reality. Item 16 of this law-equivalent interpretation stated that 'after the expiry of the labour contract, it should be regarded as of mutual agreement by the two parties to continue their original labour contract if the labourer continued working for the employer without the employer's objection' (Supreme People's Court 2001).

The second issue of interest to the study is the formal application of the term 'dissolution of the labour relationship'. It is significant because terminating the labour contract in the Chinese legal system impacts workers' entitlement to certain welfare benefits. In this case, the right to a lump-sum subsidy for employment disability was at stake.

On 4 December, Hou sued his employer again, and the principal argument was whether he was eligible to receive a lump-sum subsidy due to his occupational injury, which had resulted in his disability. This claim therefore put the formal application of the rule of dissolution of contracts to the test and received two divergent judgements by two courts.

The first-instance court refuted his claim by referring to Article 41 of the Shanghai Measures for the Implementation of the Occupational Injury Insurance, in which the rule stated that a lump-sum subsidy was granted if the labour contract was ended either because of the expiration of the labour contract or at the request of the employee. By strictly applying the rules, the court argued that because the employer had lawfully ended the labour relationship in dispute, the plaintiff was denied the subsidy—the way the labour contract ended was not the situation in which the law stipulated that the subsidy should be received—a rather obvious ground. Thus, the court took a very formalistic view of the substantive rule. However, this decision was overturned by the appellate court after Hou appealed.

The appellate court ruled in favour of the plaintiff. The ground for such a ruling, as the reasoning process shows, had three levels of consideration. First, the court resorted to the specific rule of distributing employment disability subsidies and argued that it was to remedy and compensate the employee's damages during working time. Thus, the distribution of the subsidy should not be influenced by the factual reason for the dissolution of the labour relationship. Second, the court drew support from another higher-ranking law, the Social Insurance Law. Quoting Article 39 of this law,[21] the court argued that the distribution of the subsidy should be conditioned on the termination of the labour contract, and the specific reasons for ending the labour contract should have no influence. This argument was backed by para. 3 of the Article, which stated that 'lump-sum subsidies for disability employment eligible by employees upon termination or rescinding of labour contracts'. Thus, the employer should pay lump-sum subsidies to employees after their labour relationship ends. In other words, as long as the labour relationship has formally ended, the concrete factors that brought it to an end should not impact the allocation of subsidies—the law seeks only formal characteristics of ending the labour relationship, and the substantive reason behind the termination is irrelevant. Third, in an effort to re-explain the rules that the first-instance court used to support its ruling, the appellate court reasoned on the basis of common sense. It argued that if the employer should pay the lump-sum subsidy when the employee requested an end to the labour contract, then it was a matter of course that the employer should pay the subsidy when the contract was ended at the employer's will. The court ruled in favour of the plaintiff for the claim of the subsidy.

Taken together, the two legal concerns that arose in the case demonstrate that social concerns have an evident footprint in how Chinese courts apply the law. The first issue demonstrates the reconciliation of the formal application of the law with the social reality of Chinese society, where strict implementation of a written form of labour contract was still an unrealistic hope at the time. In a similar vein, the second issue exhibits (taking the final ruling as the case) the pursuit of social purpose in circumventing the strict rules. As shown, the appellate court adopted several tools—resorting to the purpose of the rule, referring to the structure of related rules, and even appealing to common sense to reinterpret the rule that appeared to disfavour the plaintiff's situation to prevent the plaintiff from losing employment disability subsidies.

6.3 The Reformulation of Legal Education

If 'expansion' is the term to describe the admission of law students in the 1990s, then 'explosion' is the right word to frame the growing pace of law student enrolments in the first decade of the twenty-first century. This was partly due to a general expansion policy endorsed by the central government, which aimed to significantly expand the scale of its higher education in general by the end of the century (CCCCP and State Council 1999, pp. 37–51). It was partly a response to the adoption of the 'rule of law' policy by the Jiang administration in 1997, which, for many, implied a prosperous advancement of legal professionals. Either way, the double-digit increase in law enrolment lasted for many years (Yang 2008, pp. 262–263).

6.3.1 The Crisis of the Legal Profession

Two decades of development in legal education made China's law schools spring up like mushrooms. From 1981 to 2010, the number of departments and institutions offering legal education jumped from 20 to 2194 (Editorial of China Education Yearbook 1986, p. 120). Unsurprisingly, the labour market for law graduates was abundant. From 1990 to 1998, 10 to 20,000 law graduates entered the market each year (National Bureau of Statistics of China 1999, pp. 91–92). Whereas the rising number of legal professionals appeared to show China's growing orientation towards the 'rule of law' and legal modernity, as both are conditioned on the existence of a large number of legal professionals, the bleak reality of the employment ratio of law students tells another story. It has been reported that the employment rate of law majors was one of the worst among university graduates (MyCOS Institute 2012).

Hence, around 2010, there was an odd relationship between the law and the economy in China. While both the economy and legal education were proliferating, the economy could not absorb the expanding body of legal professionals. In other words, the growing supply of legal services was simply mismatched with actual demand. Another perspective is that while the economy was expanding and reasonably becoming more complicated, legal services on the market were not well consumed by society. It is an odd phenomenon, given that the growing complexity of the economy would trigger more disputes to be solved or require preventive legal advice and therefore would give rise to demands for legal services. Hence, the asymmetric supply and demand of legal services begs the question of just what was the role of law in the years of China's economic expansion, given that society seemed to have little interest in the law (Huang 2010).[22]

Before delving into the reasons for the high unemployment ratio, let us first consider career possibilities for law students after graduation. By and large, job opportunities open to law graduates are concentrated in three areas: law firms, the legal departments of enterprises, and the judicial system, such as courts and procuratorates. Judge and prosecutor jobs, as governmental positions, require applicants to pass the civil service examination in addition to being qualified as legal professionals,[23]and typically only a handful of positions are available each year. Therefore, the majority of law graduates must work either as lawyers in law firms or as in-house legal consultants for enterprises.

Much discussion of unemployment has focused on the issue that there are simply too many law graduates for the country, referring to the supply exceeding the actual demand; additionally, some have suggested that the poor quality of legal education, resulting in unqualified law graduates, may be a reason for the low rate of employment (Su 2006; Zhu 2009). As relevant as these issues might be, the low market demand for legal services, especially in the private sector, as Professor Huang Yasheng (Huang 2010) pointed out, may be the deciding factor behind the difficulties faced by many law graduates.

As the majority of law graduates must locate positions either in law firms or in enterprises, the demand for legal services from the business field, especially private enterprises, since there are many of them, are weighted significantly towards offering job opportunities for legal experts. However, such needs in China are minimal. In economic terms, the majority of the private sector cannot afford to hire regular legal professionals. The in-house legal department is a luxury that exists mainly in large groups, SOEs, or prosperous businesses. From the perspective of necessity, given that China grew into a world factory, the business models do not seem complex enough to need regular legal consultants. This leaves law graduates with few choices; the standard choice is to find a position in a law firm, and the significant demand for legal services in China is, in essence, ex post facto.

Therefore, it is not unfair to say that the crisis of legal employment was due partly to the economy's structure, as the Chinese economy grew upon business models that entail a large amount of manual work and exporting labour-intensive products (Huang 2010). Therefore, it is unfair to blame universities or students for the predicament of the job market. The economic structure that China developed, to a certain extent, was one of the reasons that constrained the need for legal services.

That said, a widely accepted diagnosis of China's legal education and the difficulties its graduates face lies in the gap between university education and practical work. Universities have been accused of focusing too much on the law in the book and not preparing students to use legal skills in the real world (Zhu 2009). Therefore, several measures were implemented to address the problem. First, the authority decided to curb the growth of legal education after the early 2000s, and the number of law graduates consequently shrank. Second, a group of elite universities, aided by the Ford Foundation, launched the Formal Clinical Initiative in 1999 with the aim of reforming Chinese legal education, which is the concern of the next section.

6.3.2 *Reform of the Teaching Method*

The traditional style of education in China encourages memorizing knowledge points such as particular historical events and famous sayings. The embodiment of this style in legal education was that Chinese law classes preferred to praise students' ability to memorize a broad scope of black-letter laws and legal concepts, principles, and provisions written in their textbooks (Phan 2005, p. 127). This style can be likened to training legal technicians who would learn basic knowledge about the law but would not learn to put it to use in reality (Phan 2005, p. 127). Therefore, it is unsurprising that many Chinese law school graduates were inexperienced in critical thinking, legal reasoning, and communication skills (Phan 2005, p. 135). In other words, they lacked basic abilities in real-world legal situations, as the primary task of their university study was to passively receive hard legal knowledge. It did not take long to see that such an educational style did not bear fruit in a field such as law where active reasoning ability and similar qualities are essential working abilities. As a result, clinical legal education, along with the social purposes of addressing injustice and promoting legal aid, was introduced.

In 1999, funded by the Ford Foundation, Fudan and Donghua Universities pioneered this effort by launching the Formal Clinical Initiative in Shanghai in cooperation with the government (Phan 2005, pp. 128–129). Shortly afterwards, in 2000, the group expanded to seven, with Tsinghua University, Peking University, Renmin University, Wuhan University, and Zhongnan University of Economics and Law joining it. Three more followed suit in 2001—Sun Yat-sen University, Xibei University of Politics and Law, and Sichuan University Therefore, in the initial years, ten law schools started to experiment with clinical legal education, taking on the mission of training students in practical skills and correcting social injustice.

Forms of Clinical Legal Education

As acclaimed as it has been, clinical legal education has not become a part of the regular curriculum. Instead, it is a program-based special elective, open only to a handful of interested students or, more precisely, selected students (Phan 2005, p. 141). Therefore, the exact number of students trained in such programs has been somewhat limited. For instance, the three clinical education programmes hosted by Peking University combined recruited only approximately 50 students a year.[24] Students who benefited from such training were only a tiny part of the large student body of law schools. Therefore, the real impact would be difficult to estimate, an issue that is revisited soon. For now, let us examine the functional system of clinical legal education in China.

Currently, clinical legal education is practised in several law schools. While the mode of clinical education varies among law schools (2007, pp. 2148–2154), a common mode is to combine in-class skill teaching and real case practice, both taught by teachers with practical experience. For instance, the clinical legal education programme in the law school of Zhejiang University includes lecturing on theories of communication, negotiation, skills in court trials, etc., and practising real case legal consulting, drafting legal documents, presenting legal aid cases, etc. in cooperation with local law firms, the judicial bureau, and some local courts.[25] The course is open to students in the senior year of their undergraduate or second year of master's studies (Zhejiang University Guanghua Law School 2009).[26] In 2008, the first year of the programme, 20 spots were open for application, and knowledge of civil law, economic law, labour law, administrative law, and legal procedures was a prerequisite. According to the curriculum design, the programme has six major components: a general introduction to clinical legal education, theories of interviewing clients, case investigation, skills of negotiation, procedures of litigation and other dispute settlements, and court trial skills. Each section is taught with a combination of lecturing, group discussion, and role-playing, and there are seven weeks for actual case representation under the supervision of teachers. Given that legal practical training is not a prerequisite for a Chinese law degree, some real case experience is helpful for those who participate.[27]

This is the typical practice of clinical legal education (2007, p. 2149). The purposes are threefold, as stated by the university: bridging university studies and social practices, improving teaching quality, and helping the disadvantaged. Such case-based clinical education is single-case justice-oriented, and some programmes have a broader agenda. A typical example is the Centre for Clinical Legal Education of Peking University, which has established three separate modules: clinics of civil and administrative lawsuits, public policy and legislation, and microenterprises.[28]

These courses are open to third-year undergraduates and master's students to cultivate high-level legal talent and innovate legal teaching. The civil and administrative lawsuit clinic adopts a teaching system similar to that of Zhejiang University, also combining in-class lecturing on essential skills of legal practice, in-office legal consulting, and representing real-world legal-aid cases under the supervision of tutors. The other two modules are more ambitious and interesting, with an obvious purpose beyond training students' case-handling skills and single-case justice. Specifically, the public policy and legislation clinic has three subclinics: clinics for labourers and nurses and Beijing's legislation and public policy clinic. While the case-focused clinic was established in 2000, the legislation and public policy clinics came into being only ten years later, in 2011 and 2014, respectively. The main purpose of this clinic is to study legislation with a specific focus on labour-related issues. Based on literature studies, comparative research, and social investigation, it aims to develop legislative proposals for better labour protection.

The clinic for microenterprises trains students in practical skills related to legal issues for businesses and provides legal services for start-ups, which usually lack funds for hiring lawyers in the early stage of business. Hence, the teaching syllabus is filled with business and finance-related topics and skills, including, to name but a few, legal services for financing transactions for small companies, simulation training for business negotiations, contract drafting, legal practices concerning human resources, intellectual property, shareholder rights, and corporate governance.

An Essential Dose of Practical Legal Skills and Legal Consciousness

To date, China's clinical legal education has a footprint in many major universities in each province. Irrespective of its multidimensional goals, the 20 years of development have made a real difference to China's traditional teaching style, at least for students who have received such training. Moreover, the widespread use of such real-world practice has also helped diffuse the idea of law, or the idea of the 'rule of law', among groups that were mostly denied legal services for many reasons.

For the legal profession or legal education as a whole, the results of China's clinical legal education, while significant, still made a minimal level of differences. The single most crucial factor is the small size of the classes. Although the mode and areas of law are far-reaching compared to the vast programmes, the ratio of students who benefited from such practice was too small to make a real difference. As briefly mentioned above, these clinics normally accept only approximately 20–30 students each semester. Even in law schools as resourceful as Peking University, only approximately 800 students received clinical training from 2000 to 2013 (Peking University Law School 2014). Each year, only 50–60 students who graduated from Peking University were exposed to practical training before joining the legal profession.[29] While this was a welcome innovation to the traditional teaching model, even though it had some benefits at the individual level, it could hardly be claimed that it made a real difference to the overall educational results of legal studies, given the minimal number of participants. In other words, clinical legal education is still a luxury available only to small numbers of students, leaving the majority of law graduates without such training. Hence, the real influence of such training on the entire legal profession may well be irrelevant to improving the overall quality of lawyers.

On the societal front, however, it might serve as a vehicle for cultivating a legal culture (or a 'culture of law') in Chinese society (Burman 2002, p. 100). While the external function of clinical legal education emphasizes seeking social justice for disadvantaged groups, the social consequences may extend well beyond initial expectations. By bringing legal services to socially or economically disadvantaged groups, clinical legal education, in addition to exposing students to social injustice, has also introduced the role of law in correcting social injustice to groups that may have the least concept of the law and its functions. Speaking broadly, it has helped create a culture of law in Chinese society as a whole. Additionally, with legislative programmes such as the one at Peking University, clinical legal education also invites China's younger generation of legal professionals to reflect on the current legal system and prepares them for further legal evolution.

Nevertheless, at the outset, American scholars warned that the impression of legal imperialism should be avoided while aiding China's development of clinical legal education (Baskir 2012, p. 194). This concern was justified given that the blind transplantation of foreign legal institutions would not bear fruit, as seen in the Law and Development Movement (Gardner 1981). Noting that the reform was initiated by China rather than pushed by the U.S., Erie (2009) argued against the concern of 'legal imperialism' (p. 62), an opinion that was shared by Baskir (2012, p. 195). Additionally, it was suggested that the initiators should refrain from transplanting

American legal institutions without considering local needs (2007, p. 2155). On the Chinese side, concerns over the transplantation of educational modes concentrated mainly on China's limited number of qualified faculty, insufficient funding, or the necessity of developing clinical legal education for practical purposes (Chen 2005; Mou 2002; Wang 2005).

While it may be too soon to judge the concern of cultural imperialism, the current programme design of China's clinical legal education indicates minimal impact of the legal thought of the common law tradition because the training is conducted mostly by faculty members and lawyers who themselves have barely any training in these concepts. It is safe to say that these programmes are primarily intended to develop students' practical legal skills and prepare them for real-world cases.

6.3.3 *Reform of the Bar Exam*

On the other hand, China made a major reform in its evaluation system for legal professionals in 2002, the bar exam. Before we consider the details of the change, let us first present some data regarding the passing ratio of the new bar exam. The first unified judicial examination was held in March 2002; that year, 360,000 applied to take the exam, and 24,000 passed, accounting for 6.68% of the participants (Gao and Jiang 2020, p. 74). This unified examination was held for 16 years until further reform took place in 2018. Within these 16 years, nationally, over five million participants took the exam, and 980,000 of them received legal professional certificates (Gao and Jiang 2020, p. 74).

Whereas the unified form of the examination appears to be a notable feature, the change went far beyond the form. To understand the critical aspects of the change, it is helpful to start with a brief overview of the unified bar exam. In general, the examination was open to people with a formal university education; their major was irrelevant. To receive the certificate of the bar exam, a candidate had to sit for four written examinations continuously over two days, with a half-day dedicated to each test. The examination tested candidates on hundreds of laws and regulations over the two days.

Three of the examinations were composed of 100 multiple-choice questions covering all substantial and procedural laws, general knowledge of international laws, Chinese legal history, professional ethics, etc. Each lasted for three hours without interruption. The fourth examination was designed with subjective questions; typical questions included interpretation of legal terms, case analysis, and essay questions, and the test lasted for three and a half hours.[30] In total, the four exams were worth 600 points, and those scoring 360 out of 600 would receive the credentials of the legal profession.[31]

Although both the unified bar exam and the earlier lawyers' qualification exam were made up of four written exams, the degree of difficulty increased greatly, which could be a clear indication that it was becoming visibly and decisively more difficult to join the legal profession.

First, the qualification for taking the examination was significantly raised. In the 1990s, the lawyers' qualification exam was open to people with three types of educational background: law majors with a junior college education or above; non-law major applicants with an undergraduate education or above; and applicants who had graduated from the correspondence legal education programme hosted by the Ministry of Justice (Bureau) (1994). The eligible group for the exam was narrowed down after the reform, making the bar exam open only to people with an undergraduate education, regardless of their major.[32] In other words, people without a formal university education were excluded from taking the exam. However, non-law graduates were still eligible for the time being.[33]

Second, while the basic structure of the exam, four written tests, was the same as that of its predecessor and both took the same period to finish, all lasting for approximately three hours, the quantities of questions significantly increased. The lawyers' qualification test held in the 1990s had only 10–20 questions for each exam, mostly in the form of multiple-choice questions, yes-or-no questions, and short-answer questions. In the unified bar exam, however, except for the fourth exam, which was designed for subjective questions and had seven or eight cases for analysis, the remaining three tests were all composed of a hundred multiple-choice questions, the majority of which were case scenarios, and aimed to examine the applicants' ability to develop legal solutions. Therefore, within the same three-hour period, the number of questions was nearly five times that of the previous test.[34]

The bar exam attracted high-profile attention in Chinese society owing to the degree of difficulty: extensive coverage of laws and the pinpointing nature of the questions. Those who passed the written exam move on to the next stage of training—one year of internship in a law firm. Then, they will in principle automatically receive the lawyer qualification certificate and started to work as a licenced lawyer. Although the quality has been greatly improved, the examination has nevertheless been criticized for its strong emphasis on the knowledge of legal articles in the book, indicating that it cannot reflect applicants' practical ability to apply the law in reality (Fu 2014).

6.4 The Integrative Role of Law and the Welfare Economy

After two decades of expansion, the legal education system had produced too many legal professionals, and the market equilibrium between supply and demand for legal services was broken. Consequently, unemployment ensued as the economy entered the third decade of transformation. As the legal demand from society withered, the diagnosis of the authorities was that China's legal education placed too much stress on academic training, and law students were not sufficiently trained in law schools. In other words, the low employment rate among law graduates was due to their undertraining in legal skills. Hence, changes were made regarding teaching methods in this decade.

As the much-criticized academic training was imported from the civil law tradition, this time, the authority asked common law countries for help. Clinical legal education from the U.S. was introduced to help law students become familiar with practical skills in the real world. Good intentions notwithstanding, the real difference made by the programme, if not negligible, was hardly substantial in terms of the overall influence on legal education and the compatibility of the common law reasoning technique with China's civil law system. Its limited effect was also partly due to the elite educational mode that was (and is) available only to a handful of students.

The more substantial change regarding the legal profession in this period was the critical reform of the bar exam. First, the new bar exam abolished the three parallel exams for different legal professions and substituted a unified judicial exam for people interested in legal careers. Second, eligibility to participate in the exam was further limited, and people without an undergraduate education were excluded from sitting for the exam. Third, the degree of difficulty of the exam was significantly increased, as was seen in the significant increase in the number of questions and the stresses on reasoning skills. The unification of the bar exam marked China's latest effort to formalize its legal profession. By then, from education to evaluation, Chinese legal education had made its full turn towards formalizing the training and selection system, which would be crucial for the formation of group status and the role of law professionals in society as a whole.

On the other hand, the state made a progressive transformation to address social inequalities resulting from two decades of unbalanced development. The laws that emerged in this period were a social response, as the normalized social rights, such as labour rights and social insurance, in a concentrated manner. Whereas the legal system underwent a formalization change in this decade, it showed a substantive orientation in this period. There were two aspects of this. First, the areas of legislation demonstrated the pursuit of particular social results via the law. For instance, the Labour Contract Law (2007) and the Labour Dispute Mediation and Arbitration Law (2008) were promulgated back-to-back, regardless of related issues that had already been normalized in the Labour Law (1994). Second, taking the Labour Contract Law as an example, the characteristics of the rules diverge between different issues—formal rules are common for issues concerning the validity of critical stages of contractual behaviours, such as formulating, changing, and dissolving labour contracts. Substantive rules are primarily for issues that generally would bring a contract to an end, whether it is actively dissolved by the two parties or ends for other reasons.

These selective areas of lawmaking and the subtly differentiated use of formal and substantive rules imply that the state, by deploring a substantive turn in the law, was attempting to balance the effects of a formal approach to the law and to reassume its interventional role in the market. The law was thus built for specific social outcomes. Such a substantive turn of law is not surprising given that the twenty years of regionally biased economic development had resulted in the formation of backwards regions and marginalized groups and hence an unintegrated Chinese society. As the reform entered the third decade, the authority wanted to rectify via the law—legislation was oriented towards correcting social inequalities and addressing social welfare concerns, revealing the law's socially integrative role in the emerging welfare economy.

For example, to protect rural labourers from constant wage default as well as other concerns, the Labour Contract Law was put into force; to integrate the segmented rural and urban society, administrative rules gradually dismantled the *hukou* institution; and to fill the gap in welfare benefits among different professions, the government developed a welfare system with national coverage, encompassing people from all regions and all walks of life, which was formally legalized with the promulgation of the Social Insurance Law in 2010. Thus, the law was making an effort to assist social integration by eliminating social and economic gaps.

In summary, after some significant economic reforms, Chinese society experienced an expanding gap among its people. The disadvantaged group, mostly rural residents, was marginalized, and the social inequality was in desperate need of correction. The state restructured welfare institutions to eliminate the harm caused by the unintended market results, and the law responded by substantively legalizing social issues and creating flexible rules oriented towards particular social results, i.e., prioritizing labourers' rights over those of employers. These legal phenomena suggest that the law has purposively wielded its social functions to relieve the damage caused by the widely divided society and institutionalized the course of social integration.

Notes

1. The 'three rural issues' are the livelihood of peasants, the development of agriculture, and the social advancement of rural areas. For an assessment of the 'three rural issues' and China's approaches to address them, see Hong (2016, pp. 171–183).
2. The meaning of 'harmonious society' in the Chinese context was perhaps most revealing in discussions of China's petition letter system, as Chinese Professor Tang (2010, p. 87) argued: 'Citizens shall not maintain their lawful rights at the cost of social stability, and the fact that we respect petitioners does not necessarily mean that we will echo whatever issues they raise'.
3. Household status was granted to people at birth, and their status was decided in conformity with their parents' hukou status. Hence, the location of birth and the exact place of residence were irrelevant to people's initial hukou status.
4. Article 17 of the Provisional Regulation of the Shanghai Blue-stamp Hukou (1993).
5. Article 12 of the Provisional Regulation of the Shanghai Blue-stamp Hukou (1993).
6. The majority have to leave their children in rural areas to be taken care of by the children's grandparents. This became such a common social phenomenon that the term 'left-behind children' was coined to describe these children. The study of Guo and Zhao (2019) further suggested the impact of hukou status on education equality.
7. Article 9–10 of the Regulation of the Basic Pension Insurance of Zhejiang Province. The actual ratio of contribution to the fund pool was within the purview of the provincial government and was subject to change according to the local economic situation.
8. People employed in the public sector were exempted from paying into individual accounts, which the state supported. The central government ended this privilege in 2015.
9. For instance, the experiment took place in three northeast provinces to find possible solutions for empty personal accounts.
10. It is difficult to merge the social funding pool at the national level due to local protectionism, especially in economically advanced regions that have little incentive to share their funds with poorer regions.

11. As Guo's study showed, the scale of empty personal accounts was estimated at 14 billion in 1997 and 200 billion in 2000 and was increasing at a pace of 100 billion per year.
12. Empty personal accounts are the personal accounts of older generations who joined the workforce before the pension system was established and thus had limited time and few or no contributions to their personal accounts.
13. Data presented by the Ministry of Human Resources and Social Security of the PRC, available at http://www.mohrss.gov.cn/xxgk2020/fdzdgknr/zcjd/zcjdwz/202107/t20210713_418347.html. Accessed 21 Sept 2021.
14. Individuals could choose from different contribution amounts, ranging from 100 to 500 yuan per year.
15. The state would deposit 55 yuan per person per month in the account. This was subject to change based on the economic and price situation.
16. The report of the Ministry of the Human Resources and Social Security, available at http://www.mohrss.gov.cn/SYrlzyhshbzb/dongtaixinwen/dfdt/201112/t20111229_94499.html. Accessed 29 Sept 2021.
17. Regulation of Labour Insurance 1951, and Detailed Implementing Rules of the Regulation of Labour Insurance 1953.
18. Provisional Regulations of Hainan Public Health Insurance for the Employees of Enterprises 1991; Provisional Regulations of Shenzhen Basic Health Insurance for the Employees of Enterprises 1996.
19. Also Articles 2 and 14 of the Regulations on Unemployment Insurance (1999).
20. For an official introduction to the promulgation of the Labour Contract Law, consult Quanguo renda changweihiu fagongwei jiedu laodong hetong fa/The interpretation of the labour contract law by the Legislative Affair Committee of the Standing Committee of the National People's Congress. Available at http://www.law-lib.com/fzdt/newshtml/21/20070702105540.htm. Accessed 28 Sept 2021.
21. Article 39 of the law reads, 'The following expenses incurred for work injury shall be payable by the employer per national provisions: (1) Wages and welfare expenses for the duration of work injury treatment; (2) Disability allowances paid each month to disabled employees of degrees five and six; and (3) Lump-sum subsidies for disability employment eligible by employees upon termination or rescinding of labour contracts'.
22. The discussion of the economic structure and the role of law in the economy was inspired by the interview conducted by Yasheng Huang (2010) on the issue of Chinese college degrees.
23. The national exam for civil servants started in 2002.
24. The course introduction of the programme is available at https://www.law.pku.edu.cn/xwzx/ggtz/15732.htm. Accessed 29 Sept 2021.
25. As a case study, the introduction of clinical legal education of Zhejiang University is available at http://www.cliniclaw.cn/hyschool.asp?school=%D5%E3%BD%AD%B4%F3%D1%A7. Accessed 21 Sept 2021.
26. As the university announced, preference was given to students who had secured their master's degree studies through a postgraduate recommendation system.
27. However, one year of practical training in a law firm after passing the bar exam is a precondition for applying for a lawyer's licence. See Article 5 of the Lawyer's Law of the PRC.
28. The introduction of clinical legal education at Peking University is available at https://en.law.pku.edu.cn/academics/announcements/21888.htm. Accessed 28 Sept 2021.
29. A similar scale of clinical training is common at other elite universities; for instance, from 2000 to 2009, Renmin University, another top Chinese university, claimed that it had trained 486 students in clinical education, which amounted to approximately 50 students each year. Available at http://www.law.ruc.edu.cn/flzs/ShowArticle.asp?20618.html. Accessed 22 Sept 2021.
30. See various versions of the announcements of the exam and test syllabus issued by the Ministry of Justice.
31. A lower passing score was possible for western regions, which lacked legal professionals.

32. See various versions of the Announcement by the Ministry of Justice for the Judicial Exam. Available at http://www.moj.gov.cn/jgsz/jgszzsdw/zsdwgjsfkszx/. Accessed 18 Mar 2023.
33. In 2018, a further reform of the bar exam took place, since when the bar exam is open only to people either with a law degree or trained in other disciplines but with three years of law-related work experience. Detailed requirements for taking the exam are available at http://www.moj.gov.cn/news/content/2018-06/08/zlk_20640.html. Accessed 22 Sept 2021.
34. The comparison is based on the lawyers' qualification test in 1993 and the unified judicial exam in 2008. The structure of the former is introduced in chapter five, and the original exam papers of the 2008 bar exam are available at http://www.cnsikao.com/html/zhenti/linianzhenti/index_3.html. Accessed 22 Sept 2021.

References

(1994) 1994 Nian quanguo lüshi zige kaoshi de youguan guiding/Relevant provisions of the 1994 national exam of lawyers' qualification. China Lawyer 6:3

(2007) Adopting and adapting: clinical legal education and access to justice in China. Harvard Law Review 120(8):2134–2155

Baskir CE (2012) Crossing borders: creating an American law clinic in China. Clinical Law Review 19(1):163–206

Bian YJ (1994) Guanxi and the allocation of urban jobs in China. China Quarterly 140:971-999

Burman JM (2002) The role of clinical legal education in developing the rule of law in Russia. Wyoming Law Review 2(1):89-118

CCCCP (1965) Guanyu ba weisheng gongzuo zhongdian fangdao nongcun de baogao/The report on focusing the public health work in rural areas

CCCCP (2003) Guanyu wanshan shehuizhuyi shichang jingji tizhi ruogan wenti de jueding/Decisions on several issues about completing the system of socialist market economy. In: CPC Party Literature Research Office (ed) (2004) Shiliuda yilai zhongyao wenxian xuanbian, shang/Selected key documents since the 16th National Congress of the CCP, vol 1. Central Party Literature Press, Beijing

CCCCP and State Council (1999) Guanyu shenhua jiaoyu gaige quanmian tuijin suzhi jiaoyu de jueding/Decisions on deepening educational reform and comprehensively promoting quality education. In: CPC Party Literature Research Office (ed) (2001) Shiwuda yilai zhongyao wenxian xuanbian, Zhong, zhong/Selected key documents since the 15th National Congress of the CCP, vol 2. Central Party Literature Press, Beijing

CCCCP and State Council (2002) Guanyu jinyibu jiaqiang nongcun weisehng gongzuo de jueding/Decisions on further strengthening rural public health work. In: CPC Party Literature Research Office (ed) (2003) Shiwuda yilai zhongyao wenxian xuanbian, xia/Selected key documents since the 15th National Congress of the CCP, vol 3. Central Party Literature Press, Beijing

Chan KW and Zhang L (1999) The hukou system and rural-urban migration in China: Processes and Changes. China Quarterly 160:818-855

Chen JM (2005) Cong faxue jiaoyu de mubiao shenshi zhensuo falü jiaoyu de diwei he zuoyong/Assessing the importance and function of clinical legal education from the perspective of the purposes of legal education. Global Law Review 3:281–287

Congressional Research Service (2016) China's hukou system: overview, reform, and economic implications. Available at https://www.everycrsreport.com/files/2016-01-07_IF10344_90e25c2b4c5b85546abd876c58bd96164f0d2dd5.pdf. Accessed 15 Mar 2023

Deng DS and Liu CP (2007) Xinnongcun shehui baozhang tixi yanjiu/Studies on the neo social security system for rural society. People's Publishing House, Beijing

Dong BH (2007) Lun woguo wuguding qixian laodong hetong/A discussion on the non-fixed term labour contracts in China. Studies in Law and Business 6:53–60

Dong WJ (2008a) Woguo laodonghetongfa zhong de qingxie baohu yu liyi pingheng/Tilted protection and balance of interest of China's labour contract law. Contemporary Law Review 3:106–110
Dong KY (ed) (2008b) Zhongguo jingji gaige 30 nian: zhehui baozhang juan/China's 30 year of economic reform: social security. Chongqing University Press, Chongqing
Editorial of China Education Yearbook (1986) Zhongguo jiaoyu nianjian 1982–1984/China education yearbook 1982-1984. Hunan Education Publishing House, Changsha
Erie MS (2009) Legal education reform in China through U.S.- inspired transplants. Journal of Legal Education 59(1):60–96
Fan C and Chen C (2014) The new-generation migrant workers in China. In: Wu FL, Zhang FZ, and Webster C (eds) Rural migrations in urban China: enclaves and transient urbanism. Routledge, London
Fan XY and Qie SF (2002) Nongcun laodongli zhuanyi zhuangkuang yu tezheng/The situations and characteristics of the transfer of rural labour force. China Statistics 7:26–27
Fu CR (2012) China's hukou reform: the Guangdong and Shanghai cases. In: Wang GW and Zheng YN (eds) China: development and governance. World Scientific, Singapore
Fu ZT (2014) Gaige sifa kaoshi zhidu, tuijin guojia zhili fazhihua xiandaihua/Reform the judicial exam system, push forward the legalization and modernization of governance. Law and Social Development 20(5):68–70
Gao YF and Jiang W (2020) Falü zhiye zige kaoshi gaige de huigu yu sikao/Review and reflection on the reform of Bar Exam. Public Security Science Journal—Journal of Zhejiang Police College 3:72–78
Gardner JA (1981) Legal imperialism: American lawyers and foreign aid in Latin America. The University of Wisconsin Press, Madison
Giles JT et al. (2021) One country, two systems: evidence on retirement patterns in China. World Bank Group Policy Research Working Paper 9650. Available at https://www.iza.org/publications/dp/14725/one-country-two-systems-evidence-on-retirement-patterns-in-china. Accessed 23 March 2022
Goldmann M (2020) The European economic constitution after the PPSP judgment: towards integrative liberalism. German Law Journal 21(5):1058–1077
Gu T et al. (1998) Nongcun yiliao baoxian zhidu xiangguan wenti fenxi ji zhengce jianyi/Analysis of issues of rural health insurance system and policy suggestions. China Health Economics 4:42–43
Guo XS (2003) Woguo jiben yanglao baoxian geren zhanghu kongzhang wenti yanjiu/The study on the issue of empty personal account of the basic pension system. On Economic Problems 3:37–39
Guo Y and Zhao LQ (2019) The impact of Chinese hukou reforms on migrant students' cognitive and non-cognitive outcomes. Children and Youth Service Review 101:341–351
Halegua A (2008) Getting paid: processing the labour disputes of China's migrant workers. Berkeley Journal of International Law 26(1):254–322
Han AG (2008) Building a harmonious society and achieving individual harmony. In: Guo SJ and Guo BG (eds) China in search of a harmonious society. Lexington Books, Lanham
He P (1997) Guoyou qiye gaige zhong de shehui baoxian/The social insurance issue in the SOEs reform. Economic Science Press, Beijing
Hong YX (2016) The China path to economic transition and development (trans: Yin X-h). Springer, Heidelberg
Hu JT (2003) Shuli he luoshi kexue fazhanguan/Establish and fulfil the scientific view of development. In: CPC Party Literature Research Office (ed) (2004) Shiliuida yilai zhongyao wenxian xuanbian, shang / Selected key documents since the 16th National Congress of the CCP, vol 1. Central Party Literature Press, Beijing
Huang YS (2010) What is a college degree worth in China. New York Times 2 December 2010. Available at http://www.nytime.com. Accessed 15 Feb 2023
Hurst W (2009) The Chinese worker after socialism. Cambridge University Press, Cambridge

Leung JCB and Xu YB (2015) China's social welfare: the third turning point. Polity Press, Cambridge

Li WP (2002) Zhognguo nongcun jiankang baozhang de xuanze/The options for China's rural health security system. Chinese Financial and Economic Publishing House, Beijing

Lin JYF, Wang GW, and Zhao YH (2004) Regional inequality and labour transfers in China. Economic Development and Cultural Change 52(3):587–603

Mahoney JG (2008) On the way to harmony: marxism, Confucianism, and Hu Jintao's *hexie* concept. In: Guo SJ and Guo BG (eds) China in search of a harmonious society. Lexingtong Books, Lanham

Ministry of Civil Affairs (1992) Xianji nongcun shehui yanglao baoxian jiben fangan/General planning of the county level rural social pension insurance

Ministry of Civil Affairs (1997) 1997 Minzheng shiye fazhan tongji baogao/The 1997 statistic report of the development of civil affairs

Ministry of Finance (1969) Guanyu guoying qiye caiwu gongzuo zhong de jixiang zhidu gaige de yijian/Opinions on the reform of some regulation for the financial work of SOEs

Ministry of Health (2012) Zhongguo weisheng tongji nianjian 2012/The statistic yearbook of public health of China 2012. Peking Union Medical College Press, Beijing

Ministry of Labour (1950) Jiuji shiye gongzuo zanxing banfa/Interim measures of reliving laid-off workers 1950

Ministry of Labour (1996) Qiye zhigong gongshang baoxian shixing banfa/Interim measures of occupational injury insurance for enterprises workers

Ministry of Labour and Social Security (2003) Guanyu renzhen zuohao dangqian nogcun shehui yanglao baoxian gongzuo de tongzhi/Circular on conscientiously implementing the work of rural social pension insurance

Ministry of Labour and Social Security (2004) Guanyu nognmingong canjia gongshang baoxian de youguan tongzhi/Circular on rural migrant workers joining occupational injury insurance

Ministry of Labour and Social Security (2005) 2005 Niandu laodong he shehui baozhang shiye fazhan tongji gongbao/The 2005 statistic communique of the development of labour and social security affairs

Ministry of Public Health (1957) Zhiyebing fangwei he zhiye huanzhe chuli banfa de guiding/ Stipulations on the range of occupational diseases and the treatment of patients with occupational diseases

Ministry of Public Health and Ministry of Finance (1965) Guanyu gaijin gongfei yiliao wenti de tongzhi/Circular on issues of improving the management of state-funded public medical system

Ministry of Public Health and Ministry of Finance (2008) Guanyu zuohao 2008 nian xinxing nongcun hezuo yiliao gongzuo de tongzhi/Circular on work on 2008 neo rural cooperative medical system

Ministry of Public Health, Ministry of Finance, and Ministry of Civil Affairs (2012) Guanyu zuohao 2012 nian xinxing nongcun hezuo yiliao gongzuo de tongzhi/Circular on work on 2012 neo rural cooperative medical system

Ministry of Public Security (1992) Guanyu shishi dangdi youxiao cehngzhen jumin hukou zhidu de tongzhi/Circular on the implementation of effective local urban hukou system

Ministry of Public Security (1997) Xiachengzhen huji zhidu daige shidian fangan/Executive plan of reforming hukou system in towns and small-sized cities

Mou XY (2002) Falü yuanzhu zhidu yu zhensuo falü jiaoyu/Legal aid system and clinical legal education. Law Science 8:26–30

MyCOS Institute (2012) 2011 Zhongguo daxuesheng jiuye baogao/ annual report of employment of Chinese college graduates 2011. Social Sciences Academic Press (China), Beijing

National Bureau of Statistics and Ministry of Labour and Social Security (2005) Zhongguo laodong tongji nianjian/China labour statistical yearbook. China Statistics Press, Beijing

National Bureau of Statistics and Ministry of Labour and Social Security (2006) Zhongguo laodong tongji nianjian/China labour statistical yearbook. China Statistics Press, Beijing

National Bureau of Statistics of China (1999) Xinzhongguo wushinian tongji ziliao huibian/Comprehensive statistical data and materials of new China's fifty years. China Statistical Press, Beijing
National Bureau of Statistics of China (2003) Zhongguo tongji nianjian/Statistical yearbook of China. China Statistics Press, Beijing
Naughton B (2018) The Chinese economy: adaption and growth, 2nd edn. The MIT Press, Cambridge
Perking University Law School (2014) Centre for Clinical Legal Education of Peking University. Available at https://en.law.pku.edu.cn/alumni/alumniassociations/23410.htm. Accessed 28 Sept 2021
Phan PN (2005) Clinical legal education in China: in pursuit of a culture of law and a mission of social justice. Yale Human Rights & Development Law Journal 8:117–152
Qian WY (2002) Jianguohou tudi yu nongmin shehui baozhang wenti de lishi yanbian/The historical evolvement of land and social security system for peasants since the establishment of the new China. Historical Research in Anhui 3:80–83
Roberts C (2012) Far from a harmonious society: employment discrimination in China. Santa Clara Law Review 52(4):1531–1560
Saich T (2004) Governance and politics of China, 2nd edn. Palgrave Macmillan, London
Shanghai Government (1993) Shanghaishi lanyin hukou zanxing guanli guiding/Provisional regulation of the Shanghai blue-stamp hukou
State Commission for Restructuring et al. (1994) Guanyu zhigong yiliao zhidu gaige de shidian yijian/Opinions on the pilot program of reforming the public health system for the employees of enterprises
State Council (1957a) Guanyu quxiao suijunjiashu gongfei yiliao daiyu de pifu/Approval on abolishing the government-sponsored public medical service for the relatives of military personnel
State Council (1957b) Guanyu laodongli tiaoji gongzuozhong de jige wenti de tongzhi/Circular on several issues of labour force adjustment
State Council (1986) Guoying qiye zhigong daiye baoxian zanxing guiding/Provisional stipulations on unemployed SOE workers
State Council (1991) Guanyu qiye zhigong yanglao baoxian zhidu gaige de jueding/Decisions on the reform of the pension system for the employees of enterprises
State Council (1993) Guoying qiye zhigong daiye baoxian guiding/Stipulations on unemployed SOE workers
State Council (1995) Guanyu shehua qiye zhigong yanglao baoxian zhidu gaige de tongzhi/Circular on deepening the institutional reform of the pension system for the employees of enterprises
State Council (1997) Guanyu jianyi tongyi de qiye zhigong jiben yanglao baoxian zhidu de jueding/Decisions on constructing a uniform pension system for the employees of enterprises
State Council (1998) Guanyu jianli chengzhen zhigong jiben yiliao baoxian zhidu de jueding/Decisions on building up basic health insurance for urban enterprises workers
State Council (1999) Zhuanpi zhengdun baoxianye gongzuo xiaozu baoxianye zhengdun yu gaige fangan de tongzhi/Circular on approving the rectify and reform measures for insurance industry proposed by the working team of consolidating insurance industry
State Council (2001) Guanyu zhengdun he guifang shichang jingji zhixu de jueding/Decisions on rectifying and normalizing the order of the market economy. In: CPC Party Literature Research Office (ed) (2003) Shiwuda yilai zhongyao wenxian xuanbian, xia/Selected key documents since the 15th National Congress of the CCP, vol 3. Central Party Literature Press, Beijing
State Council (2003a) Guanyu guifan guoyou qiye gaizhi gongzuo de yijian/Opinions on normalizing the reform of the SOEs
State Council (2003b) Guanyu jianli xinxing nongcun hezuo yiliao zhidu de yijian/Opinions on building up neo health cooperative medical system for rural areas
State Council (2004a) Guanyu tuijin ziben shichang gaige kaifang he wending fazhan de ruogan yijian/Opinions on deepening the reform of the capital market and stabilizing the development.

In: CPC Party Literature Research Office (ed) (2004) Shiliuda yilai zhongyao wenxian xuanbian, shang/Selected key documents since the 16th National Congress of the CCP, vol 1. Central Party Literature Press, Beijing
State Council (2004b) Guanyu touzi tizhi gaige de jueding/Decisions on the reform of the investment system
State Council (2005a) Guanyu guli zhichi he yindao geti siying deng feigongyouzhi jingji fazhan de ruogan yijian/Opinions on encouraging, supporting, and guiding the development of non-public economies like individual businesses and private enterprises. In: CPC Party Literature Research Office (ed) (2006) Shiliuda yilai zhongyao wenxian xuanbian, zhong/Selected key documents since the 16th National Congress of the CCP, vol 2. Central Party Literature Press, Beijing
State Council (2005b) Guanyu wanshan qiye zhigong jieben yanglao baoxian zhidu de jueding/ Decisions on improving the basic pension system for the employees of enterprises
State Council (2005c) Guanyu kaizhan chengzhen jumin shehui yanglao baoxian shidian de zhidao yijian/Guiding opinions on launching pilot project of social pension system for urban residents
State Council (2007) Guanyu kaizhan chengzhen jumin jiben yiliao baoxian shidian zhidao yijian/ Guiding opinions on the pilot program of implementing basic health insurance for urban residents
State Council (2009) Guanyu kaizhan xinxing nongcun shehui yanglao baoxian shidian de zhidao yijian/Guiding opinions on carrying out a pilot project of neo rural social pension insurance
State Council (2015) Guanyu jiguanshiye danwei gongzuo renyuan yanglaobaoxian zhidu gaige de jueding/Decisions on the institutional reform of the pension system for employees of government departments and public institutes
Statistical Information Centre of the Ministry of Public Health (2005) Disanci guojia weisheng fuwu diaocha fenxi baogao/The report of the investigation and analysis of the third national public health service. Chinese Hospitals 1:3–11
Su L (2006) Dangdai zhongguo faxue jiaoyu de tiaozhan yu jiyu/The challenge and opportunities of China's contemporary legal education. Law Science 2:3–21
Supreme People's Court (2001) Guanyu Shenli laodong Zhengyi anjian shiyong falü ruogan wenti de jieshi/Explanations on the application of the laws in hearing labour dispute cases
Supreme People's Court (2015) Hou Hongjun su shanghai longmao jianzhu zhuanghuang youxian gongsi laodong hetong jiufen an/Hou hongjun sue shanghai longmao decoration co. on labour contract dispute. Communique of the Supreme People's Court, vol 11. Available at http://gongbao.court.gov.cn/Details/8280bb0fe8bc0be7e9b6bfb7600818.html. Accessed 28 September 2021.
Tang XT (2010) Reforms in the petition letter and visit system of China and construction of a harmonious society. Frontiers of Law in China 5(1):77–90
Wang JY (2005) Zhensuoshi falü jiaoyu bentuhua de sikao/Consideration of localizating clinical form of legal education. Hebei Law Science 3:82–84
Wang QX and Huang K (2008) Wugudingqixian laodonghetong de shiyufei/The rights and wrongs of the non-fixed term labour contracts. The Jurist 2:13–18
Wen JB (2005) Guanyu zhiding guomin jingji he shehui fazhan dishiyige wujian guihua de jianyi/ Suggestions on the 11th five-year plan of the national economic and social development. In: CPC Party Literature Research Office (ed) (2006) Shiliuda yilai zhongyao wenxian xuanbian/ Selected key documents since the 16th National Congress of the CCP, vol 2. Central Party Literature Press, Beijing
Wen JB (2008a) Guanyu shenru guanche luoshi kexuefazhanguan de tuogan zhongda wenti/On several key issues about deepening the implementation of the scientific view of development. In: CPC Party Literature Research Office (ed) (2009) Shiqida yilai zhongyao wenxian xuanbian, shang/Selected key documents since the 17th National Congress of the CCP, vol 1. Central Party Literature Press, Beijing
Wen JB (2008b) Zhengfu gongzuo baogao/The report of the government work. In: CPC Party Literature Research Office (ed) Shiqida yilai zhongyao wenxian xuanbian/Selected key documents since the 17th National Congress of the CCP, vol 1. Central Party Literature Press, Beijing

Xu YY, Li BQ, and Huang XX (2021) Outsiders to urban-centric growth: the dual social exclusion of migrant tenant farmers in China. Third World Quarterly 42(6):1314–1329

Yang DP (2008) Gaodeng jiaoyu gonggong zhengce de yanbian/Changes of public policy in higher education. In: Zhang XL (ed) Zhongguo jiaoyu fazhan yu zhengce 30 nian/China's education development and policy 1978–2008. Social Sciences Academic Press, Beijing

Young J (2013) China's hukou system: markets, migrants and institutional change. Palgrave Macmillan, London

Zhang L and Li M (2018) Acquired but unvested welfare rights: migration and entitlement barriers in reform-era China. China Quarterly 235:669–692

Zhang ZK et al. (1994) Guanyu woguo nongcun hezuo yiliao baojian zhidu de huiguxing yanjiu/ A retrospect study on rural cooperative medical care system. Chinese Rural Health Service Administration 6:4–10

Zhao DG (2002) Nongcun yanglao baoxian gongzuo huigu yu tansuo/Review and exploration of rural pension system. Population and Family Planning 5:23–27

Zhejiang University Guanghua Law School (2009) Guanyu falü zhensuo de xuanke shuoming/ Explanation on selecting the courses of clinical legal education. Available at http://www.ghls.zju.edu.cn/ghlscn/2009/0406/c13718a1106637/page.htm. Accessed 21 Sept 2021

Zhu RJ (2001) Guanyu zhiding guomin jingji he shehui fazhan de shige wunian jihua de jianyi / Suggestions for the 10th five-year plan of the national economic and social development. In: CPC Party Literature Research Office (ed) (2001) Shiwuda yilai zhongyao wenxian xuanbian, zhong/Selected key documents since the 15th National Congress of the CCP, vol 2. Central Party Literature Press, Beijing

Zhu SL (2009) An institutional inquiry into legal skills education in China. Global Business and Development Law Journal 22(1):75–92

Chapter 7
Conclusion

Abstract The conclusion summarizes the coevolution of the relationship between the law and the economy in China's thirty years of development and highlights the key features of the law and the political economy in the process. From there, it moves to the concluding implications, advocates a contextualized approach to the law and the economy, and rejects a straightforward understanding of their interactions.

With a historical overview of China's 30 years of development, this research contributes to the law and development debate and argues against modernization theory and determinism, which would anticipate similar results globally, independent of context. Therefore, the present book aims to counter a perception that law is static in relation to the economy and to reveal the complexity of the role of law in different political and economic pursuits.

As has been shown, the role of law in the Chinese economy was not uniform over the years. Driven by political will, it changed from a parent-like role providing instruction in great and small issues alike to a facilitative role assisting economic growth and finally to an integrative role to bridge the unintegrated society. The coevolution of the law and the political economy in the Chinese context signals the probability of a mutually entrenched relationship between these spheres and delineates an institutionally integrative future development of law and the economy.

In the Chinese context, the paradigm of the law and political economy is often indicated in the political agenda announced in the debut of each generation of leadership. Law, as an institution deeply intertwined with politics, is deployed by the state to achieve goals, whether political, as when the judicial system was used to punish counterrevolutionaries in the early years, or economic, as when the law is employed to shape economic behaviours. That said, the role of law in economic affairs is unavoidably constrained by the economic environment of a given society. This means that the material condition of the economy, or the developmental stages of society in general, and the specific economic system that the society employs—centrally planned or market-oriented—will define the role of law in the economy.

China's 30 years of economic transformation have not followed a straightforward path. The economy has experienced much back-and-forth over economic strategies,

J. Hu, *The Role of Law in China's Economic Development, 1978–2011*,
https://doi.org/10.1007/978-981-99-9911-8_7

has had momentous long-term growth, and has undergone hesitation and corrective actions. The Chinese legal system passed through these ups and downs with the economy and has made its own transformation.

While the economy had yet to embrace market rules and planned economic strategies were dominant, the rule system showed a substantive approach to the economic sphere, especially in reform areas. When the aim was to accelerate the market reform of the economy, the rule system made a timely formalization of the laws and thus appeared qualified for a facilitative role in the economic transformation. When Chinese society became unintegrated and social and economic inequality were rampant, the law took a social turn and responded by emphasizing the rights of disadvantaged groups and social welfare. In short, the functions of the law altered as the external social and economic environment changed.

However, the change in the law's external role could not be achieved independently. In other words, the external function of the law relies on certain conditions; among them are the role of the state in the economy and the internal characteristics of law. Retrospectively, one can see that the Chinese government employed a mixture of formal laws and policy papers to achieve direct control over the market in the 1980s, and this direction then evolved into one that featured a retreating from state intervention and reliance on formal and rational laws to navigate the economy. Then, the state reclaimed its master role in correcting economic consequences, and the law took a slight substantive turn in its formal rule system. Each of these stages of legal development was associated with a reciprocal external social and economic environment—a correspondence of the relationship between the state and the market via different types of law.

By exposing China's adaptation of Western theories, the study shows that the relationship between law and economic development is contingent. The interaction of the two implies their dependence on specific contexts, and no apparent progress narrative can be told; nor would a straightforward shift towards the rule of law ensure development. This result therefore indicates the need to integrate studies on the relationship between the economy and the corresponding legal changes to avoid a fragmented and partial understanding of China's economic development. Therefore, we dismiss the suggestion that China directly transplanted Western legal institutions and instead find that it took a localization approach to legal and economic ideas that grew out of advanced economies.

With such empirical evidence, this study challenges the conventional view that the autonomy of law is a prerequisite for economic development—a prevailing perception that assumes that a free market, the rule of law, and a democratic political structure are the pillars underpinning economic development. Although this study does not negate this view, it does provide an alternative perspective.

GPSR Compliance
The European Union's (EU) General Product Safety Regulation (GPSR) is a set of rules that requires consumer products to be safe and our obligations to ensure this.

If you have any concerns about our products, you can contact us on

ProductSafety@springernature.com

In case Publisher is established outside the EU, the EU authorized representative is:

Springer Nature Customer Service Center GmbH
Europaplatz 3
69115 Heidelberg, Germany

www.ingramcontent.com/pod-product-compliance
Ingram Content Group UK Ltd.
Pitfield, Milton Keynes, MK11 3LW, UK
UKHW022211051026
15624UKWH00001B/112

* 9 7 8 9 8 1 9 9 9 9 1 0 1 *